PRO TOOLS
for Musicians and Songwriters

Gina Fant-Saez

Peachpit
Press

Pro Tools for Musicians and Songwriters

Gina Fant-Saez

Peachpit Press
1249 Eighth Street
Berkeley, CA 94710
510/524-2178
800/283-9444
510/524-2221 (fax)

Find us on the World Wide Web at: www.peachpit.com
To report errors, please send a note to errata@peachpit.com

Peachpit Press is a division of Pearson Education
Copyright © 2006 by Gina Fant-Saez

Development Editor: Jim Aikin
Peachpit Editor: Cary Norsworthy
Production Editor: Lisa Brazieal
Copyeditor: Carol Henry
Compositor: Owen Wolfson
Indexer: Joy Dean Lee
Cover design: Mimi Heft
Cover production: Andreas Schueller
Interior design: Yvo Riezebos, Yvo Design

ISBN 0-321-33703-4

9 8 7 6 5 4 3 2 1

Printed and bound in the United States of America

For 15 years of cheerleading, wisdom, blind faith, patience, tolerance, humor, forgiveness and unconditional love, this book is dedicated to my better half, Pamela.

Acknowledgements

Thank you to Peachpit for the opportunity to write this book, to Cary Norsworthy for her patience and flexibility, to Jim Aikin for his wisdom and experience, to Lisa for the extra hours and hard work, to Owen for the great layout, to Pamela for feeding me and allowing me to type until 4 A.M. without complaint, to Wisdom for barking me away from my computer to play ball, to Kevin for his brilliant support and guidance, to Ryan for being wise and talented beyond his years, to Wee Wee for being the best brother on the planet, to Mom Saez for always believing in me, and to all those who had the faith in buying this book.

CONTENTS

3: THE EDIT WINDOW 50

4: PLAYLISTS & MARKERS 96

5: USING PLUG-INS 124

6: INSERTS & BUSSES 146

7: MIDI TRACKS 180

11: AUTOMATE & MIX 346

12: EXPORT YOUR SONG 420

A: HELP YOURSELF 490

B: INTERNET COLLABORATION   502

INDEX   511

INTRODUCTION

Do you ever wake up in the morning, turn on the coffee pot and think, "Hey, I wonder how this machine works?" and then decide to take it apart and figure it out? Me neither. I simply want to turn on the machine and drink my coffee.

I find the same thing in recording my music. I don't want to be a technician; I simply want to be a musician and songwriter. That's the premise of *Pro Tools for Musicians and Songwriters*. If you want to sit down and be creative, and make music without being overwhelmed with technical details, then you made a wise choice in picking up this book.

So many new users of computer-based audio systems are intimidated by the technology and overwhelmed at the thought of setting up and learning it. If you feel that way, you're not alone. I always remind new users that at some point in their lives, the knobs and buttons on the dishwasher or washing machine looked complicated too—but now they're common knowledge. That's the comfort zone where I hope this book will take you. I believe this book will make it possible for songwriters and musicians to learn Pro Tools in a fun, unintimidating way. My goal is to turn even the staunchest technophobes into download-savvy Pro Tools whizzes. So, make a fresh pot of coffee and let's get started.

I'm Going to Assume...

...that musicians already know how to play their instruments and that songwriters already know how to write songs. I'm going to assume that all of you understand common song structure, as well as tempo and meter. But other than that, you'll need to know almost nothing about making music with your computer in order to read and learn from this book. You won't need to know much about the computer itself beyond how to turn it on, and the difference between clicking and double-clicking.

And You're Going to Need...

- A computer with an Internet connection
- A Pro Tools interface, such as
  - Digidesign's Mbox
  - Digi 002 or 002 Rack
  - Any Pro Tools–compatible M-Audio interface
- Pro Tools LE 7 or M-Powered Pro Tools 7
- A separate, external hard drive to record to
- A MIDI keyboard
- A microphone, your instrument, and cables
- Headphones and/or speakers
- A CD burner and CD burning application

A computer with an Internet connection. It's *very* important to have an Internet connection on the computer that you'll be recording with. This book will require many downloads from the Internet throughout the various chapters, with the specific goal of helping you become more comfortable using the Internet to download and import audio files. In today's professional music industry, a basic understanding of the Internet and of how to upload and download files will open up your world as a writer and musician. The Internet provides a limitless palette of sounds, musicians, and resources for your music.

A Pro Tools interface. Until very recently, there were only two hardware choices for Pro Tools LE—Digidesign's Mbox and the Digi 002. Now that M-Audio has become part of the Avid/Digidesign family, the choice of interfaces has drastically expanded. M-Audio supports 11 different interfaces that work with Pro Tools LE. Four that I recommend are the Ozonic Interface and Controller, the FireWire Solo, the FireWire 410, and the FireWire 1814.

If you buy an Mbox or Digi 002, the Pro Tools software is included. However, if you buy an M-Audio interface, you'll also have to buy Pro Tools M-Powered software. Take note that an M-Audio FireWire Solo combined with Pro Tools M-Powered software costs almost exactly the same as an Mbox. Given the choice, I would definitely choose the FireWire Solo because it uses a FireWire connection and also provides MIDI functionality; the Mbox uses USB and does not support MIDI. I personally find FireWire to be much faster and more reliable to work with. That said, I'd choose a Digi 002 or 002Rack over the M-Audio FireWire 1814 because I find the Digi 002 to be a sturdier, more substantial piece of gear.

A separate, external hard drive to record to. A common question I get from new users is, "Doesn't the computer have a hard drive? Why do I need another one?" The answer is: Your *computer's* hard drive is for the programs you use; the *external* hard drive will be the one onto which you record your music. In other words, the computer is the tape machine, and the external hard drive is the reel of tape.

The hard drive that came with your computer is already running your operating system, as well as your applications. If you force it to do all that, and also record and play back multiple audio tracks, you're going to have nothing but headaches. So do yourself a favor *before* you get started with Pro Tools—invest $100 in a 7200 RPM FireWire hard drive.

What's a Hard Drive, Anyway?

Remember 45 records? They were called 45s because they rotated at 45 RPMs (revolutions per minute). Hard drives work the same way. Inside the metal case of a hard drive is simply a disk that looks almost exactly like an old record album—but it's spinning thousands of times faster. Just as the old records turned at 45 or 33 RPM, hard drives come in different speeds. Pro Tools requires the hard drive used for recording to spin at a minimum of 7200 RPM. So make sure when you buy a hard drive for Pro Tools that the speed is sufficient to allow problem-free playback and recording.

Platters ———
Spindle ———

Head
Arm

I recommend using an external drive because it is much more convenient for moving around, working at another studio or with other musicians. Simply unplug your hard drive and go. If you ever replace your computer, you have all your songs ready to move with you. I recommend FireWire drives because they are the simplest and best hard-drive solution for Pro Tools.

Since all new Macintosh computers come with a FireWire port, hooking up an external drive is fast and easy. Windows users may need to add a FireWire card, but it is worth the extra money and effort in order to work with a FireWire drive, because external USB 2.0 drives are not supported by Digidesign at this time and may have playback issues.

Rename Your External Hard Drive

I always recommend renaming the hard drive used for recording, changing it to "Audio Drive" so that it's very clear which hard drive you are recording to and saving to. To rename a hard drive on the Macintosh, click the drive's name (below its icon) on the desktop. When you click once on the name, it will turn into a type-able field. In Windows, your hard drives are found under My Computer, and also in Windows Explorer. Rename the drive by right-clicking it and choosing Rename.

This is my System Hard Drive

Macintosh HD

This is the hard drive I record to

Audio Drive

Open
Explore
Search...
Scan with SpySubtract...
Sharing and Security...
Scan with Norton AntiVirus
Format...
Copy
Create Shortcut
Rename
Properties

A MIDI keyboard. If you're a keyboard player, this is a must—and if you're not a keyboard player, it's still a must. So many people say, "I don't want to use MIDI, I just want to record audio." That's what you think now. But I promise that you'll find many creative uses for a MIDI keyboard. And if you're intimidated by MIDI, this book will change all that and will teach you MIDI simply and painlessly.

A microphone, your instrument, and the proper cables. A few exercises in this book require the use of a microphone. Make sure that you use a real microphone cable, known as an XLR cable. It's very common for inexperienced users to try to use a 1/4" cable for a microphone. If you want to have proper volume levels and less noise, use a professional microphone cable. If you play keyboard, bass, or guitar, have a 1/4" cable on hand for that, too.

Headphones and/or speakers. Ideally, you'll have both headphones and speakers. When you record, you turn the speakers down and put the headphones on. When you're mixing, you use the speakers. Sony 7506 headphones are very popular. KRK speakers are an affordable, quality choice found in many personal studios.

A CD burner and CD-burning application. These days, most computers come with a CD burner (writer) installed. If yours didn't, you're going to need one. You'll also need a special application for burning the CDs. You can use what comes with your computer, but I recommend Roxio Toast and/or Jam for Mac, and Roxio Easy Media Creator for Windows. These applications make possible the reordering or changing of your songs' audio level, where the stock applications don't. These applications will be invaluable not only for burning your audio CDs but for backing up your data, as well.

Why This Book?

This book takes an unconventional approach by teaching Pro Tools from the musician's and songwriter's perspective. The chapters comprise a series of step-by-step exercises. Each step is followed by a screenshot—a picture of what you'll see on your monitor—that allows you to follow along visually. The exercises will increase your skill gradually, demonstrating Pro Tools and helping you acquire the knowledge you need to use this application—not as a technician, but as a musician and/or songwriter.

The Pro Tools manual is extremely informative, but it's written as a reference guide rather than a tutorial and has an overwhelming amount of information. Since Pro Tools is such a versatile program, it's used not only for music production but also for film and video production, sound design, radio production, mastering, and more. There are many Pro Tools functions that you, as a musician, will simply never use. So think of this book as your shortcut to the information that you need, and a way around the information that you don't.

By the end of the book, you'll be comfortable importing audio, recording, editing, automating, mixing, and bouncing. You'll know the keyboard shortcuts for many common commands, and you'll have learned lots of tips and tricks for becoming fast and effective using Pro Tools. The goal of this book is to give you the skills that you need so that you can concentrate more on your music and less on the technology required to record.

Working in Bars and Beats

If you're a musician or songwriter and you're going to learn Pro Tools (or any music software), and create your songs without a click track and without a designated meter and tempo, then you may as well be using a 20-year-old analog tape machine. The greatest strength of Pro Tools for creating music is using it in *Bars and Beats* mode.

In Bars and Beats, you specify a fixed tempo for your song and record to a click track. As a result of this fixed tempo, your song is displayed on a linear timeline and divided visually into bars and beats, providing a grid to work with as you edit. Bars and Beats mode gives you complete musical freedom to copy and paste one section to another and edit the arrangement of your songs. Using Bars and Beats ensures that your edits will be perfectly synchronized with other tracks, and provides a seamless solution for bringing your work to other players and other studios. When you present a Pro Tools session recorded to a click track to other musicians, they have the same luxury of being able to move, edit, and copy and paste any new parts to and from any bar. You and your fellow musicians become more flexible and efficient, only making your songs better in the end.

Note

Every exercise in this book will be done using Bars and Beats.

I can honestly say that 99 percent of every professional piece of music recorded in Pro Tools is recorded to a click track or drum loop. Most every piece of music that I've had the honor to work on over my 15-year career as a studio owner and Pro Tools engineer—whether it was pop, country, rock, metal, new age, world, techno, R & B—was created using a click track and Bars and Beats. Some of you may be unaccustomed to working with a click track, and may even argue that it makes music "sterile." But a click track doesn't have to be just a rim shot or cowbell—it can be a shaker or tambourine loop or even a drum loop. I find it much easier to play to something musical other than just a click track. You'll learn how to do this in Chapter 1.

I promise that our journey using Bars and Beats will take your music to the next level.

"My Drummer Won't Play to a Click Track"

Over the years, numerous artists and bands have played their demos for me. Many of these are extremely well produced, but their tempo drifts: Verses feel slow, choruses feel rushed. What I call "1970s drum fills" are everywhere, further varying the tempo. All this makes the demo sound unprofessional. When I gently suggest they should have recorded the song to a click track, a common answer is, "My drummer won't play to a click track."

I'm going to piss off a lot of drummers out there, but I'm going to say this anyway: A drummer in a modern studio who refuses to play to a metronome shouldn't be recording. Get another drummer immediately. Any drummer playing today's music and recording with today's technology *must* be able to record to a metronome. There are definitely exceptions to working with a metronome, but a studio drummer should actually *prefer* working with a click track whenever possible.

I've heard some sob stories about bands who finally achieved that record deal—but once they got into the studio with a professional producer, the drummer couldn't or wouldn't play or practice to a click track. Many, many times, though, producers will only let the band's drummer play in live concerts and will hire a session drummer to record the album.

Why Did I Write This Book?

My father was a gadget addict. Back in the early '70s when the first calculators and tape recorders became available, he continually brought home the latest technological toys. He also traveled to Japan quite frequently, and he returned from every trip with some kind of electronic gadget that we would both sit down and figure out how to use. He often gave up in frustration, and I would take the gadget to my room and learn how to use it. Then I would go and teach my father. It always felt like such a victory when I conquered a new piece of gear, and I got double the satisfaction teaching him how to use it.

Over the years, I, too, became a gadget addict, and to this day I have an odd assortment of old and new electronic toys. Today it includes PDAs, Game Boys, digital video cameras, iPods—not to mention mountains of software. I started playing piano and guitar and writing songs around the age of 11. With my "high-tech" Japanese tape machines, I began creating some very terrible demos. I started working in recording studios at the age of 18 and opened my first studio, Blue World Music, in 1992 in New York City. With every job I was hired to engineer, I bought and sold gear to stay up with the latest technologies. When I purchased my first digital audio system in 1992, it changed my life as a songwriter, musician, and engineer. I was, and still am, passionate about the endless creative possibilities a digital audio system has provided for me.

For many years, when I wasn't working in my own studio, I was consulting, installing, and training for other studios, advertising agencies, game design companies, musicians, song-writers, producers, and engineers—helping as many as I could to also make the transition into the digital world. I've received enormous personal satisfaction in seeing the huge difference this knowledge has made in the lives of so many creative individuals. Training people to use Pro Tools has become second nature to me.

At present, I'm in the process of creating eSession.com, which I optimistically anticipate will mean my doing more and more training and support. Fortunately and unfortunately, I can no longer keep up with the numbers of people buying personal studios. So, with a little urging from clients and family, I decided to write a book. What better way to reach a large number of people and to make an even bigger difference than with one-on-one training?

I hope you find my approach as a writer and musician valuable in turning the usual struggle of learning software into a fun, unintimidating, and musically captivating experience.

GETTING STARTED

1

In this chapter you'll learn some important basics on your journey toward recording. You should now be sitting in front of your computer with Pro Tools installed and ready to go.

You'll set up your first Pro Tools session and learn where your files are located and exactly where you're saving your sessions. It's important to have an understanding about how Pro Tools manages your files. You need to know where your files are located and what hard drive you are recording to—otherwise, you could have playback problems later.

Working in your new Pro Tools session, you'll create your first track and learn how to insert a plug-in. The first plug-in that you'll create is a click, or metronome. Using this metronome, you'll learn how to use Pro Tools in Bars and Beats mode—a timing reference that allows you to record your music to a grid. This grid further allows you to edit entire song arrangements and easily copy and paste tracks anywhere in your music. As you work in Bars and Beats, you'll begin to appreciate the importance of the grid in creating professional music.

The First Step

This may not be the most exciting chapter in the book, but it's important that we cover the basics so that you have a strong foundation to build your music on. When learning to drive a car, you wouldn't just get behind the wheel and head down the West Side Highway in New York City without any instruction. So here at the beginning, try to have patience and faith in our purpose. Learning all these exercises will pay off in the end.

EXERCISE 1:

Start a New Session

Before we can create a new song—or what Pro Tools calls a *session*—we need to open Pro Tools. Where is it? Pro Tools is installed on your system's hard drive, meaning the hard drive that came installed in your computer. However, that's not where you'll want to save your newly created project files.

Let's walk through the process of finding and opening Pro Tools, starting a new file, naming it, and saving it to your external audio drive.

1]

Find Pro Tools. Mac users: Open your internal hard drive, and open your Applications folder. Inside there is a folder called Digidesign. Inside that folder is another one called Pro Tools, which contains the Pro Tools application. If you haven't already, drag the Pro Tools application to your Dock.

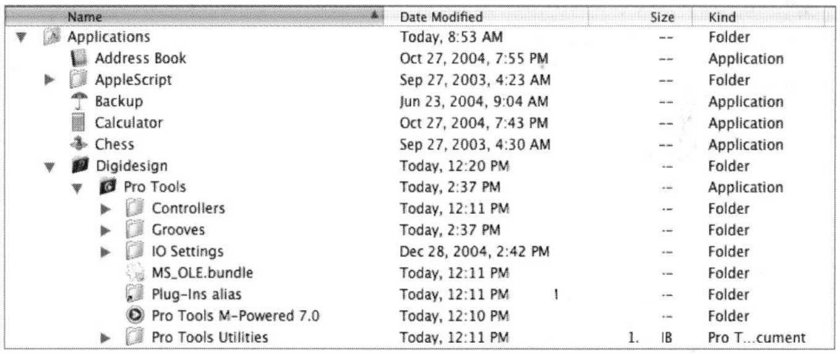

Windows users: If you're curious, open My Computer or launch Windows Explorer. Open your local drive (usually C:) and and then the folder called Program Files. Inside that is the Digidesign folder, which contains the Pro Tools folder, which contains the ProTools.exe application. When you install Pro Tools in Windows, a desktop shortcut is automatically made for you, so you should seldom need to access anything in Program Files yourself.

Name	Date Modified	Size	Kind
▼ 🗐 Applications	Today, 8:53 AM	--	Folder
📓 Address Book	Oct 27, 2004, 7:55 PM	--	Application
► 📋 AppleScript	Sep 27, 2003, 4:23 AM	--	Folder
🖥 Backup	Jun 23, 2004, 9:04 AM	--	Application
🖩 Calculator	Oct 27, 2004, 7:43 PM	--	Application
♣ Chess	Sep 27, 2003, 4:30 AM	--	Application
▼ 📁 Digidesign	Today, 12:20 PM	--	Folder
▼ 📁 Pro Tools	Today, 2:37 PM	--	Application
► 📁 Controllers	Today, 12:11 PM	--	Folder
► 📁 Grooves	Today, 2:37 PM	--	Folder
► 📁 IO Settings	Dec 28, 2004, 2:42 PM	--	Folder
📄 MS_OLE.bundle	Today, 12:11 PM	--	Folder
📄 Plug-Ins alias	Today, 12:11 PM	1	Folder
⊙ Pro Tools M-Powered 7.0	Today, 12:10 PM	--	Folder
► 📁 Pro Tools Utilities	Today, 12:11 PM	1. IB	Pro T...cument

Warning

For both Mac and Windows users, **never** *take the Pro Tools application out of the Pro Tools folder. The folder contains files that the Pro Tools application needs in order to operate.*

"I never know where anything is on my hard drive!"

The most common confusion I encounter with new computer users is that they never fully grasp where things are located. They don't understand where they are saving their files, and so they often don't know how to find things again.

If I asked you, "Where are your socks?" you might say, "in my dresser." If you had to tell me where to go to find your socks, you might say, "Go to my house, open the front door, open the bedroom door, open the closet door, open the dresser drawer, and find my socks."

File structure is a lot like that. The hard drive is your house. To find Pro Tools, for example, you open the house's front door—the hard drive. You open the bedroom door—the Applications (Mac) or Program Files (Windows) folder. You open the closet door—the Digidesign folder. Then you open the dresser drawer—the Pro Tools folder—and inside is exactly what you're looking for.

In this book, the / character indicates the *path* you'll take to find something. For instance, I'd explain the path to the Macintosh Pro Tools folder this way: Hard Drive/Applications/Digidesign/Pro Tools.

2] **Launch Pro Tools.** In Windows, double-click your Pro Tools desktop shortcut. On a Mac, click Pro Tools in your Dock. On the Mac, the menus at the top of your screen will become the Pro Tools menus.

3] **Start a new session.** Under the File menu, choose New Session. You'll get a window, or *dialog box,* full of choices. This window is asking you, "How do you want to work? Do you want your song to be a 16-bit or 24-bit file? Do you want to work with WAV files or AIFFs?" The good news is that there are really no wrong choices. Choose 24-bit, 44.1, AIFF (a very common file type)—but *don't* click Save yet.

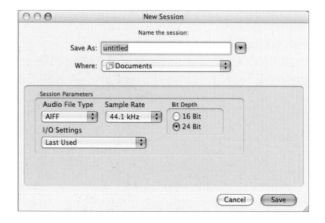

Sample Rate and Bit Depth, in Plain English

Digital photos are made up of tiny squares called *pixels*. A pixel is one dot on the computer screen. The more pixels per square inch, the clearer the picture; also, the more pixels, the larger the file. In photography, these pixels are measured in dpi, or dots per inch. So, a 72 dpi photo is a smaller file but has less detail than a 300 dpi file. Make sense?

If that makes sense to you, then *sample rate* will be simple. Instead of tiny pixels representing a piece of a picture, think of tiny samples or pieces of sound making up one second of audio. The more samples per second, the clearer the sound; but again, more samples make a larger file.

The 44.1 kHz setting simply means that your audio is being sampled or recorded 44,100 times per second. About 75 percent of my work is done at 44.1, but 48 kHz is very common. Higher sample rates such as 96 and 192 kHz are being used more and more these days. There is no wrong choice. For important projects, world-class engineers suggest you always work in the highest sample rate available; but they have fast computers and huge hard drives. The higher the sample rate, the harder your computer will have to work, and the more storage space you'll need for the tracks you record.

Bit depth is a little more complicated, but not much. Digital photos have shades of color, and the shades are represented by bits. If you have only one bit to represent whether a pixel is red or not, another bit for green, and another bit for blue, your photo will have three-bit color resolution, with no subtle shades at all. The more bits we add, the more shadings we can see in the picture. In audio as well, the higher the bit depth, the more accurate the audio sound being represented digitally and, yet again, the larger the file.

A word about large files: Hard drives are so affordable these days that worrying about using too much disk space is like worrying about where to place a broom in a four-car garage. Most likely you will have more space than you need, so go for quality and don't be miserly with disk space.

4] **Name your session.** This dialog box is also where you *name* your song and tell the computer where to save it. In the box where the file's name currently says Untitled, type "Learning PT." But then wait—*don't* click Save yet! This dialog box is also where you decide how and where to save the files. Mac users: See the blue triangle with the black arrow pointing down? Click that. The arrow will now point up. Windows users will see a drop-down menu when you click on the drop-down menu at the top of the box. This expands your view and shows you every hard drive connected to your computer, as well as the folders within your drives. Whenever you see a Save window like this one, get in the habit of expanding your window so you can see where you're saving your files.

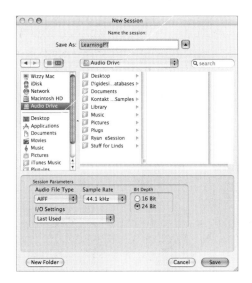

5] **Save your session.** Make sure that you're saving your session file onto your external audio drive, which you should be able to select in this dialog box. Click your external hard drive to select it—and *now* you can click Save.

Now you'll see a big empty window.

"So many audio formats—which one should I use?"

The good news is, there's really no wrong choice:

SDII is the Sound Designer 2 format and is the native audio format of Digidesign, which makes SDII less compatible with some other programs. Some experienced audio users use this format for specific technical reasons, but for the sake of compatibility, I would suggest new users not choose SDII as a format.

AIFF stands for Audio Interchange File Format. It was initially created for Macs but has become cross-platform over the years and is more and more prevalent. Being a Mac user myself, I typically use AIFF as my default format, but I've recently been told by a few prominent engineers that broadcast WAV is slowly becoming the format of choice.

WAV (Windows Audio/Visual) files are also called **BWF** or **broadcast WAV** files. Though initially developed for Windows, this is also now a cross-platform format and very common among Windows and Mac users.

So, where is your session? Before we get started making music, let's find your new session and see what has happened on your hard drive.

6 | **Hide Pro Tools.** On the Mac, from the Pro Tools menu, choose Hide Pro Tools. In Windows, you can minimize the Pro Tools window or, if Windows Explorer is running in the background, simply click on it in the Task Bar at the bottom of the screen to bring it to the front.

7] **Open your session folder.** Open your external hard drive, and you should see a folder called Learning PT.

Double-click on the folder to open it and see what's inside.

When you make a new session, Pro Tools creates a folder with your song's name. Inside this folder, which contains your session file or song, Pro Tools creates four other folders, called Audio Files, Fade Files, Region Groups, and Session File Backups. You may also see a WaveCache.wfm file. This file helps redraw your audio waveforms faster.

◆ Everything you record in this song will be created as audio files and put into the Audio Files folder.

◆ Anytime you create a fade or a cross-fade, it will go into the Fade Files folder.

◆ Anytime you create a Region Group (more about these in a later chapter), that group is saved into the Region Groups folder.

◆ Last but not least is the very important Session File Backups folder. Pro Tools will make a safety copy of your song every 5 minutes and keep the last 10 versions. This is extremely helpful if you forget to save and the computer crashes. Simply open this Backups folder and open the last saved version. It's also helpful if you accidentally edit something incorrectly; you can always go back to a previous version and work with that.

8] **Go back to Pro Tools.** On a Mac, click the Pro Tools icon in your Dock. In Windows, maximize Pro Tools by clicking on it in the Task Bar at the bottom of the screen. This brings Pro Tools back to the front, with your big empty window.

Fasten Your Seatbelts

Now we're back to our big, empty window. It's empty because we haven't created any tracks yet. So, it's time to do that.

EXERCISE 2:
Create Your First Track

1] **Create an audio track.** Under the Track menu, choose New Track. A dialog box opens, asking about the kind of track you want to create.

Tip

You'll want to get used to using the keyboard shortcut for Track > New Track, which is ⌘+Shift+N for Mac, and Ctrl+Shift+N for Windows.

2] **Choose the type of track.** If you click each menu option in the dialog box, you'll notice that you have a few choices in each field. You can choose the number of tracks you want to create, whether to record in mono or stereo, and what kind of track it is. We'll eventually try all of them, but to start out just create one Mono Audio track, which is the default. Where the menu currently says Samples, select Ticks. (I'll explain why later.)

Click Create to create your new track.

The Mix and Edit Windows

There are only two prominent windows in Pro Tools. One is the Mix window, which will act as your mixing console, and the other is the Edit window, which you will use to edit your music. To toggle between the two windows, use the keyboard shortcut Command+= (Mac) or Ctrl+= (Win).

If you're going to use Pro Tools a lot, an ideal solution is to have two monitors and put the Mix and Edit windows each on its own monitor. You can also resize the two windows to fit on the same screen. Below I've put the Edit screen on the left and the Mix window on the right.

If for some reason you don't see both windows automatically when you open a session, you can turn them on by selecting Show Mix or Show Edit in the Window menu.

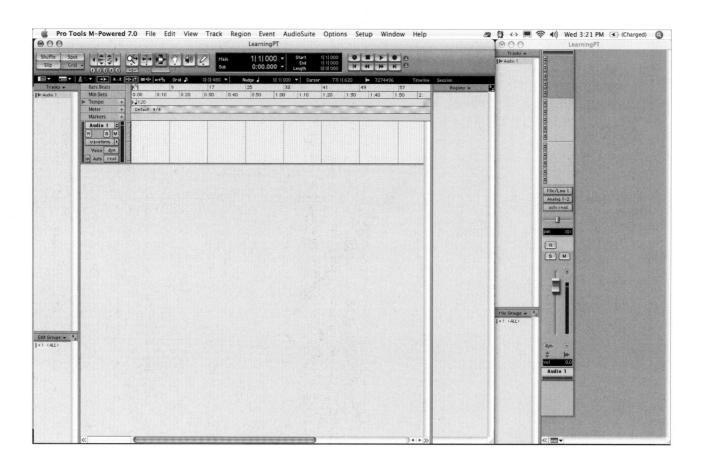

3] **Rename the fader.** Now that you've created your first track, you'll see your first fader in the Mix window. The fader is at the bottom of a vertical column called a channel strip. The new channel is named Audio 1. Notice the same name in the Edit window.

To rename the track (in Pro Tools, tracks and channels are basically the same thing), double-click the track name Audio 1 in either the Mix window or the Edit window. A small window opens. There, type "Click" for the new name and then click OK.

So, our first track is going to become a click track, also known as a metronome.

EXERCISE 3:

Add Your First Plug-in

When someone says "plug-in," you probably think of an effect or a compressor or EQ—but instruments are plug-ins, too, and since a click uses a sound, it is considered an instrument plug-in. We're going to work with other plug-in instruments such as synths and pianos later in the book, but for now we're going to use a plug-in instrument that generates a click sound, so you'll have a metronome to work with.

1] **Turn on Bars and Beats.** First, make sure that Pro Tools is set to display in Bars and Beats. Under the View menu, go to the Main Counter submenu, and if Bars and Beats is not checked, select it to turn it on.

2] **Find Inserts and Sends.** In the Mix window at the top of the channel strip, you'll see five little buttons with tiny up and down arrows. This section of the channel strip is called Inserts. Below that are two identical-looking sections called Sends. For now, we'll concentrate on Inserts only. This is the place where you put, or *insert,* your click instrument (and eventually your cool effects plug-ins and instruments).

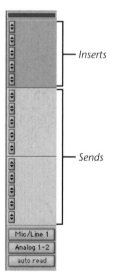

3] **Insert a click.** At the top of your channel strip, click on the top Insert arrow, which reveals a pull-down menu. Choose Plug-in, and notice that Pro Tools categorizes all the plug-ins according to what they do. As I mentioned, the Click plug-in is considered an instrument, so scroll down to Instrument and choose Click.

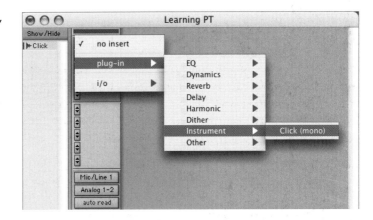

4] **Open the Transport window.** Under the Window menu, choose Transport.

5] **Turn on the metronome.** On the far-right side of the Transport window you'll see a metronome icon. Make sure that it's highlighted, which indicates that the metronome is on. You can also turn it on and off by pressing 7 on your numeric keypad.

6] **Play the click.** Now it's time to hear our click track. Press the spacebar to play, and press it again to stop. (You can also click the play and stop buttons in the Transport window.)

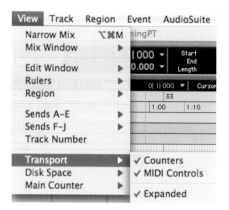

Note

If your Transport window looks different from what you see illustrated here, or if some icons are missing from your display, go to the View menu and choose Transport to enable everything.

EXERCISE 4:

Change the Click Sound and Volume

When you first play the Click plug-in, you'll hear the default click sound, which is a computer-generated sound that I find to be a bit sterile. Let's make it more interesting.

We're going to change the click sound to something more musical. Then we'll explore some of the plug-in's other options.

1] **Open the plug-in:** To see the Click plug-in window, click the Click insert on your channel strip in the Mix window. The plug-in window opens.

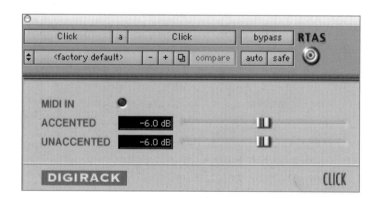

2] **Choose a new click sound.** Click Factory Default, and you'll be given a menu of sounds to play for the click track. I use Marimba 2 for most things.

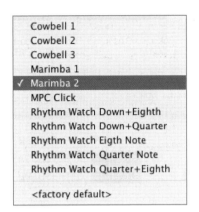

3] **Audition the click.** Now press the spacebar to play. You should hear a new click sound.

Try changing to a few other click sounds to become familiar with the choices.

4] **Change the accent.** Notice how the first beat is louder than all the rest? This is because some people like to work with Beat 1 accented, or louder than the other three beats.

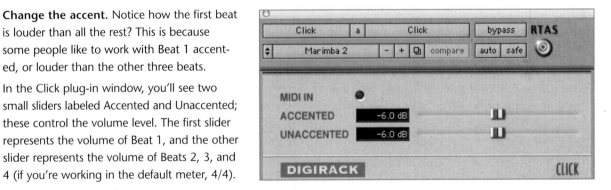

In the Click plug-in window, you'll see two small sliders labeled Accented and Unaccented; these control the volume level. The first slider represents the volume of Beat 1, and the other slider represents the volume of Beats 2, 3, and 4 (if you're working in the default meter, 4/4).

If you try to set these fader levels at the same volume, you'll find it's not very easy to be exact. One quick way to put all beats at the same volume is to hold down the Option key (Mac) or the Alt key (Win) and click both sliders. The levels will go to 0, and both sliders will be at the same level.

Clicking while holding the Option key (Mac) or the Alt key (Win) sets most everything in Pro Tools to the default setting. Try it: Go to the Mix window and move your fader's volume slider up or down. Now Option+click (Mac) or Alt+click (Win) on the fader to reset it to 0.

5] **Save your metronome setting.** Click the two tiny up and down arrows to the left of the name Marimba 2, and choose Save Setting As. Name it "My Click."

Now that you've saved this setting, the next time you create a song, you can open your saved Click instrument by choosing My Click from the menu.

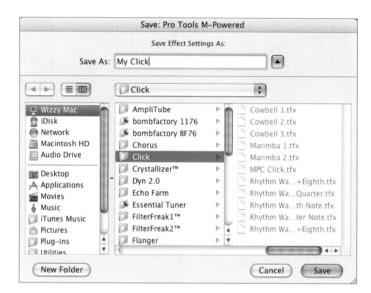

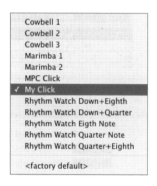

6] **Save the session.** Under the File menu, choose Save. Or get in the habit of using the shortcut Command+S (Mac) or Ctrl+S (Win).

EXERCISE 5:

Change the Tempo

Now that you've created your own click, you'll want to be able to use it at different tempos.

1] **Open the Transport window.** The Transport window may still be open. If it's not, select Window > Transport again. Or use the shortcut Command+1 (Mac) or Ctrl+1 (Win), using the 1 on your numeric keypad.

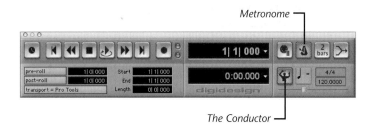

Metronome

The Conductor

2] **Turn off the Conductor.** See the little icon of the man conducting in the Transport window? That's the Conductor, which you'll learn more about in Chapter 10. Click the Conductor icon to turn it off for now.

3] **Set a manual tempo.** When your Conductor is off, Pro Tools uses the manual tempo setting. At the far right in the Transport window is the Manual Tempo field.

The default tempo is 120 BPM. Type your desired tempo into this field—100 (for 100 beats per minute), for example—and press Return/Enter.

Tempo Field

Warning

You must press Return or Enter. If you don't, the tempo will not change.

4 **Play the click.** Press spacebar. Your click track
should be playing more slowly now.

Setting the Tempo with a Finger Tap

If you're sitting with your guitar or piano and you have a song but no idea what the tempo
is, it's very handy to be able to tap your own tempo. To enter your own tempo by tapping,
first make sure the Conductor is turned off. Move the cursor to highlight the Tempo field,
and then repeatedly tap the T key on your keyboard to the beat of your song. Watch the
Tempo field and see the number change as you tap.

EXERCISE 6:

Get to Know the Ruler Timeline

Open the Edit window and maximize it to make it larger. At the top is a long rulerlike section called the Timebase Ruler (or Ruler view), which displays your song from beginning to
end, in various measurements. You can completely customize the selection of rulers you see
on the screen, so let's first get to know which ones we need; then we'll remove the ones we
won't be using.

Working with music, you'll mostly use the Bars and Beats, Minutes and Seconds, Markers,
Tempo, and Meter rulers.

◆ The Bars and Beats ruler shows your song measured and divided into bars made up of
beats. This allows you to keep everything in sync as you edit arrangements quickly and
easily. Looking at the Bars and Beats ruler, it's easy to tell that the chorus starts at Bar
32, or that the song ends at Bar 99.

◆ The Minutes and Seconds ruler helps you keep tabs on your song's length, or at what
point a certain section of a song (such as a verse or chorus) begins and ends. I use the
Minutes and Seconds ruler to make sure that my song isn't running too long, or that I
don't have two minutes of intro before the first verse, and so forth.

◆ With the Marker ruler, you can label each section of the song with names like Verse 1,
Chorus 2, or Bridge, so it's easy to know where you are at all times.

◆ The Tempo ruler displays the tempo of your song, and any changes to the tempo—
in this case, 100 BPM.

◆ The Meter ruler displays the meter (or time signature) of your song, such as 4/4 or 6/8,
and allows you to insert meter changes.

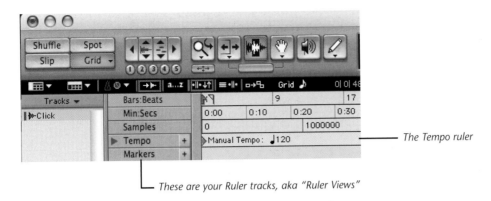

The Tempo ruler

These are your Ruler tracks, aka "Ruler Views"

In this exercise, you're going to turn off the Ruler views you don't need and get them out of your way, because every inch of screen space is important in using Pro Tools. The more room you have to work with on screen, the better.

1] **Choose your rulers.** Go to the View menu, and choose Rulers. This is where you tell Pro Tools which rulers you'd like to see in your song.

2] **Turn off what you don't need.** In the Rulers submenu, click to turn Meter on and Samples off. Meter should be checked, and Samples should not. (The Samples ruler is for precise, microscopic editing, which we won't be doing.)

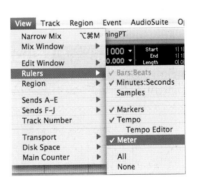

Wrap Up

So you've made it through the first chapter. From here, you have a few more back roads to cover before you head down the highway—but at least you're behind the wheel and starting to cover some serious ground. Hang in there; it only gets better from here.

LOOPS & RECORDING

2

In this chapter, you'll be using the same Learning PT session that you created in Chapter 1. You'll download and import some drum loops from the Internet and learn how easy it is to import audio into Pro Tools.

After we place the drum loops into the session, we will learn how to resize and move tracks around. We will also take a brief look at the Mix screen and then repeat our one-bar drum loops to make 50 bars so that we have more audio to work with. We'll then begin an introduction to recording. Our final exercise will teach you how to record using punch-in and punch-out settings, so you can correct any mistakes made during recording.

The Upside of Downloading

You should always keep the Internet connected to your Pro Tools computer. The Internet's resources are invaluable when you need to update your software, find answers to technical questions, and download drum loops. You can even use interactive applications to work with other musicians.

Current music is all about the use of drum loops. It's important to understand how to work with loops, how to import and duplicate them, and eventually how to create your own custom loops. If you're going to be recording using Bars and Beats like a professional, it's so much easier to play your guitar or keyboard parts to real drum loops as opposed to a typical static metronome that only clicks on each quarter note. Drum loops can also be a great source of inspiration when you're writing songs. In the first exercise you'll be downloading some loops. If you already have some loops on your hard drive you can use them instead, but this exercise will teach you some other skills as well, so it's worth going through it.

EXERCISE 1:
Download Loops

1] **Hide Pro Tools.** In the Pro Tools menu (Mac), choose Hide Pro Tools. In Windows, minimize it by clicking the horizontal line button in the top right corner.

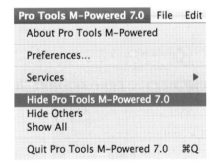

2] **Open your Web browser.** In the Internet location field, type this Web address (known as a URL): "www.protoolsformusicians.com" and press Return (Mac) or Enter (Win).

3] **Download the loops.** On the Pro Tools for Musicians website, there is a section called "Chapter 2 Downloads." Click the icon to the left of Chapter2Loops.zip to download the file.

On a Mac, this file will automatically download to your designated download folder or to your desktop. In Windows, you'll get a window asking you whether to open this file or save it. I always choose to save because I like to keep copies of the files I download. Choose to save this file to your Audio Drive. After the files download, choose to Open Folder. You'll be directed to the Audio Drive and see the downloaded file.

4] **Hide or quit your browser.** We no longer need the browser—but it's a good idea to bookmark this Web page or make it a Favorite because we'll be downloading other files from this same page. Then quit or hide your browser.

5] **Locate the downloaded file.** Windows users, if you chose Open Folder in Step 3, you'll see Chapter2Loops.zip on your audio drive. Mac users will find the file already uncompressed on the desktop if you're using Safari. You can skip the next step if the zip file is already uncompressed.

"What's a .sit or .zip file?"

A file with the filename extension .sitx, .sit, or .zip is a file that's compressed. Compression can be used to make a file smaller, to keep files organized together, and to keep file contents from getting corrupted in transit. When you write a letter on several 8½ x 11" sheets of paper, you fold them all up to fit into one envelope. In this case, numerous drum loops have been folded into one file, which saves disk space and download time by allowing you to download one compressed file as opposed to three uncompressed drum loops.

You uncompress a file using StuffIt Expander or WinZip (Windows only). Windows users can also right-click on the .zip file in Windows Explorer and choose Explore. Just double-click the compressed file, and Stuffit or WinZip should automatically launch and uncompress it. If that doesn't happen, launch the application and choose Open from the File menu. You'll learn how to create .sit and .zip files in Chapter 12.

6] **Uncompress the files.** Mac users, if you have a Chapter2Loops.zip file on your desktop, double-click it to uncompress it using Stuffit Expander and copy the uncompressed Loops folder to your Audio Drive. You should delete this file from your desktop after copying it.

Windows users should right click on the Chapter2Loops.zip file and choose Extract to Here. This will unzip this file and create an unzipped folder in the same place you are in, which should be the root directory of your audio drive.

EXERCISE 2:
Import Loops into Pro Tools

You'll have to import these loops in order to play them.

1]

Import the loops. If you haven't already, go back to Pro Tools. Go to the File menu and choose Import > Audio to Track.

➤ **IMPORT AUDIO:**
  Reference Guide, p. 122

2]

Locate the loops. An Import Audio window opens and wants to know, "OK, where is the audio you want to import?" Choose your external audio drive/Learning PT/Chapter 2 Loops folder. You should see the folder selected with a list of files inside of it.

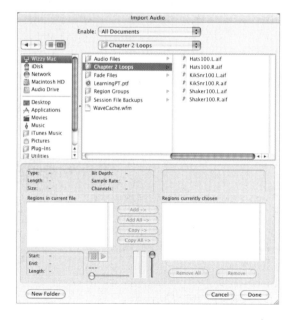

3] **Import all the loops.** You don't need to import these one at a time. To get them all at once, hold the Shift key and click every loop in the list. Make sure every loop is highlighted. On the Mac, at the bottom of the window, you'll see four buttons: Add, Add All, Copy, and Copy All. Click Copy All. In Windows, there are two buttons: Add Files and Copy Files. Click Copy All or Copy Files. This will put all the highlighted loops into the right side of the window with the word *Copy* next to them. Click Done.

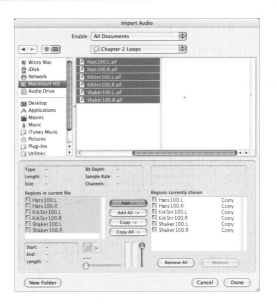

4] **Copy the loops into your Audio Files folder.** A Choose Folder window comes up; it's asking, "OK, where do you want to copy these files?" Pro Tools automatically chooses the Audio Files folder for you. Click Choose (Mac) or Use Current Folder (Win).

"What's with the .L and .R files?"

Notice how each audio file is separated into two parts, as in Shaker100.L and Shaker100.R. Even though Pro Tools records in stereo, it doesn't create stereo files. Instead it creates what's called Multiple Mono or Dual Mono files, which are really two separate files—one for the left channel and one for the right. Additionally, when you import a stereo file, Pro Tools will separate it into two pieces, as you see here.

EXERCISE 2: IMPORT LOOPS INTO PRO TOOLS **25**

5] **View your new tracks.** Besides your click track, you now have three additional tracks. Your Mix and Edit windows should look like this:

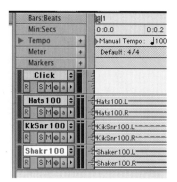

Edit window

Mix window

6] **Play the tracks.** Click the play button in the Transport window or press the spacebar, and you should hear one bar of the drum loop.

EXERCISE 3:

Resize and Move Tracks

These new tracks are probably very small in your Edit window. Let's resize them to make them larger so it's easier to see the audio waveforms. Tracks are much easier to edit if you can see clearly what you're doing. This exercise also helps you learn the important skill of moving tracks to better organize your sessions.

1] **Click the Resize ruler.** In the Edit window, there's a small vertical ruler that you can use to resize the tracks. It's at the left of the beginning of each waveform and to the right of the track name. Click on that ruler and you'll see a list of track size options.

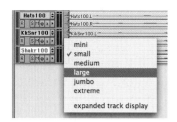

2] **Change the track size.** Set the Hats100 track to large.

➤ **TRACK HEIGHT:** *Reference Guide, p. 224*

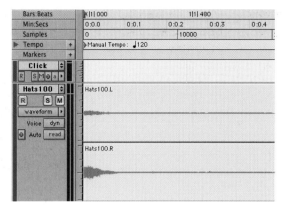

3] **Resize all tracks.** Holding down the Option key (Mac) or Alt key (Win) while resizing a single track changes all tracks to the size you choose. Do that now: Option-click or Alt-click any track's Resize ruler and choose medium to set the view of all tracks to medium size.

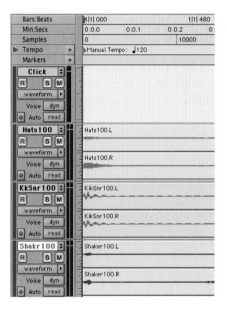

The Option Key (Mac) or Alt Key (PC)

The Option key on the Mac and the Alt key for Windows users are important in Pro Tools. These keys serve quite a few functions. For example, holding down Option or Alt when you change a setting on a track will make that change to every track. Hold Option or Alt and click the letter M (for mute) on one track, and all tracks will be muted. Click again to unmute the tracks. Option-clicking or Alt-clicking will reset any fader or slider to its default setting, as we did in Chapter 1 to reset the volume slider.

4] **Move tracks.** Let's put the KikSnr100 track below the Click track. In either the Mix or Edit window, click on the KikSnr100 track name and hold down your mouse button. Now drag the track in between Click and Hats100, until you see a faint dashed line. Release the mouse button, and your KikSnr100 track is repositioned between the Click and Hats100 tracks. It may take a little practice to get the hang of this, so keep trying if the track doesn't move at first. Remember to look for the faint little line.

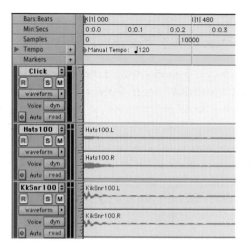

After you've moved the track, your Edit window should look like this:

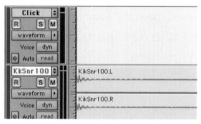

5] **Move multiple tracks.** You can move multiple tracks by holding the Shift key and clicking the track names of all the tracks you want to move, to highlight them. Then click and hold one of the highlighted track names and drag it; they'll all move. Move all three loops above the Click track now.

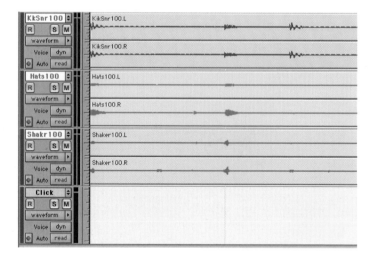

EXERCISE 4:
Mute, Solo, Pan, and Volume

Let's get more familiar with the channel strips in the Mix window. Each channel strip has the same controls down in the lower half. The large slider controls the track's volume. The S button above that will solo this track (play this track by itself). The M button is for mute, which turns this track's audio off. The R button will enable the track to record.

Above the buttons are two numeric fields topped by two small sliders. These fields and sliders are for controlling your *panning* levels. The top tiny slider controls the panning for the left channel, and the one below controls the right channel. When both sliders are panned as far as they can go, it means that the track will have the widest possible stereo image.

1]
Select and maximize the Mix window.
You should see four tracks, as shown here.

Notice that the first three volume sliders have two black lines to the right of them and two panning sliders above—except for the Click track, which has only one indicator and one slider. This tells you that every loop track is stereo and the Click track is mono.

2] **Solo one track.** Let's solo the Shaker track—click the S button. Notice that this automatically mutes the other tracks. Now press the space-bar to play and hear the shaker alone. Click the S button again to unsolo the track. You can solo as many tracks as you want.

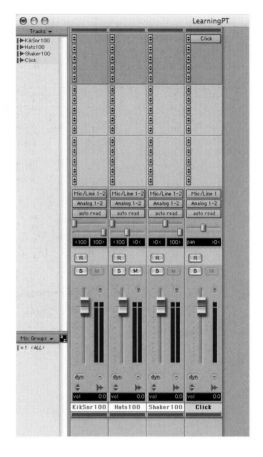

3] **Pan tracks.** Next, try panning the hi-hat track a bit to the left, and then pan the shaker a bit to the right. In the Hats100 channel strip, drag the lower (right channel) slider to the middle; or Option-click (Mac)/Alt-click (Win) it to make the slider jump there automatically. In the Shaker100 channel strip, set the upper (left channel) slider to the middle.

4] **Mute a track.** Let's also mute the Click track—just click the M button to turn off the audio.

5] **Adjust volume.** Play your tracks, and drag the volume slider for each channel strip to suit your own preferences.

EXERCISE 5:
Repeat Audio Loops

We imported three one-bar drum loops, right? That's not much to work with, so now we're going to repeat them in the Edit window to give ourselves more bars. The first step is using the necessary tool: the Grabber.

1] **Choose the Grabber tool.** To turn your cursor into the Grabber tool, click the hand icon at the top of the Edit window or hit F8 on your keyboard. The hand is part of a row of icons that represent your Edit tools, which we'll cover in depth in Chapter 3.

2] **Select all tracks.** Using the Grabber in the Edit window, click the first loop's waveform, which will highlight it. Now hold the Shift key and click each one of your other loops until they're all highlighted.

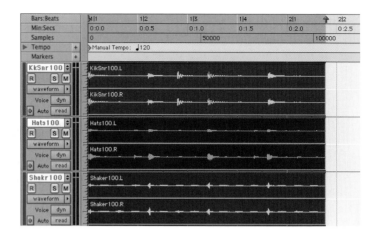

3] **Repeat all tracks.** Go to the Edit menu and choose Repeat. The shortcut is Option+R (Mac) or Alt+R (Win).

4] **Choose the number of repeats.** A small window comes up asking you how many times you want to repeat these highlighted waveforms. Type in "50" and click OK.

5] **Zoom out.** You now have 51 bars of drums loops, but you probably can't see them—you need to zoom out. To zoom out and see an entire song, simply press Option+A (Mac) or Alt+A (Win). You should see all 51 bars now.

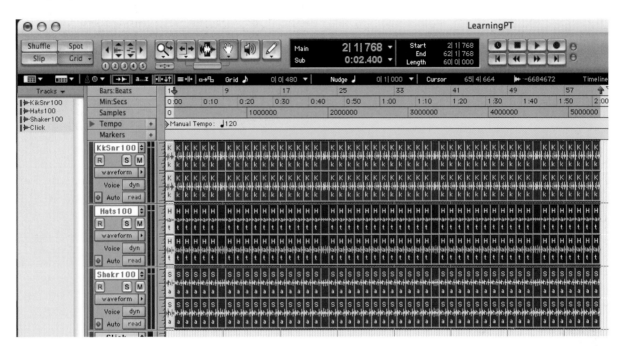

6] **Rewind and play.** Press Return (Mac) or Enter (Win). This moves your cursor to the beginning of the song. Press the spacebar to play. You should now hear 51 bars—almost two minutes of a loop to play to.

Intro to Recording

Now that we have an extended rhythm track to work with, we're going to plug in a microphone or instrument and learn how to record by playing or singing along with the drum loop.

Plug a microphone or instrument into the first input of your Pro Tools interface. Make sure you're plugged into Input 1—if you're using an Mbox, it's labeled Source 1. If you're using a microphone, please use a professional microphone cable. If you're plugging in a guitar or keyboard, a 1/4" cable is best.

Make sure that you've chosen the correct input setting on your interface or mic pre. For example, on an Mbox you can choose Mic, Line, or Instrument. On an M-Audio FireWire 410, the choices are simply Mic or Line. It's pretty straightforward: If you have a mic, set it to Mic, and if you have an instrument, set it to Instrument or Line.

Using an External Mic Pre

Although the Digidesign and M-Audio built-in mic preamplifiers are very good, they are obviously not of the same quality you'd find in a state-of-the-art console. However, you can buy mono and stereo mic pres that are exactly like having one or two channels of a Neve or API console. If you're serious about creating professional music, you may want to invest in an external mic pre for vocals and other important tracks that require a more pristine sound. There are some great boutique audio companies making affordable Class A mic pre's, including Brent Averill, Daking, Universal Audio, Grace Design, Langevin and Manley, and API.

If you're going to use an external mic pre, here are the steps for connecting it to your Pro Tools interface:

1. Connect the microphone into the external mic pre and make sure you are getting level—meaning the mic is picking up sound. (Most professional mic pres come with a level meter.)

2. Connect the output of the external mic pre to Input 1 of your Pro Tools interface.

3. Set your interface to Line input, not to Mic.

EXERCISE 6:

Prepare to Record

The first thing to do before you record is create the track or tracks you're going to record to. In this case, we need one mono audio track.

1] **Make a new track.** In the Track menu, choose New; or use the shortcut ⌘+Shift+N (Mac) or Ctrl+Shift+N (Win). In the New Tracks dialog box that pops up, select 1 mono audio track and click Create.

2] **Resize your tracks.** It's always a good idea to enlarge the track you're working with and reduce the size of others. Go to the Edit window and reduce the size of the loops' tracks to make them small. Remember that you can use the Option or Alt key to make them all small at once.

Now make the new audio track large.

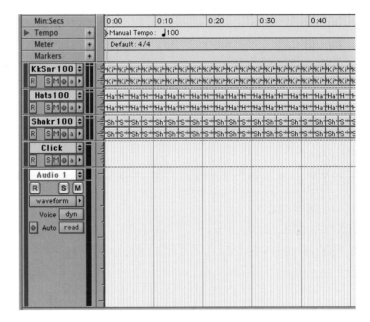

3] **Name your new track.** Double-click on the track name in either the Edit or Mix window, and call it "Testing."

4] **Set the input.** You can't start recording until you've set up your input in Pro Tools. In the Mix window, above the small panning sliders on every channel strip, you'll see three buttons. From top to bottom, these buttons are the Input, Output, and Automation settings (those last two you'll learn about later).

Make sure your mic or instrument is plugged into the first input of the Pro Tools interface and that the interface's input is set to either Mic or Line. Then choose Mic/Line 1 in the Input settings.

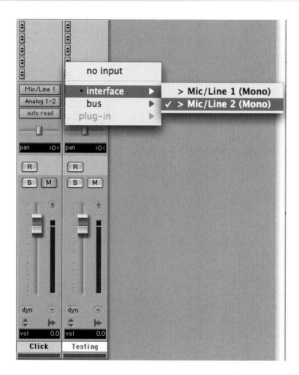

5] **Put your track in Record mode.** You might want to turn down your speakers and put on some headphones at this point. If you put a track in Record with the speakers up and a mic connected, you could be the victim of painful feedback.

On the Testing channel strip in the Mix window, click on the R button to record-enable this track. The R will turn red, and you should now see level on your channel strip.

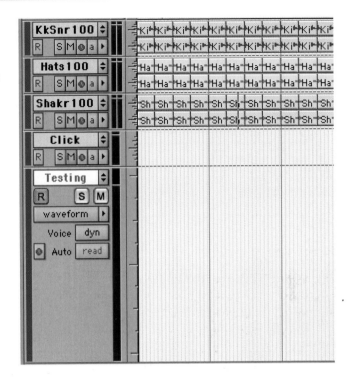

"I don't have any %#!^@#$& volume level!"

If for some reason you don't see a recording level when your track is in Record, here's a troubleshooting list to help you figure out the problem:

◆ Double-check your connections. Make sure the input you set in Pro Tools is the same input you're plugged into.

◆ Does your microphone need phantom power? Some mics, specifically condenser microphones, require an additional 48 volts of power in order to work. All external mic preamps and most Pro Tools interfaces provide a 48V switch. Look for the 48V button on your Mbox, M-Audio interface, 002 Rack, or mic pre, and make sure the button is pressed in if you have a mic that requires phantom power.

◆ Make sure that you've selected the correct input source on your Pro Tools interface or mic pre.

◆ Keep in mind that your computer's system preferences, control panels, and internal sound settings do not affect the operation of Pro Tools. Pro Tools uses its own drivers and its own hardware.

6] **Set your recording (input) level.** Whether you're using an external mic pre or one built into your Pro Tools interface, the Input knob on your mic pre is what affects the level being recorded. The fader volume in the Mix window has no impact on the recording level; it affects only what you hear (the output volume), not what you are recording. The colored strip to the right of the volume slider is what shows your input level. As you talk or sing, the lights rise through green and yellow and into red.

Turn your mic pre's Input knob up or down until you have a good amount of level—without hitting the red peak indicator. As a rule, a healthy level is in the yellow area.

Caution

Try to avoid the red peaks whenever possible. A red peak doesn't necessarily mean that a track will be distorted, but to be safe, keep the peaks down to a minimum. If you do hit a red peak, lower the input level and click on the red peak indicator to reset it.

7] **Compensate for latency.** Speak into your mic or play a few notes—if you notice a delay while monitoring the input live, that's called *latency*. Latency is caused by the time it takes an audio signal to pass through the computer. It's usually a problem only when you're recording. You can reduce it by adjusting the Playback Engine settings.

Go to the Setup menu and select Playback Engine. In the dialog box, set the Buffer Size to 256 if you're using an Mbox, or 128 if you're using an M-Audio interface. As a rule, choose the lowest setting you can for recording. You should increase the setting only if the sound coming from Pro Tools starts to break up. This can happen at low latency settings if the computer is being forced to work too hard.

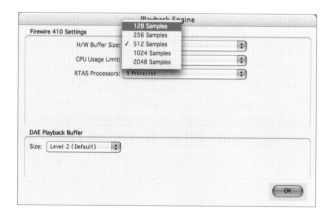

➤ **LATENCY:** *Reference Guide, p. 156-157*

8] **Adjust the count-in.** *Count-in* (which Pro Tools calls "Countoff") is the number of bars you want Pro Tools to click before starting to record. The default is two bars, so when you begin recording, you'll hear two bars of click and then Pro Tools will record.

Open the Transport window and double-click the metronome icon. This opens the Click/Countoff Options window. See at the very bottom? This is where you tell Pro Tools how many bars of count-in you want, and whether count-in should occur all the time or only during recording.

You're now ready to record.

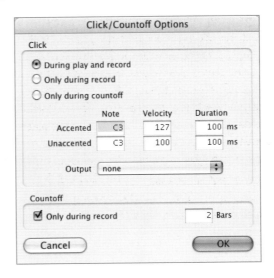

The Playback Engine

The Playback Engine is the part of the Pro Tools application that controls how much of your computer's processing power to designate for playback. The Playback Engine is found under the Setup menu.

◆ H/W Buffer Size. The hardware buffer size tells Pro Tools how much of the hardware to use for functions such as recording or using plug-ins. You should always set it to the lowest setting while recording and to the highest level when mixing. A lower hardware buffer setting reduces the amount of delay that you hear in your headphones; a larger setting allows you to use more plug-ins.

◆ CPU Usage Limit is where you tell Pro Tools to use as much (or as little) of your computer's power as possible. I keep mine up to the max setting, which allows me to run larger sessions with many tracks and also to use more plug-ins. The maximum value for CPU Usage will depend on which Pro Tools system you are using, and whether you are using a single- or multiprocessor computer.

◆ DAE Playback Buffer lets you set the amount of memory that Pro Tools uses to access your hard drive (DAE stands for digital audio engine). A simple rule is to always leave this set to Level 2, the default.

EXERCISE 7:

Record Your Track

1] **Start recording.** Make sure that you are starting at the beginning of the song by pressing Return or Enter, and then press ⌘+spacebar (Mac) or Ctrl+spacebar (Win) to record. Your track should start turning red and you'll see the waveforms created as you record, indicating that recording is occurring.

Say "Test 1 2 3," or record anything you choose.

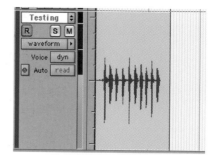

2] **Stop recording.** Press the spacebar (just the spacebar, without ⌘ or Ctrl) to stop recording.

3] **Play it back.** Hit Return or Enter to go back to the beginning of your tracks; then press spacebar to play back what you recorded. There's no need to disable Record mode in the track to listen to it.

4] **Record take 2.** Press ⌘+spacebar or Ctrl+spacebar again, and record over what you previously recorded.

You get the idea. Spend a bit of time recording a few takes. If you do something you like, be sure to save (⌘/Ctrl + S or choose Save in the File menu).

5] **Add a new track.** Press ⌘/Ctrl + Shift + N (or choose File > New Tracks). Create a new mono audio track. In the Edit window, make the size large, and name it "Testing 2." In the Mix window, set the Input button to Mic/Line 1, and click the R button to enable recording.

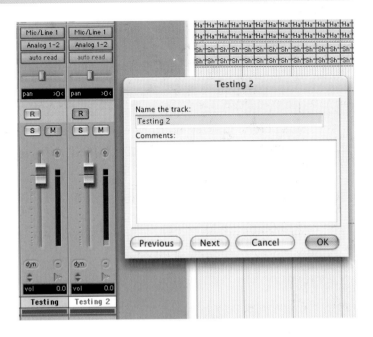

6] **Record another track.** Press ⌘+spacebar or Ctrl+spacebar to record in the new track. You can choose to mute your previous track (click the M button in the track's Mix channel strip), or keep it playing and play along with it.

Practice making some other new tracks and setting the correct input until you are comfortable with the process of creating new tracks and recording takes.

Tip

Pearl of Wisdom: If you're really serious about learning Pro Tools, then you must start memorizing and using keyboard shortcuts. In the Help menu, there is a guide showing all of the keyboard shortcuts in Pro Tools.

Help
DigiBase Guide...
DigiRack Plug-Ins Guide...
Keyboard Shortcuts...
Digidesign FAQ...
Pro Tools Menus Guide...
Pro Tools Reference Guide...

Note to Mac Users: Recording in Tiger

For Mac users in OS 10.4 ("Tiger"), ⌘+spacebar is now the default for opening Spotlight (Apple's search engine) and overrides the Pro Tools shortcut to enable recording. When you first install Pro Tools 7, you are warned that certain Tiger key commands must be turned off.

To turn off the Spotlight key command, go to System Preferences > Spotlight. At the bottom of the Spotlight window, you can assign a keyboard shortcut for the Spotlight menu.

Click inside the field and type a keystroke of your choice. Be sure not to change it to one of your F keys, because you're also going to need those for Pro Tools. I changed mine to Control+S.

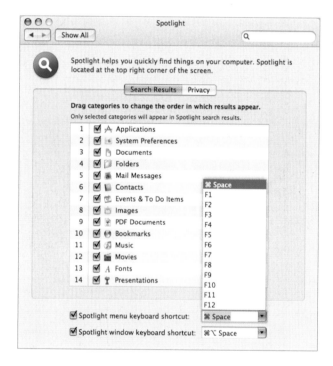
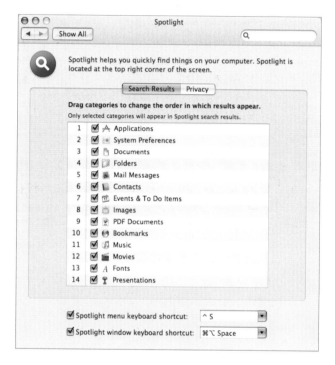

Listening with Auto Input or Input Only Monitoring

When recording, you have two choices for hearing what you record: Auto Input and Input Only Monitoring.

In the Track menu, you'll see the option called Input Only Monitoring. You should leave this *unchecked* most of the time. When Input Only Monitoring is *not* checked, you are using the default, called Auto Input.

Auto Input Monitoring means that you'll hear what is playing back on a track until you begin recording; then Pro Tools will automatically go into Input, and then you'll hear what you're recording. If a track is in Record (the Record button on a track is red) and then you play the song without pressing the Record button on the Transport, you'll hear what's on the track (if anything) and not what you are recording. In Auto Input, you *must* press Record in order to hear what you are recording.

Auto Input Monitoring is used when you're punching in (which we'll do in Exercise 8). Pro Tools will play back the track to the point where you're punching in, and then you'll hear the input of what you're recording until you punch out. Then you'll hear the recorded track again from the point where you punched out.

Input Only Monitoring means that if a track is in Record and you press play, you will *not* hear what is playing back on the track. You will only hear what is coming into the input.

Input Only is useful when you're setting levels before recording and you don't want to waste disk space by recording while you're setting the levels. So you put your track in Record, set Pro Tools to Input Only Monitoring, and press play, *not* record. Then you'll hear the musician or singer without recording the audio. This way you can set your levels or get your sounds before recording. When you are ready to record, set Pro Tools back to Auto Input.

EXERCISE 8:

Punch In and Punch Out Manually

Nobody's perfect, so it's a good thing you can go back and re-record over mistakes. This is known as *punching in* and *punching out*.

1] **Enable QuickPunch.** In the Options menu, you'll find an option called QuickPunch. Make sure it's checked. This is the *only* setting you need to enable punch-in and punch-out.

QuickPunch allows you to use ⌘+spacebar (Mac) or Ctrl+spacebar (Win) to punch in and out while a track is playing back.

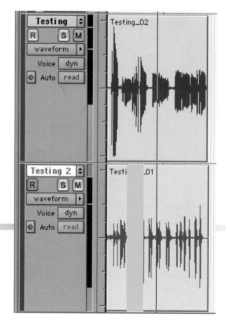

2] **Punch in.** Put one of your Testing tracks into Record. Rewind to the top of the song, and press spacebar to play. When the track plays to the spot you want to record over, press ⌘+spacebar or Ctrl+spacebar to punch in and begin recording. As you play, sing, or otherwise make noise, you can see the track turn red from the spot where you punched in and onward.

➤ **PUNCH RECORDING:**
Reference Guide, p. 176

3] **Punch out.** Press ⌘+spacebar or Ctrl+space-bar again when you're ready to punch out. Your song will continue to play, and only the portion of the track between where you punched in and punched out will be red.

4] **Punch in and out again.** Using either the same track or an additional track, perfect your recording by punching in and out as you need to. And get comfortable with the ⌘+spacebar/Ctrl+spacebar shortcut!

You may have noticed in this exercise that every time you punch in and out manually, Pro Tools creates a new audio region. Punching manually creates audio file on top of audio file, and causes pops and clicks and many problems if you punch in too many times. Fortunately, Pro Tools offers *automated punching,* which lets you punch into the exact same spot as many times as you need without creating overlapping audio regions.

EXERCISE 9:
Automated Punch-In and Punch-Out

Automated punching is a far better and more professional method than using manual punching, for several reasons. Often it's much faster and more accurate to tell Pro Tools where you want to punch in and out and then let it do the punching for you. And, of course, if you're playing your own parts while simultaneously engineering, it's physically impossible to play guitar and punch at the same time. Or if you're running in and out of the studio to go into a vocal booth to sing, manual punching can be quite a challenge.

Before you can use automated punch, you'll need to do a little bit of setup.

Note

Pre-roll and post-roll are studio terms from back in the old days when they would literally roll tape. When musicians needed to hear more of the music before they punched in to record, they would say, "Hey, gimme a little more pre-roll."

1] **Set pre-roll and post-roll.** Pre-roll is the number of bars Pro Tools will play before punching in, and post-roll is the number of bars it plays after punching out. Open the Transport window; in the bottom-left corner you'll see the pre-roll and post-roll fields. Since we're using Pro Tools in Bars and Beats mode, both these fields are in Bars and Beats as well. (I'll explain more about Bars and Beats in Chapter 3.)

Click on the first number in the pre-roll time field, type "2," and press Return or Enter. You *must* press Return or Enter, or the new number will not remain. Now you have created a two-bar pre-roll. Do the same thing in the post-roll field below, and create a two-bar post-roll. Make sure the pre-roll and post-roll indicators to the left of the fields in the Transport window are highlighted.

Tip

The keyboard shortcut to turn pre- and post-roll on and off is ⌘+K (Mac) or Ctrl+K (Win).

2] **Get the Selector tool.** You can click on it once or use F7 to activate the Selector. This is the most frequently used tool in Pro Tools.

3] **Set your punch-in point.** To tell Pro Tools where to punch in, go to the Edit window and simply click with the Selector tool on the spot in your track where you want to punch in.

4] **Record.** You first hear two bars of what you previously recorded, and then the track will begin recording. Since you did not yet specify a punch-out point, Pro Tools will keep recording to the end of the song or until you manually punch out.

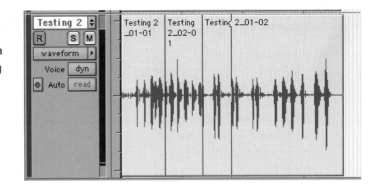

5] **Set your punch-out point.** Using the Selector tool, click and drag in the track from your punch-in point to your punch-out point. The portion of the track where you are going to record is now highlighted.

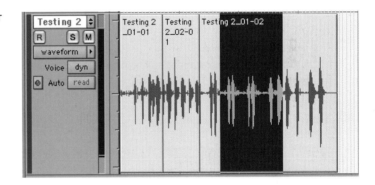

6] **Record.** Press ⌘+spacebar or Ctrl+spacebar to record. You'll hear two bars of your previously recorded track. Then Pro Tools will punch in, record until your punch-out point, and then play two more bars of your recorded track.

7] **Save.** Press ⌘+S or Ctrl+S, or choose File > Save to save your session.

8] **Close the session.** After you've saved your Pro Tools session, close it by either choosing File > Close Session or using the shortcut ⌘+Shift+W (Mac) or Ctrl+Shift+W (Win). Pro Tools remains open but with no session loaded—the big empty window you started with.

A Cautionary Word About Closing Pro Tools Sessions

In order to open another session or to make a new one, you *must* first close any open session. Pro Tools does not allow multiple sessions to be open at the same time. There's a right way and a wrong way to do this.

So many who are new to computers think that closing their Internet browser window or closing a document also closes the related program. In the Macintosh, it doesn't. It leaves the program open, using your computer's memory to no purpose. It's like turning your washer and dryer on without putting any clothes inside, wasting energy and water. When you're done using any program, always quit or exit. Most every application made, including Pro Tools, supports ⌘+Q or Ctrl+Q to quit.

When using Pro Tools, there will be many times when you won't want to Quit but want to simply close the song or session so you can open another one or start a new one. But watch out: If you close *both* the Mix and Edit windows in Pro Tools, it will close the session and ask you if you want to Save. Do *not* get in the habit of closing sessions this way. Try to always close your sessions from the File menu or using the shortcut ⌘+Shift+W (Mac) or Ctrl+Shift+W (Win).

Why? There are two reasons: First, closing windows to exit is in general a bad habit when you're using any program. Second, the next time you open the Pro Tools session, the only window you'll see is the last window that you closed. So if you have your Mix and Edit windows set up as you like them and then you close your session by closing windows, the session isn't going to look the way you want it to when you next open it. Trust me—close your sessions from the File menu.

Wrap Up

The absolute best way to learn Pro Tools is by repetition. Create a few new tracks. Record or punch in and out. Become comfortable with the process of recording.

Start learning your keyboard shortcuts, too—or keep a cheat sheet next to your computer until you have them memorized. In the next chapter, we'll work our way toward editing.

THE EDIT WINDOW

3

The majority of your time in Pro Tools will be spent in the Edit window. This chapter gives you a brief overview of this window and gets you familiar with the Edit modes and Edit tools. We'll download and import a few new drum samples as we explore the Edit window's functionality. At the same time, we'll begin to delve into Bars and Beats using Grid mode, and start using the Edit modes and tools to place a few drum samples at the correct beats in order to create a custom drum loop.

Import Audio a New Way

In Pro Tools, there are often several ways to perform similar functions. Just as you may sometimes take the highway to get home, and sometimes the back way, both routes get you where you're going—but they serve different purposes, as well. As you continue working with Pro Tools, gradually you'll begin to understand which functions to use when.

There are a few different ways to import audio into Pro Tools, so this time we'll use another method: importing to the Region bin.

1] **Launch Pro Tools.** You should have just the big empty window we started with in Chapter 1. If you already have a Pro Tools session open, save and close the session (rember the ⌘/Alt+Shift+W shortcut).

2] **Download and uncompress new samples.** With Pro Tools open, start your Web browser, go to www.protoolsformusicians.com, and click on the Chapter 3 link. Control-click or right-click to download Chapter3Samples.zip. As always, make sure you know the destination location to which you're downloading these files.

Uncompress the file; you'll have a folder containing five samples.

3] **Make a new session.** Go back to Pro Tools (you can quit or hide your Web browser if you like), and select File > New Session or use ⌘+N or Ctrl+N. Name your session "Chapter3Tutorial."

To make things fast and simple, we're going to use the default tempo of 120, but feel free to change the tempo in the Transport window to anything you want. Remember that you have to turn off the Conductor icon in order to type in a tempo.

4] **Import to the Region bin.** Go to the File menu. Under Import, choose Import Audio to Region List. The shortcut is ⌘+Shift+I (Mac) or Ctrl+Shift+I (Win). This places your imported audio into the Region bin, but it's up to you to create a track and place the audio regions at the correct places.

Remember, last time we imported audio files, we used the command File > Import Audio to Track. Either way, the same Import Audio window opens.

5] **Choose the samples to import.** We've seen this window once before, and it's asking the same question: "Where are the files?" Find where you downloaded your Chapter3Samples folder, and import all five samples by holding down the Shift key and selecting them all. When all five samples are in the bottom-left window (Regions in Current File), click the bottom button, Copy All.

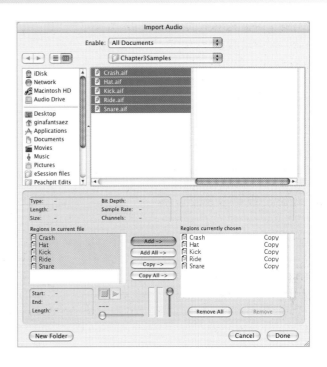

6] **Choose a folder.** When you choose Copy All, as opposed to Add All, Pro Tools makes a copy of the audio you're importing and then conveniently places the copied files into your Audio Files folder. So now you just tell Pro Tools where to put the copies.

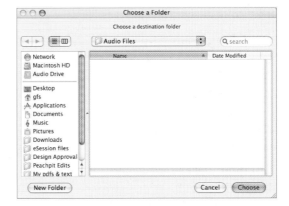

Warning

If you had chosen Add All rather than Copy All, Pro Tools would not make a copy but would use the samples where you put them on your drive. Using Add All can be very dangerous, because your audio files will be in various folders on your hard drive rather than inside the Audio Files folder where they should be. So get in the habit of choosing Copy when you import; it's best never to use Add All.

7] **Find the samples in the Region bin.** You'll now see all five samples in the Region bin.

If you don't see the Region bin in the Edit window, click the tiny arrow at the lower right-hand corner of the window.

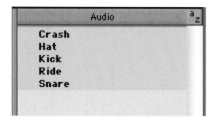

The Edit Window Explained

Now that we have some samples to work with, let's learn how we begin editing.

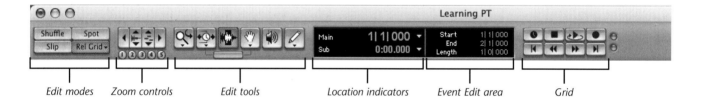

The most important items in the Edit window are the four Edit modes and six Edit tools. To start learning to edit, you'll need to first understand these modes and tools. Let's start with the Edit tools.

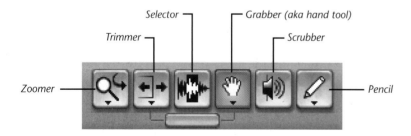

EXERCISE 2:
Use the Zoomer

1] **Create one new track.** Create one new mono audio track (you *have* memorized the shortcut ⌘+Shift+N/Ctrl+Shift+N by now, right?) Make sure you set it to Ticks, and name it "Kick."

Here's a shortcut for this step and Step 3: Make sure the kick sample is the only one highlighted in the Region bin, and drag it to the Tracks list. This will create a track with the correct name and place the audio at bar 1, beat 1. If you do this, you'll need to set the track to Ticks by clicking the track's Time Base selector button.

2] **Make it jumbo size.** Click on the Track Height selector beside the Kick track and choose jumbo.

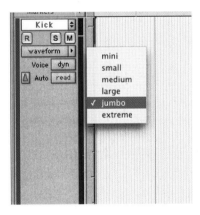

3] **Drag the sample to the Edit window.**
In the Region bin on the right side of the
Edit window, you'll see the five drum samples.
Click the kick sample and drag it to the beginning of your Kick track. Don't worry about
being exact, we'll fix things later. After you
drag the sample to the window, you'll probably barely be able to see it because it's very
small. This is because we're zoomed very far
out and the sample is only one beat long.

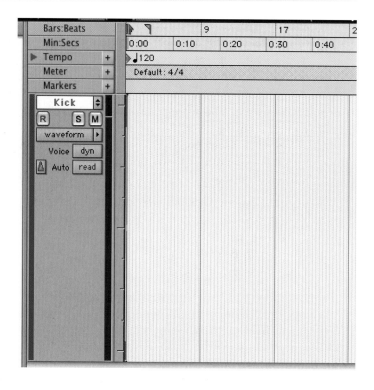

4] **Select the Zoomer.** We're going to use the
Zoomer tool (aka the magnifying glass) first.
Click and hold on the magnifying glass icon,
and you'll see two menu options, Normal
Zoom and Single Zoom. Normal Zoom means
that when you activate the Zoomer, you'll be
using the Zoomer until you choose another
tool. Single Zoom lets you use the Zoomer
tool once, and then it automatically switches
back to whatever tool you were using before.
To practice with the Zoomer, you may want to
leave it set to Normal Zoom; after you become
more comfortable with the tool, you'll begin
to appreciate Single Zoom.

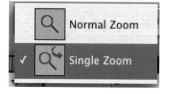

5] **Zoom in.** Make sure the Zoomer tool is selected and that your cursor is now a magnifying glass. Clicking with the Zoomer will zoom in one level each time you click. That's pretty imprecise, so I always tell new users to draw a box with the Zoomer around the area they want to Zoom into. Also, it's a good idea to develop the habit of dragging from right to left rather than left to right. You'll find it's just much easier that way.

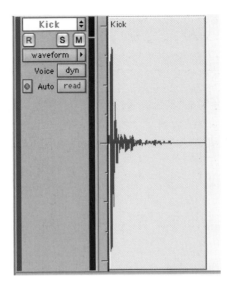

Using the Zoomer, click and hold and drag from Bar 9 to Bar 1. You'll see the faint lines of a box being created by the Zoomer tool. When you let go of the mouse button, Pro Tools zooms into that boxed area.

Note

Below the Zoomer tool, notice the small button with tiny up-and-down and left-and-right arrows—that's the Zoom Toggle. It's hard to show you how Zoom Toggle works with only one track, so we'll save Zoom Toggle for a later chapter when we have more tracks to work with.

6] **Zoom out.** Make sure the Zoomer is selected. To Zoom out, hold the Option (Mac) or Alt (Win) key and notice that the magnifying glass cursor now has a minus (–) sign (it's normally a plus sign). Clicking while holding Option/Alt will zoom out one level each time you click.

Tip

Shortcut: You can also zoom in using the keyboard shortcut ⌘+] (Mac) or Ctrl+] (Win), and zoom out using ⌘+[(Mac) or Ctrl+[(Win). As I've mentioned, it's a good idea to get in the habit now of using these shortcuts. Zooming in and out is something you will do constantly, and it's generally much faster to hit ⌘+] or Ctrl+] rather than choosing the Zoomer tool and dragging.

7] **The Zoom settings.** To the left of the Edit tools are the Zoom settings. The left arrow zooms out. The right arrow zooms in. The up arrow increases the size of the audio waveform, and the down arrow decreases it. Play with each setting to get familiar with it (but I still prefer to use the keyboard shortcuts ⌘+[and Ctrl+[, and ⌘+] and Ctrl+]).

8] **The Zoom Presets.** The five tiny buttons below the Zoom settings are the Zoom Presets. With these you can save the way a track is zoomed, so you can go back to specific zoom settings. To create a Zoom Preset, find a zoom setting that you like, hold down the ⌘ or Ctrl key, and click on any preset number. To recall that zoom anytime, just click on the preset number.

9] **Zoom out to view entire song.** To zoom out in order to see an entire song, double-click on the Zoomer.

I use this command constantly throughout editing. You may notice that when you double-click on the Zoomer, you see our one Kick sample zoomed in close up. Since our song only consists only of that one beat right now, you're seeing the entire song, which is a one-beat kick drum sample. This double-click Zoomer command will come in handy when we have a three-minute song and need to zoom out quickly.

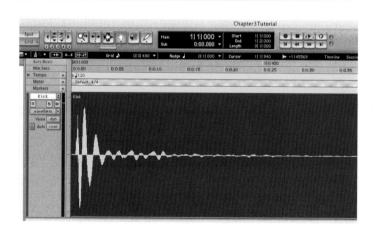

10] **Zoom out again.** Using ⌘+[or Ctrl+[, zoom
out to where you can see at least five or
six bars.

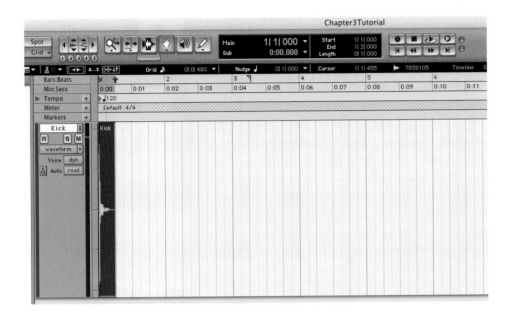

To the right of the Zoomer are five more tools: the Trimmer, the Selector, the Grabber, the
Scrubber, and the Pencil. The tools you'll use primarily while editing are the Selector,
Grabber, Trimmer, and Zoomer.

EXERCISE 3:

Use the Grabber in Grid Mode

We're going to skip the Trimmer and the already familiar Selector for now, and move on to what most users call "the hand tool" but what the Pro Tools manual calls the Grabber. You already used it a bit in Chapter 2, but now you'll see some other things it can do.

Clicking and holding on the Grabber reveals a pull-down menu with the choices Time, Separation, and Object. The standard mode is Time. When you use the Grabber in Time mode, you can move audio regions in time on the same track or drag them to another track. We'll be working with the Time Grabber throughout most of the book.

In case you want to know, Separation mode for the Grabber is used like this: You highlight a portion of an audio region with the Selector, then choose the Separation Grabber, and click your highlighted area. This will make the area into its own separate region. The Object Grabber is used when you need to highlight regions that are not connected, or regions on multiple tracks.

At the top-left of the Edit window are the four Edit modes: Shuffle, Spot, Grid, and Slip. The most common modes for music are Grid and Slip. We'll address the other modes in the last exercise of this chapter, but for this exercise we'll use the Time Grabber tool in conjunction with Grid mode.

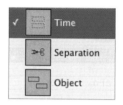

1] **Choose Grid mode.** Click Grid mode. (It might already be selected.)

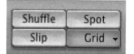

Grid mode is the mode you will use most for arranging and editing music. While in Grid mode, all of your editing will be done to the beat of your specified tempo. The cursor will now only move to exact beats. With Grid mode turned on, whatever you drag into the track will snap to a specified grid, such as quarter notes or eighth notes. Grid mode is especially helpful while creating a song arrangement, giving you the ability to copy and paste sections of your music at specific bar numbers. We will work extensively in Grid mode throughout this book.

2] **Set the grid value.** Below the Edit tools, you will see the setting of your grid value.

Click on the tiny white triangle next to the grid value. A pull-down menu shows you the options for changing your grid to another note value. Let's change it to eighth notes.

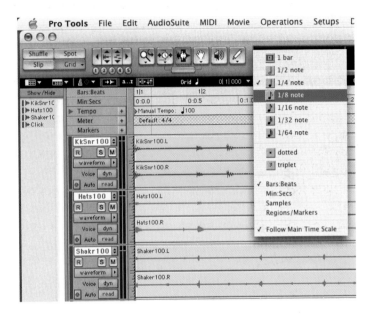

Notice how the grid lines that divide up the Edit window have increased in number. Since your grid value is smaller now, there are more lines or subdivisions of the beats. Change it back to quarter notes, which is the default. Notice the three light-blue lines and the one dark-blue line in each bar? Those lines are showing you where your quarter notes are.

Now that we're in Grid mode with the grid value set to quarter notes, let's move some Kick samples around so you get the hang of using this mode.

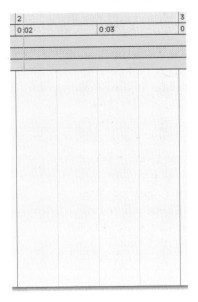

3] **Use the Grabber.** Activate the Grabber, and click the one kick drum sample. Move it anywhere in the track and let go. Drag it again with the Grabber. Notice that the kick can only be placed on exact quarter notes.

4] **Read the location indicators.** To the right of the Edit tools are the location indicators, which tell you where your cursor is in the song. Move the Kick sample to the second blue line from the beginning. This will be seen in the Main location indicator as 1/2/000, which means Bar 1, Beat 2, and zero ticks.

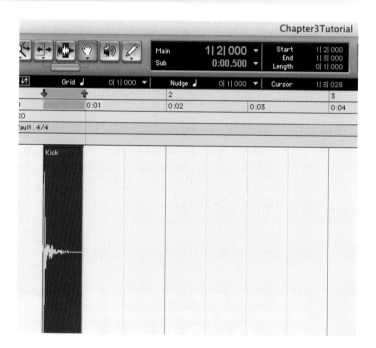

Bars, Beats, and Ticks

When you measure time in your daily life, you use hours/minutes/seconds. If a clock reads 1:30:26, you know that the 1 represents hours, the 30 represents minutes, and 26 is the number of seconds, right? To measure music in Pro Tools, you use bars/beats/ticks. Beats are made up of 960 ticks, so ticks are just a subdivision of one beat.

Here's how it works (if you're in 4/4):

- ◆ 1 bar = 4 beats
- ◆ 960 ticks = 1 quarter note or one beat
- ◆ 240 ticks = 1 sixteenth note
- ◆ 1 beat = 960 Ticks
- ◆ 480 ticks = 1 eighth note

If Pro Tools reads 2/4/480, that translates to Bar 2, the fourth beat, and the second eighth note of that beat. In musical terms, you might call it the "and" of Beat 4 in Bar 2, or perhaps the "eighth-note pickup to Bar 3."

5] **Read the Sub location indicators.** Notice that you also have a Sub location indicator below the Main location indicator. Pro Tools is simply giving you two ways to view your song. My Main location indicator is set to Bars and Beats, and my Sub location indictor is set to Minutes and Seconds (the default settings—just click the arrow to the right of the indicator to change it). With Bars and Beats, I can always tell exactly where I am in a song, while Minutes and Seconds helps me keep track of how long the song is.

6] **Duplicate the Kick sample.** Drag the Kick sample back to Beat 1. Now hold the Option (Mac) or Ctrl key (Win) and drag the kick to Bar 1, Beat 3, or 1/3/000. Hold the Option/Alt key and drag to make a copy of the waveform. Your kick should now look like this:

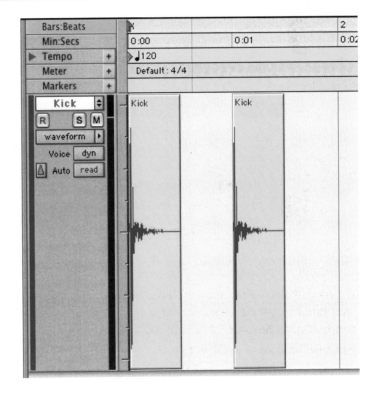

7] **Drag another kick.** From the Region bin, drag another kick sample to the track and place it at 2/1/000. Do it again, dragging another kick to 2/3/000. As you can see, these are two ways of accomplishing the same things. You can Option/Alt-drag a region, or drag more regions from the Region bin. Your Kick track should now look like this:

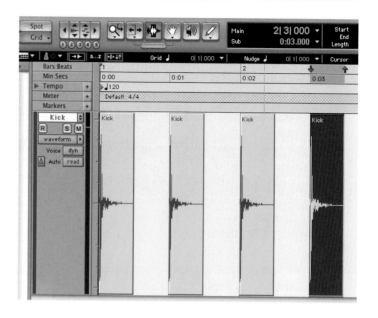

8] **Use the Selector.** Choose the Selector tool and highlight from Bar 1 to Bar 3. It's much easier to click at Bar 3 and drag left than it is to click at Bar 1 and drag right. You should have two bars of the kick highlighted now.

The Selector is the most important Edit tool and the most often used. We'll use it about 80 percent of the time. In this exercise, we'll use it to highlight regions and then copy and paste.

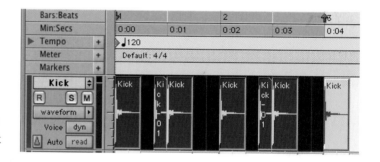

Tip

It's a good habit to always go back to the Selector tool after using any other tool.

9] **Duplicate the kick.** With the two bars of kick highlighted, we'll use the keyboard shortcut ⌘+D (Mac) or Ctrl+D (Win), or the Duplicate command on the Edit menu. The Duplicate command will take whatever is highlighted and place a copy directly behind it. Press ⌘+D or Ctrl+D four times to duplicate the kick. Since you had two bars of kick highlighted and you duplicated these two bars four times, you now have eight bars of kick from Bar 1 through Bar 9.

Note that you could have also used Edit > Repeat as you did in Chapter 2. But I think of using Repeat for something I want to continuously repeat, and Duplicate for something I just need a few copies of rather than many repeats. You can use these two commands interchangeably.

10] **Change the track size.** Now that you're done creating the Kick track, make the track smaller again. Click on the Track Height selector and choose medium.

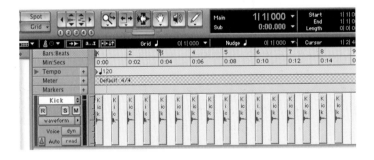

11] **Play the kick and save it.** Press spacebar to play your kick. You should now have eight bars of a kick drum that plays on Beat 1 and Beat 3 of each bar. Press ⌘+S/Ctrl+S to save your session.

EXERCISE 4:

Create a Snare Track and a Hi-Hat Track

1] **Create two new tracks.** Using the shortcut ⌘+Shift+N/Ctrl+Shift+N, make two new mono audio tracks set to Ticks. Name one "Snare" and the other "Hi Hat." Make them both large.

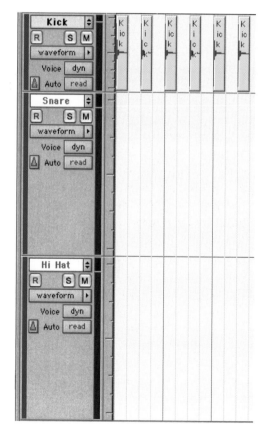

2] **Drag the Snare.** Zoom in to the first bar. Then drag two snare samples from the Region bin to Beat 2 of Bar 1, and Beat 4 of Bar 1 of the Snare track.

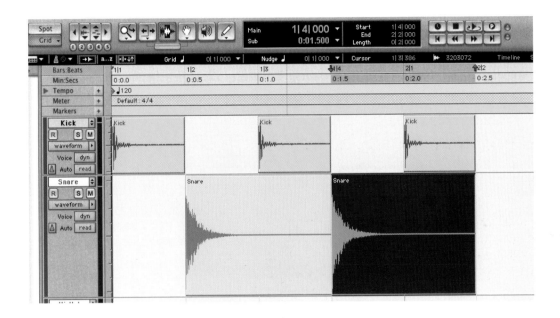

The Event Edit Area

Always keep an eye on the Event Edit area, so you can tell what you're editing or where you're placing a region. I consider this one little place the most important of all the areas in the Edit window. This is where you tell Pro Tools where an edit begins and where it ends. Below the Start and End points is the Length indicator.

Use the Selector tool and highlight any track, dragging from one bar to another. Notice that all the Event Edit numbers change according to what you highlighted. The Start and End fields show you exactly where you highlighted—from one point to the other—and the Length field tells you the exact length of your highlighted selection.

3] **Change the grid value.** Let's use eighth notes now instead of quarter notes for the grid value. Click on the tiny white triangle next to the grid value and choose 1/8 note. Notice that you have twice as many grid lines now, showing that you're working with an eighth-note grid.

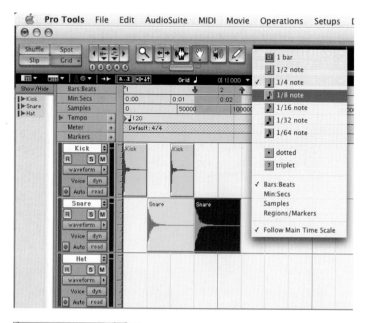

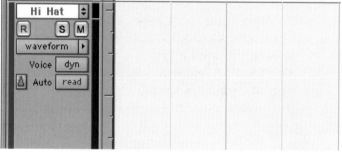

4] **Drag the Hat.** Drag one hat sample from the Region bin to Bar 1, Beat 1 of your Hi Hat track.

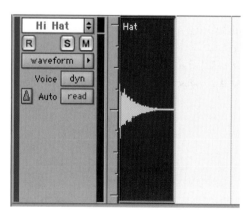

5] **Select the Hat.** Choose the Selector and highlight the Hi Hat track from Bar 1 to Bar 1/1/480. Your Event Edit area should look like this:

Notice that the length of the highlight is 480 ticks. Remember that 960 ticks equals one quarter note, so 480 ticks is half of that, or one eighth note. The location 1/1/480 is simply the first eighth note of Bar 1, Beat 1.

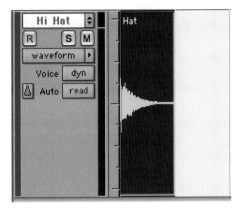

6] **Duplicate the hat.** With the one hat highlighted, hit ⌘+D/Ctrl+D to duplicate the hat seven times. You should now have eight hi-hats that fill Bar 1. This command will produce a metrically sensible rhythm only if the hi-hat audio region both starts and ends on the beat.

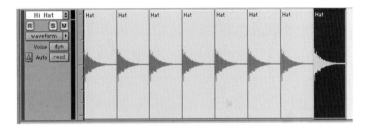

Tip

You could have also used Repeat, choosing seven repeats, rather than Duplicate. Sometimes it's helpful to use Duplicate if I'm not sure how many times I need to repeat something and I want to see my region being duplicated visually one at a time. Then I can stop pressing ⌘+D/Ctrl+D when I see that I have the number of duplicates I need.

7] **Zoom out and highlight.** Zoom out now to where you can see all eight bars. (Remember your Zoom Out shortcut, ⌘+[/Ctrl+[). With all eight bars showing, highlight the Snare track and the Hi Hat track from Bar 1 to Bar 2. To highlight both tracks, hold down the Shift key as you highlight. Notice that the decay of the snare sample is not being highlighted.

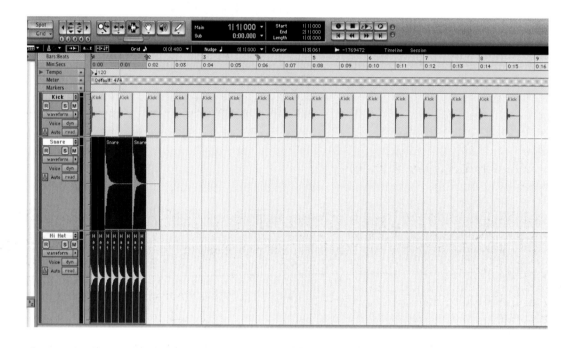

Remember to keep an eye on your Event Edit area, which should show that you have highlighted from 1/1/000 to 2/1/000 and that the highlight length is exactly one bar.

8] **Repeat the Snare and Hat.** This time, use Option+R/Alt+R or Edit > Repeat. Type "7" for the number of repeats and both selected areas will be repeated.

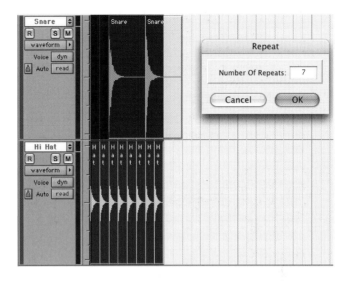

You should now have eight bars of kick, snare, and hi hat.

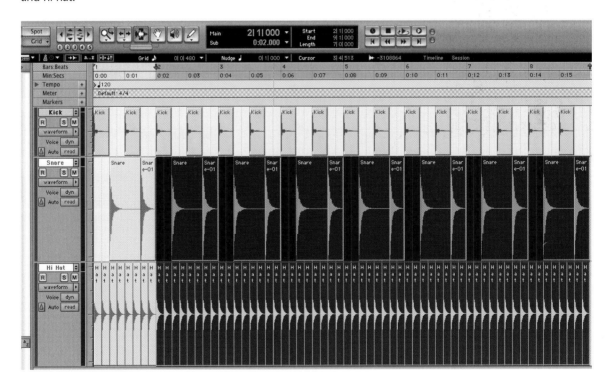

9] **Highlight all eight bars.** Another way to highlight is from the Event Edit area by typing in numbers. You *must* press the Enter key after typing in a number.

You can also use the forward slash (/)—on the numeric keypad, not the regular keyboard—as a shortcut to the Event Edit area's Start and End times. Keep pressing / to reach each number field. Using the Event Edit area, make Bar 1/1/000 the Start and then make 9/1/000 the End. Your Event Edit area should show that you have a length of eight even bars. The regions in the tracks should now be highlighted for eight bars as well.

10] **Enable Loop Playback.** With these eight bars highlighted, go to the Options menu and make sure that Loop Playback is checked. When Loop Playback is enabled, whatever you have highlighted in the Edit window will play in a continuous loop.

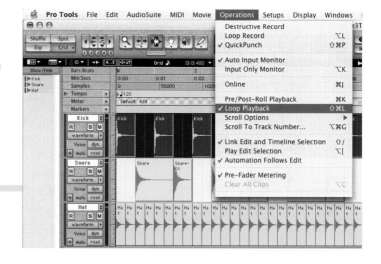

11] **Play and save.** Now you can audition your continuous loop. Hit spacebar to play. The highlighted loop will play indefinitely until you press Stop.

Now is a good time to save your project (⌘+S or Ctrl+S)—get in the habit of saving before you go on to the next task.

EXERCISE 5:

Use the Trimmer with Slip Mode and Spot Mode

The Trimmer tool has two functions, which you can see by clicking and holding on the Trimmer button. In the pull-down menu, the first choice and main function of the Trimmer is to edit the start and end points of audio regions. The second is called TCE (for Time Compression/Expansion), and we will use this to change the tempo of drum loops.

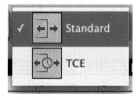

When you select the Trimmer, the cursor turns into something that looks like the letter *E* with the middle line missing. This character will be facing forward if you are at the beginning of an audio region, or backward if your cursor is at the end of an audio region. If you drag toward the audio waveform, you shorten it. If you drag away from the audio waveform, you lengthen it. You can even think of the Trimmer (provided it's in standard mode, not in TCE mode) as a tool to hide or reveal audio.

Tip

You always want to click and hold when using the Trimmer. If you click without holding on a region with the Trimmer, the tool will cut the region off where you clicked. If you accidentally do this, use the Undo shortcut—⌘+Z (Mac) or Ctrl+Z (Win).

1] **Change all track sizes.** Hold down the Option/Alt key and change one track height to medium. All the tracks will change to medium.

2]

Zoom in. Zoom in to see Bars 1 through 3.

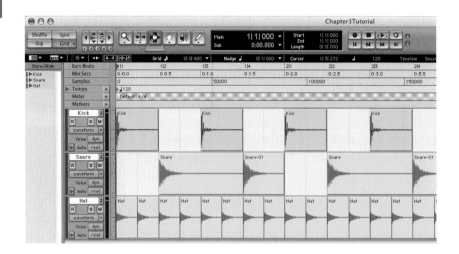

3]

Drag another kick. Make sure you're still in Grid mode with an 1/8 note grid value. Drag another kick from the Region bin and place it at 1/2/480 of your Kick track. Notice how the decay of the kick sample goes on top of the attack of the kick that starts on the downbeat of Beat 2.

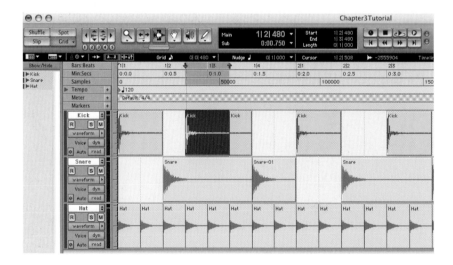

4] **Use the Trimmer in Slip mode**. Choose the Trimmer tool, and this time let's select Slip mode rather than Grid mode. With the Trimmer, grab the end of the newly placed kick sample and pull it to the left. Notice that you can now move freely. In Slip mode, you can move and copy and paste freely without adhering to a tempo-based grid.

Look at the Event Edit area and its numbers. Try to make the kick end exactly at the downbeat of Bar 2. It's not easy, is it?

➤ **EDIT MODES:** *Reference Guide, p. 246*

5] **Trim in Grid mode.** Change the Trimmer back to Grid mode, and use the tool to make the end of the kick sample end exactly at Bar 2 (2/1/000). That's much easier, right? Remember to *constantly* look at your Event Edit area. Use the Undo command (⌘+Z/Ctrl+Z) if you make any mistakes.

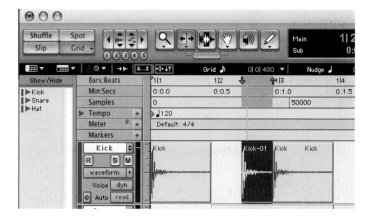

6] **In Spot mode, drag another kick.** Now try Spot mode. (You will rarely use this Trimmer mode, but it's good to understand what it does.) Choose Spot mode and again drag another kick from the Region bin, trying to place it as close to 2/2/480 as you can get. A window opens and wants to know "where exactly do you want to put this region?" Type "2/2/480" into the Start time and click OK.

The kick is put into the correct spot. Now go back to Grid mode and use the Trimmer again to pull the end of the sample back, to reveal the attack of the preceding sample.

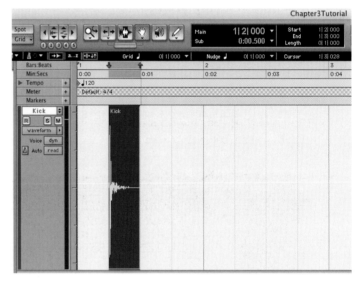

Note

Spot mode is rarely used in recording and editing music. It's used mostly for post-production audio for film and television. For example, if there's a car crash one minute into the movie soundtrack, the engineer would drag the audio file of a car crash to the Edit screen, using Spot mode, and enter one minute. This is commonly referred to as "spotting" sound effects. You can see how this would come in handy occasionally in creating music, too—when you might want to place a sound effect at a specific bar in your song, for instance.

"Why do I now have two kicks in the Region bin?"

You should have two kicks in the Region bin now, one in boldface called Kick, and one in plain text called Kick-01. Kick-01 is the edited version of your larger Kick sample. When a filename is in boldface, it means that the file is whole and unedited. When a filename is in plain text, it means that the file is an edited version of a whole file. So Kick 01 is an edited version of the entire, unedited audio file, Kick.

If you now drag-edited Kick 01, you wouldn't need to use the Trimmer, because you're using the shortened, edited version of the kick that we made in step 5.

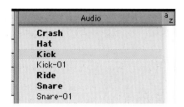

7] **Play.** Hit Return/Enter to rewind to the top and play back what you've done. You should hear a kick on the pick-up of every other beat, or on the second eighth note of every other beat.

8] **Zoom out.** Double-click the Zoomer. This shows you the entire eight bars.

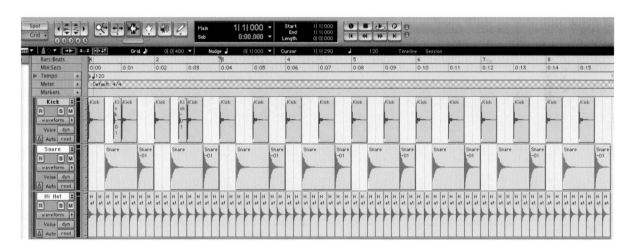

9] **Highlight the kick edits.** Since we have two bars edited correctly in our new kick drum pattern, let's make our new edit occur for the entire eight bars. Choose the Selector and highlight from Bar 1/1/000 to Bar 3/1/000.

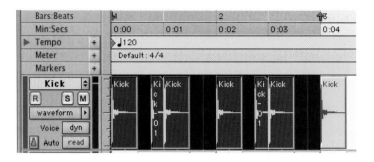

10] **Duplicate the Kick edit.** Make sure that your Event Edit area shows that you have from 1/1/000 to 3/1/000 highlighted. Then either duplicate three times with ⌘+D/Ctrl+D to fill eight bars, or use the Repeat command (Option+R/Alt+R) and repeat three times. You should now have eight bars of our edited kick pattern.

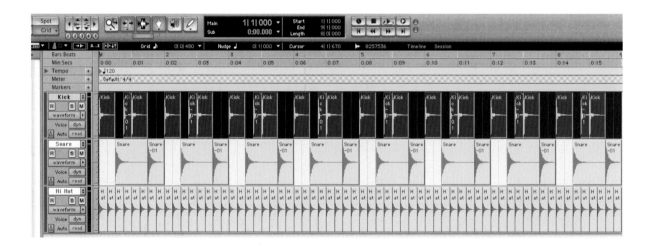

11] **Highlight the eight bars, play them, and save.** With Loop Playback enabled, highlight all eight bars and play. Press ⌘+S/Ctrl+S to save this session.

The Smart Tool

The Smart tool is a combination of the Trimmer, Selector, and Grabber. See the oval shape below the Selector tool? Click it to highlight, and now you have selected the Smart tool. This tool is used mostly by advanced users, and it works like this: If you click at the beginning or end of an audio region, the Smart tool becomes the Trimmer. Click in the middle of a region on its upper portion, and the Smart tool becomes the Selector. Click in the middle of a region in its lower portion, and you've got the Grabber.

The Smart tool also provides an easy way to create fade-ins and fade-outs by clicking on the top corners of either end of an audio region.

Many of the Edit tools have more than one function. You access these other functions by clicking on the tool until you see a pull-down menu beneath the tool. Click on the Trimmer now to access its pull-down menu. As we work through the remaining exercises, we will cover some of these additional functions.

So far, whenever you've created a new track, I've asked you to use Ticks rather than Samples as the track's timebase. Now I'm going to show you why.

EXERCISE 6:
Change Timebase

When we created our new session at the beginning of this chapter, we did not choose a tempo, which means we've been using the default tempo of 120 beats per minute.

1] **View your tempo.** Open the Transport window now and look at the Tempo field. Also look at the Tempo ruler in the Edit window. Both show you that we are using the default tempo of 120 BPM.

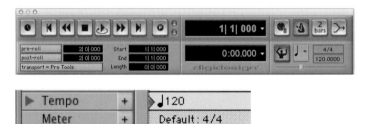

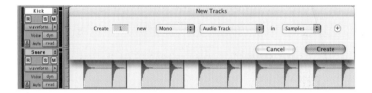

2] **Create a new track.** Highlight the Kick track's name and then create a new mono audio track—but this time, select Samples instead of Ticks as the type of track.

When you highlight a track name and then create a new track, Pro Tools places the newly created track below the one you have highlighted. Name the new track "KickTest."

Notice on the bottom-left corner of the Kick track there is a tiny green metronome. This tells us that this track is correctly set to Ticks rather than Samples. The KickTest track, on the other hand, has a tiny blue clock on the bottom-left corner. This new track is a Samples track. Make sure *all* of your tracks *except* the new KickTest track have the green metronome icon.

➤ **TRACK TIMEBASES:**
   Reference Guide, p. 234

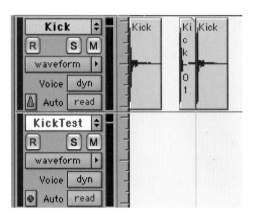

3] **Copy the kick.** Double-click the Zoomer to make sure the entire song is showing. Choose the Selector and triple-click on the first Kick track. (Triple-clicking highlights the entire track.) Now hit ⌘+C/Ctrl+C to copy this track.

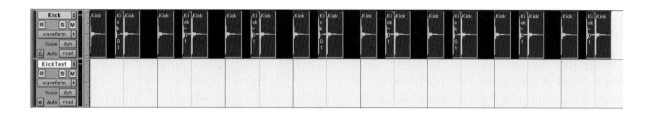

4] **Paste the Kick.** With the Selector, click on the empty KickTest track and press Return/Enter. This places your cursor at the beginning of the KickTest track. Press ⌘+V/Ctrl+V to paste. The same exact waveforms from the Kick track show up in the new KickTest track.

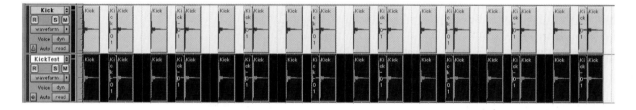

5] **Change the tempo.** In the Transport window, turn off the Conductor. Type "90" into the Tempo field and press Return/Enter. Now look at the waveforms in the Edit window. Everything has moved, *except* the new KickTest track.

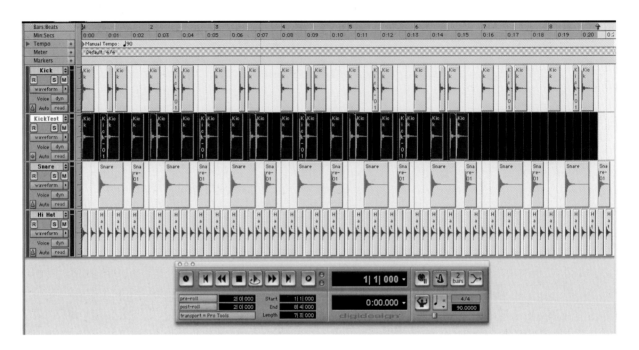

6] **Play and mute.** Play back the song and hear the slower tempo. Everything is correct, except our new Samples-based KickTest track. Mute the new track. Now everything should sound fine.

This demonstrates why we previously chose Ticks as opposed to Samples. When you create a track and make it Ticks-based, you are telling that track's regions to follow the set tempo. If you change the tempo, the regions move with the tempo change.

7] **Change KickTest to a Ticks-based track.**
Click on the blue clock icon and change this
track to Ticks. Nothing moved, right? If we
had changed the track to Ticks *before* we
made the tempo change, everything would
have been fine. But you cannot change a track
to Ticks *after* you make a tempo change and
expect the track to move.

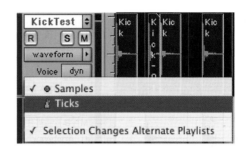

8] **Delete KickTest.** Highlight the KickTest
filename. Go to the Track menu and choose
Delete.

A window opens with a yellow Yield sign. It's
warning you, "Hey, this track has regions on
it—do you know what you're about to do?"
Go ahead, click OK. The track will disappear,
never to be seen again.

9] **Save.** As always, use ⌘+S/Ctrl+S to save
your session.

EXERCISE 7:
Use the TCE Trimmer

Skipping the Pencil and Scrubber tools for now, the last tool we use in this chapter is the Trimmer with its Time Compression/Expansion function. For this exercise, we're going to import the shaker loop from Chapter 2. This time we'll change the tempo using the Trimmer in TCE mode.

1] **Import a loop.** In the File menu, under Import, choose Audio to Track. You'll see the familiar Import Audio window. Find your Chapter 2 Loops folder, and select only the shaker files. If you hold down the Shift key, you can select both files. Choose Copy, and then click Done. This process should be getting familiar by now.

The next window allows you to select the Audio Files folder, where you'll copy these files. Then click Choose.

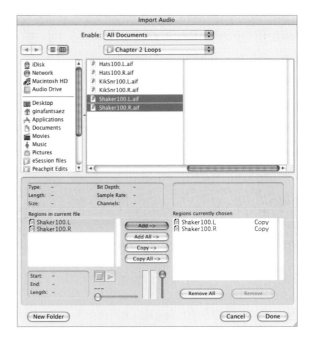

2] **Rename the track.** Double-click the track name Shaker100, and rename it to "Shaker90" (since we changed our tempo to 90 beats per minute in Exercise 6).

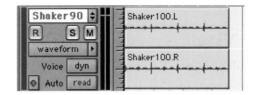

3] **Activate the TCE Trimmer in Grid mode.** Select Grid mode for the Edit window. Then click and hold on the Trimmer and choose the second option, TCE (Time Compression/Expansion).

Your Trimmer now has a clock on its icon.

➤ **TCE TRIM TOOL:**
Reference Guide, p. 255

4] **Change the loop's tempo.** With the Trimmer, click and hold the end of the Shaker loop's audio region and pull it to the left, until the Event Edit area shows you a Start time of 1/1/000 and an End time of 2/1/000, with a length of one even bar. Release the mouse button. You will very briefly see a window telling you that Pro Tools is changing the time of this audio region.

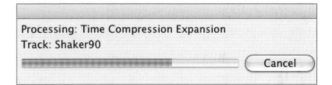

Tip

If you make a mistake, don't forget ⌘+Z/Ctrl+Z to Undo.

5] **Rename the region.** To rename a region, make sure it's highlighted. (If it isn't highlighted, the easiest way to get this done is by choosing the Grabber and then clicking on the region.) I typically use ⌘+Shift+R/Ctrl+Shift+R to rename the region. The Rename command is found in the Regions menu.

Note

Always keep the second Rename option checked, to rename both the region and the disk file. This will rename the file on the hard drive, as well as the filename in the Regions list.

As I've mentioned often, it's important to get into good habits while you're learning. For instance, I always like to know exactly what my audio regions are when I look at them on the screen. Notice that Pro Tools has renamed our region Shaker100-TCEX_02.L. To Pro Tools, this makes sense—the region was previously called Shaker100, and it has now been time-compressed (TCEX) and become edit #2 of the Shaker region. However, we really don't need to see all this information, so let's rename this region "Shaker90."

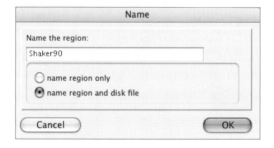

6] **Repeat the Shaker.** With the Shaker90 region highlighted, choose Option+R/Ctrl+R and specify seven repeats. You now have eight bars of each track.

7] **Save.** I probably don't even have to tell you this, by now.

The Scrubber and Pencil Tools

The Scrubber is rarely used unless you're an old analog tape user. You can click with the Scrubber on an audio region to "scrub," which is the analog term for moving the tape reels back and forth to hear where downbeats are. To use the Scrubber, simply click a track and move your mouse left and right. The faster you drag, the faster the track will play back. Slower dragging gets you a slower playback. If you drag to the right, the song plays forward, and if you drag to the left, the song plays in reverse. It would be hard to hear the results of this tool at this point, because we have very little music to play with. Try the Scrubber later on, after you have created more music.

The Pencil has a variety of uses. The first role of the Pencil tool was to help advanced users fix pops and clicks in audio files. In short, you would zoom way in to the audio waveform, find the place in the waveform where there was a pop or click, and use the Pencil to redraw the waveform to fix the flaw. Today, the Pencil has more uses, among which is to edit MIDI events. The Pencil can be very handy for custom panning, volume, or tempo curves, and for creating special effects. The Pencil has quite an extensive pull-down of options.

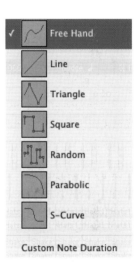

EXERCISE 8:

Use Shuffle Mode

The last Edit mode we'll examine, Shuffle mode, is used when you want to move things forward or backward in time. For example, say you have a four-bar intro and you decide to make it into an eight-bar intro. You would highlight the four-bar intro on all tracks and then duplicate them using Shuffle mode. This would insert the new four bars after the existing four bars and move ("shuffle") the whole song back four bars.

Shuffle works the same way for deleting sections of a song. Let's say you have an eight-bar intro and you want to shorten it to four bars. If you were to highlight the four bars you want to delete on all tracks in Grid mode and then hit Delete, there would be four empty bars in your arrangement. However, if you highlight the four bars in Grid mode, choose Shuffle mode, and then Delete, Pro Tools will delete the four bars you had highlighted and then move up the rest of the song, eliminating any empty space in your arrangement.

Three Types of Shortcuts to the Edit Modes and Tools

As you increase your experience with Pro Tools, you will constantly be changing around among the Edit modes and tools—and there are better and faster ways to get to them than by clicking with your mouse.

F Keys for Modes & Tools		Command/Ctrl Keys for Tools	
F1 = Shuffle	F6=Trimmer	+1 = Zoomer	+5 = Scrubber
F2 = Slip	F7 = Selector	+2 = Trimmer	+6 = Pencil
F3 = Spot	F8 = Grabber	+3 = Selector	+7 = Smart
F4 = Grid	F9 = Scrubber Tool	+4 = Grabber	
F5 = Zoomer	F10 = Pencil Tool		

And last but not least, you can scroll through the Edit modes and tools:

◆ Use the ~ (tilde) key (it's directly above the Tab key) to scroll through modes.

◆ Use the Esc key or click the center mouse button (Win) to scroll through tools (click both buttons simultaneously if you have a two-button mouse).

Try to force yourself to learn these shortcuts now. If you do, your editing keystrokes will become second nature, and you'll soon be able to focus entirely on the music rather than the technology.

Caution

Shuffle mode is all about moving things. So you want to make sure that you get out of it **immediately** *after you're done using it. If you forget, and you continue editing without realizing that you're still in Shuffle mode, the tracks you edit will have been moved accidentally— and that can be a* **huge** *mess. So think of Shuffle as a "dangerous" mode. Use it and get out.*

Suppose we want the song to start with one bar of shaker before the kick, snare, and hat come in. There are many ways to accomplish this. We could use the Selector tool to highlight the Kick, Snare, and Hi Hat tracks from Bar 1 to Bar 9, and then choose Cut and then Paste at Bar 2. But let's get familiar with Shuffle mode and use that instead.

1] **Highlight the first bar of the Kick track.** Double-click on the Zoomer to show the full song. Choose Grid mode and the Selector tool, and highlight from Bar 1 to Bar 2 on the Kick track.

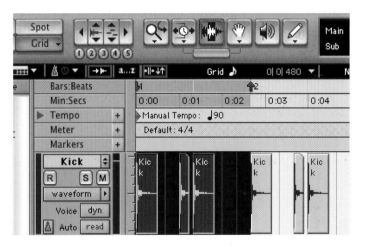

2] **Insert silence.** Choose Shuffle mode for the Edit window, and select Edit > Insert Silence.

Now you have one empty bar of the Kick track.

3] **Zoom out.** Double-click on the Zoomer again. You'll see that one extra bar of Kick extends beyond the other tracks. Shuffle mode has inserted the bar of silence and then moved the track forward one bar in time.

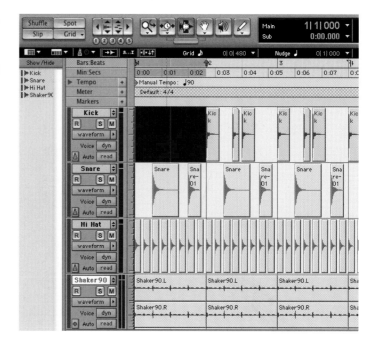

You must use Grid mode first before you use Shuffle mode. The highlighted area must be selected using Grid mode to ensure that the selection covers a precise number of bars and beats; then you can use Shuffle to move it. If you try to highlight the Snare track from Bar 1 to Bar 2 in Shuffle mode with the Selector tool, without first using Grid mode for the selection, the cursor will not snap to even bar numbers. This means you could potentially shuffle or move your tracks without a grid, and your entire song will get off tempo. Take it from me, this can be a nightmare. The best way to avoid it is by always looking at the Event Edit area before you make any edit, and making sure that the length of your edit is an even bar amount.

4] **Move the Snare forward.** Go back to Grid mode. Highlight Bar 1 to Bar 2 of the Snare track. Then choose Shuffle mode again and, rather than going to the Edit menu to insert silence, use the keyboard shortcut ⌘+Shift+E (Mac) or Ctrl+Shift+E (Win). This inserts one bar of silence into the Snare track and moves the entire track back in time one bar. You can always make sure your highlight is correct by constantly looking at your Event Edit area.

```
Start      1| 1| 000
End        2| 1| 000
Length     1| 0| 000
```

Tip

It's a bit tedious going back and forth between modes and tools to perform the same function on the next track down, right? Step 5 teaches you a trick that I use all the time.

5] **Move your highlight to another track.** Stay in Shuffle mode. The empty bar of the Snare track should still be highlighted and set to one even bar. Now use a little-known shortcut to keep the same highlight and make that highlighted area move to the Hi Hat track. You can use Control+; (semicolon) on the Mac or Start+; in Windows to move a highlight down, and Control+P (Mac) or Start+P (Win) to move a highlight up.

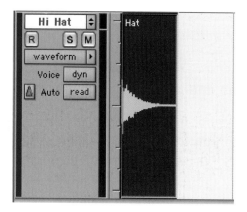

Hit Control+; or Start+; now, and your one-bar highlight should move to the track below.

6] **Insert silence on the hat.** Use ⌘+Shift+E or Ctrl+Shift+E and move the Hi Hat track forward one bar. Now all tracks except the Shaker have one extra bar.

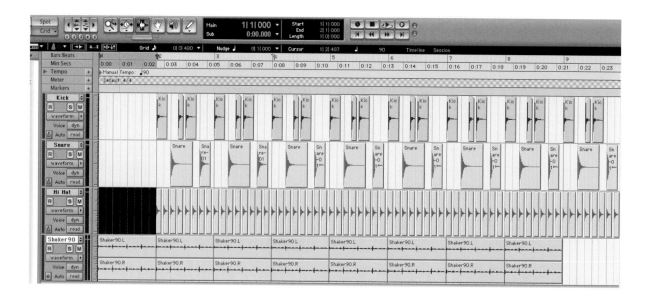

7] **Add one bar to Shaker.** Go back to Grid mode. Choose the Grabber and click on the last Shaker region at Bar 8, and hit ⌘+D/Ctrl+D to duplicate one bar of Shaker. Now all tracks end at the downbeat of Bar 10.

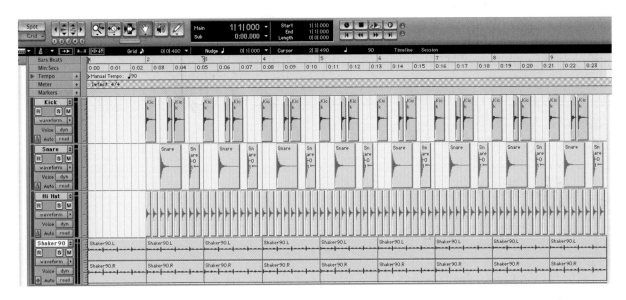

8] **Play and save.** Press Return/Enter to go back to the beginning and play back your track. Now you have one bar of shaker and eight bars of full drum kit. As always, save before you move on.

I want to mention that drums are usually not programmed as has been done in this chapter. These exercises were created to help you develop skills using each Edit mode and Edit tool. You'll thank me when it's time to edit, and you realize that you know just which tool to use for each task!

Wrap Up

We've covered a great deal of ground in this chapter. I hope you're beginning to understand how each Edit mode works, and how the Edit tools you've worked with so far can be used to create and alter your music.

It's time for a well-deserved break. When you're ready, I'll see you in Chapter 4.

PLAYLISTS & MARKERS

4

This is going to be a fun and eye-opening chapter. We're first going to learn how to create a back-up session. Then we're going to delve into one of the coolest features in Pro Tools: *playlists*. Think of playlists as little sketchpads built inside each track.

Imagine an artist, with a sketchpad, drawing a tree. He fills up page 1, but is not quite happy with the drawing. He draws another tree on page 2. Nope, still not right. So, he continues this process until he's happy with his work. He can also flip back and forth among the pages to study what he likes or doesn't like about each drawing.

Playlists are like that, only better. The sketchpad doesn't have the option of combining the best elements of each drawing into one perfect tree, but in Pro Tools you can combine all your playlists and create the perfect vocal or the perfect guitar track. This process of editing together takes is called *comping* or *compositing*.

In this chapter we're going to record numerous playlists and then see how to combine them all to make a composite vocal track. Then we'll learn the art of doubling, also making use of playlists. So, off we go...

EXERCISE 1:

Use Save Copy In

There are two ways to save a backup copy of a session. In the File menu are the two options **Save As** and **Save Copy In**.

I discourage the use of Save As for making backups. When you use Save As, you're making a backup copy of just the Pro Tools session, but not the audio files that go with it. The only time you should use Save As is when you want to create another version of the same song and you know that you're going to use the same audio files.

The Undo command is a better alternative when you want to try out an edit and then redo it if it doesn't work. You have unlimited levels of Undo in Pro Tools. Another option is your Session File Backups folder, which by default automatically backs up your session every five minutes. You can always work backward using the sessions inside the Session File Backups folder.

Save Copy In is the best way to make a copy of a session because it gives you a whole new folder, with a whole new session including all your audio files. I use Save Copy In when I want to keep a previous session intact but want to create something completely different and don't want to have to share audio files between two sessions. For example, if I have a new song called Song 1 and then I use Save As and name it Song 2, Pro Tools saves the session only—the audio files are all being used from Song 1. Which means that if I then delete audio files in Song 2 and try to open Song 1, Pro Tools will ask me, "Hey, I'm missing audio files, what did you do with them?"

However, if I use Save Copy In to name it Song 2, and also tell Pro Tools to save all the audio files, then I get a whole new folder with an independent copy of the entire session. That way, if I delete audio files in the Song 2 session, it doesn't affect Song 1 at all.

1] **Go to the File menu.** With your Chapter3Tutorial session open, go to the File menu and choose Save Copy In.

2] **Choose options for your copy.** In the Save Copy In window, you can name your new copy, as well change its format. Notice that Pro Tools has already renamed your session Copy of Chapter3Tutorial.

Click Session Format to see the options. If someone you know is using an older version of Pro Tools; this is where you could save your session into that older format. In this case, we want to keep our session format named Latest.

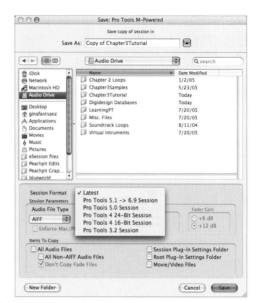

Note

Save Copy In is also used to convert sessions from one sample rate or audio file format to another. For example, suppose I'm working at 96K with .aiff files and my guitar player only works in 44.1K with .wav files. I can open my 96K session, use Save Copy In, and choose the settings that my guitar player needs.

3] **Name the session.** In the Name field, change the name to "Chapter4Tutorial" and make sure to check All Audio Files under Items To Copy. Double-check that you are saving to your Audio drive, and then click Save.

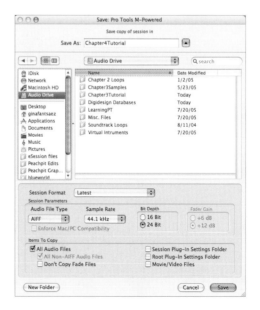

4] **Close Chapter3Tutorial.** Select File > Close Session. If Pro Tools asks you, always choose to Save before closing.

5] **Open the Chapter 4 session.** Select File > Open Session, or use the shortcut ⌘+O/ Ctrl+O. Choose your Audio drive, open the Chapter4Tutorial folder, and open the new Chapter4Tutorial.ptf.

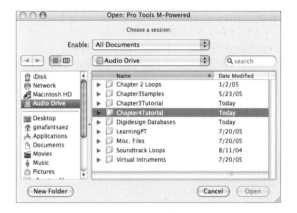

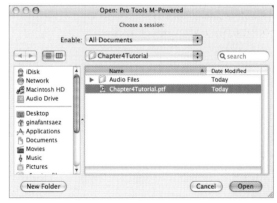

Note

When you open Chapter4Tutorial.ptf, you'll most likely see this window. It's simply telling you, "Hey, the last time I opened a session using these audio files, they were somewhere else; is that cool with you?" You don't need a report, so click No. Don't worry, nothing is wrong—you'll soon get used to seeing this message.

The original disk allocation for this session cannot be used. Check the disk allocation window to see what's changed.

Would you like to save a detailed report?

No   Yes

6] Save.

Working with Playlists

Now let's learn about playlists.

Say you've had a vocalist sing a song from beginning to end, and you want to keep the preceding performance and then have the song sung again. You could make another track, set the input, add any plug-ins, and so on—but what if the song gets repeated five or six times and you end up using only one track? Why waste the processing power and screen space making multiple tracks? Playlists let you use one track and continue recording into that same track, without recording over anything. (I promise, this will make more sense to you when we do it in the exercise.)

➤ **PLAYLISTS:** *Reference Guide, p. 236*

EXERCISE 2:
Record with Playlists

1] **Create a new track.** Make a mono track (you should be using ⌘+Shift+N/Ctrl+Shift+N regularly by now). As usual, set it to Ticks. Name this new track "Crash."

2] **Drag a crash.** Drag the Crash file from the Region bin and place it using Grid mode at Bar 2.

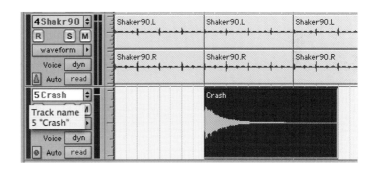

3] **Highlight one bar.** Using the Selector tool in Grid mode, highlight the crash from Bar 2 to Bar 3.

Remember to look at the Edit window's location indicators to be sure you're highlighting one bar at the correct place.

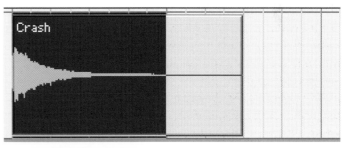

4] **Duplicate the crash.** Using ⌘+D/Ctrl+D, duplicate the crash seven times (or use ⌘+R/ Ctrl+R and repeat seven times). Now you have a crash on each beat, right?

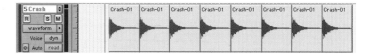

5] **Duplicate the playlist.** To the right of the track name in the Edit window are two tiny up and down arrows. This is your Playlist menu. Click the arrows to see your playlist options, and choose Duplicate to make a copy of the Crash playlist.

In the window that comes up next, name this new playlist "CrashEdit" and click OK. It may look like nothing happens, but hang in there.

Name for duplicated playlist:

CrashEdit

Cancel   OK

6] **Delete some crashes.** With the Grabber, delete every other crash. Your Crash track should now look like this:

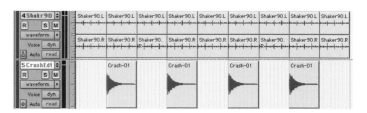

7] **Return to the original playlist.** Now click the Playlist menu, and you'll see two playlists: Crash (1) and CrashEdit (2). Choose Crash, which is your original playlist, and you'll get back your first track with a crash on each beat.

8] **Change the playlist again.** Click the Playlist menu again and choose CrashEdit. Now the edited version of the crash is back.

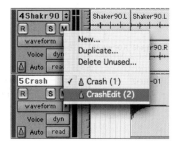

9] **Make a new playlist.** On the Playlist menu, choose New.

Name the new playlist "OneCrash." You now have an empty track.

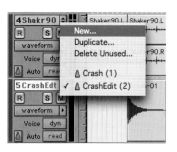

10] **Drag one crash.** In Grid mode, drag one crash from the Region bin to Bar 2.

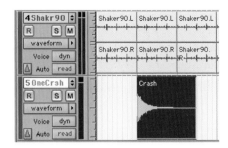

11] **Click the Playlist menu.** Your Playlist menu now has three choices.

Getting the gist now of how cool playlists are?

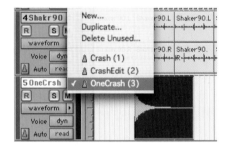

12] **Save.**

Duplicating playlists allows you to keep your original tracks intact while giving you the creative freedom to venture out and make something different. One of the main reasons I use playlists is to back up something before I edit it. For example, if I've created a guitar track that I like but I want to try improving it, I'll duplicate my playlist, name the new one GuitarEdit, and then punch into or edit that new guitar playlist. If I don't actually improve on the part, I go back to the original playlist and use that.

I also use playlists while I'm writing a song. Say I write a first verse and a second verse and then wonder how they would sound swapped around. Again, I duplicate the playlist, rename the new one, and then move the verses around in the new playlist and decide which version I like best.

Playlists can also be used so that everyone in the room feels like they get their way. When you're working with other people, there will often be many opinions about how something should be played or sung. Playlists make it easy to get everyone's favorite take and then make decisions later about which one(s) to use.

EXERCISE 3:

Record Four Playlists

My favorite use of playlists is for creating composite tracks, which is what we'll start doing now. Before we can learn how to create composite tracks, we need to record a few tracks to work with.

1] **Make all tracks small.** In your Chapter4Tutorial session, hold down Option/Alt and click in the Track Height selector of the Edit window, then set all tracks to small size.

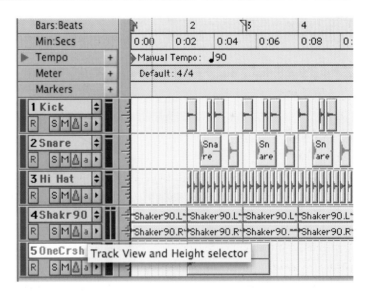

2] **Create a new track.** Using ⌘+Shift+N/ Ctrl+Shift+N, create a new mono track, name it "Scale 1," and make it medium size.

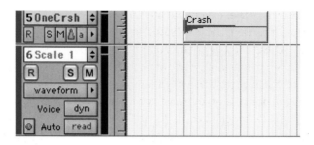

3] **Plug in a mic.** Plug a microphone into Input 1 of your interface.

4] **Set the input.** Using ⌘+=/Ctrl+=, go to the Mix window. Set your input to Input 1 and click the R button to put the track in record mode. Make sure you have level.

5] **Record a scale.** Go back to the Edit window. Start recording, using ⌘+spacebar/Ctrl+spacebar. Use the first bar of the shaker as a one-bar count-in. Starting at the downbeat of Bar 2, sing a solfège (a scale, with the syllables do, re, mi, fa, sol, la, ti, do). Sing each syllable at the downbeat of a bar.

Your waveform should look something like this. Yours will differ based on how loudly you sing or how long you hold your notes.

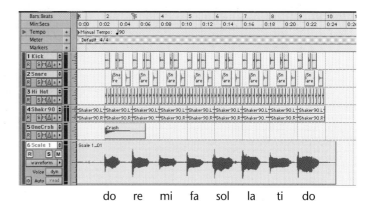

do   re   mi   fa   sol   la   ti   do

6] **Make a new playlist.** Make a new playlist and name it "Scale 2."

7] **Record a new scale.** Make your new scale just like the first one. Try to stay in the same key. If you lose your note, go back to the Scale 1 playlist and listen, then switch back to the Scale 2 playlist before you record.

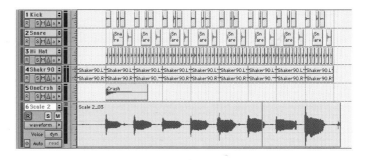

8] **Record another new playlist.** Name this third playlist "Scale 3," and record another scale. You should be getting good at this by now!

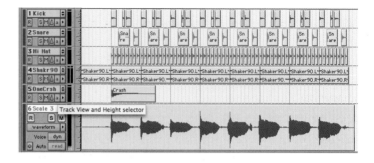

9] **Make and record one last playlist.** Name your last playlist "Scale 4" and record one final scale.

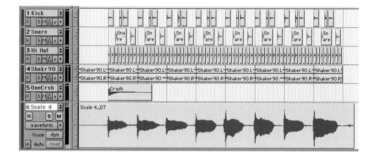

10] **Open the Playlist menu.** You should now have four playlists, Scale 1 through Scale 4.

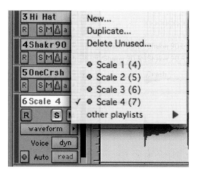

"I keep getting an error while recording!!!"

You may see this message pop up now and then and halt your recording.

This error is basically telling you that the computer is getting clogged with information. To fix it, go to the Setup menu and choose Playback Engine.

Then simply raise your H/W Buffer Size.

Remember that the higher you raise your buffer, the more latency you'll hear if you monitor the computer's input while recording. Try to keep Buffer Size as low as possible while recording, and as high as possible when mixing.

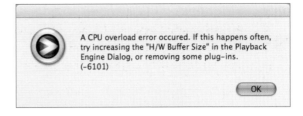

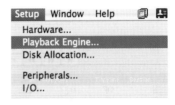

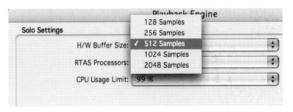

EXERCISE 4:

Create a Composite with Playlists

A composite track is the combination of many pretty-good tracks to create one excellent track, edited together into one cohesive performance. Compositing has been around since the days of recording with tape, but today's digital audio makes comping fast and easy. And playlists combined with digital audio make comping a breeze.

1] **Change your grid.** Set the Grid value to 1/4 note.

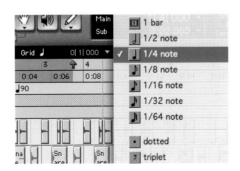

2] **Make a new playlist.** Create a new playlist named "Scale Comp."

3] **Select the Scale 1 playlist.** Go back to Scale 1.

4] **Highlight two syllables.** Using the Selector tool in Grid mode, highlight the first two syllables (do and re) from 1/4/000 to 3/4/000, which is two even bars in length.

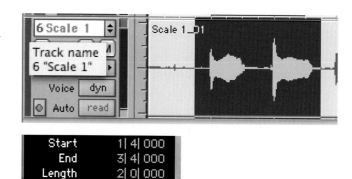

5] **Copy and paste Scale 1.** Using the shortcut ⌘+C/Ctrl+C, copy these first two syllables (you can also do this from the Edit menu). Switch to the Scale Comp playlist (which is currently empty) and paste in the syllables using ⌘+V/Ctrl+V. Now you should have the first two syllables from the first scale in your Scale Comp playlist.

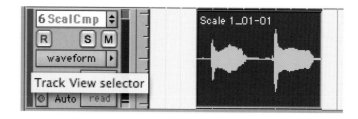

6] **Choose the Scale 2 playlist.** In the Scale 2 playlist, highlight syllables three and four (mi and fa) from 3/4/000 to 5/4/000.

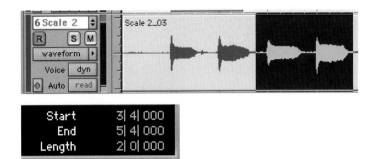

7] **Copy and paste Scale 2.** With mi and fa of Scale 2 highlighted, copy them (⌘+C/Ctrl+C), switch again to the Scale Comp playlist, and paste. You should now have four syllables in your scale: do and re from Scale 1, and mi and fa from Scale 2.

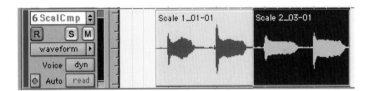

8] **Choose the Scale 3 playlist.** Go to Scale 3 and highlight syllables 5 and 6 (sol and la).

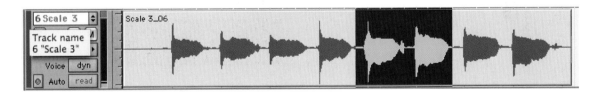

9] **Copy and paste Scale 3.** Copy the highlighted syllables on the Scale 3 playlist, and then go to the Scale Comp playlist and paste. Now you have six syllables of your scale.

I hope this is starting to make sense and that you're getting an idea of what we're doing.

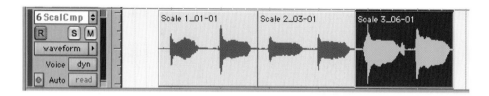

10] **Choose the Scale 4 playlist.** Go to the Scale 4 playlist and highlight syllables 7 and 8 (ti and do). You may notice on the location indicators in the illustration that I have an extra beat. This is because I held the last do syllable out a little longer.

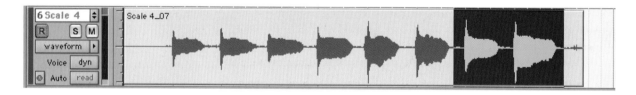

11] **Copy and paste Scale 4.** Copy your last two syllables, switch to the Scale Comp playlist, and paste.

Your scale now has all eight syllables. The first two syllables clearly came from Scale 1, the second pair came from Scale 2, the third pair came from Scale 3, and the last two syllables came from the Scale 4 playlist.

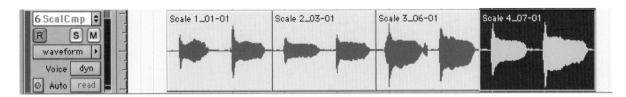

Name Your Playlists!

Let me give you a real-world example of how important it is to name your playlists. When I'm recording a real song with real vocals, I'll record numerous playlists of the vocalist until I feel that somewhere in all of the playlists lies the perfect composite. As I work, I meticulously name each playlist as Vocal 1, Vocal 2, and so on.

When I have all my playlists recorded, I make an empty playlist and name it Vocal Comp. I listen to every Vocal playlist to find either a verse or the first few lines of the song and take either written or mental note of which performance is the best. Then I go to the playlist that I like best for that line, and copy and paste it into the Vocal Comp playlist.

Moving on to the next line of song, I switch from playlist to playlist listening to the same line. I again take note of which playlist has the best performance of that line and copy it into my Vocal Comp playlist. After repeating this throughout the entire song, I can then listen to Vocal Comp from the beginning to end. I usually have a lyric sheet with me so that I can circle or highlight anything that bothers me.

Since I've been careful to name all my playlists, I can easily see where each phrase came from. My Vocal Comp track tells me exactly which lines came from which playlist. And if I have to replace something, I know what I have and haven't used.

Markers and Memory Locations

It's important to know where you are in a song and to be able to easily locate certain sections of songs. This is done by creating *markers* and *memory locations.* Memory locations are pretty much the same thing as markers, except they're used more for video postproduction, where there are many, many cues and scenes. Music usually just has markers for verses, a chorus, a bridge, and the few sections that make up a song.

EXERCISE 5:

Create and Use Markers and Memory Locations

Markers and Memory Locations are the exact same thing, but you see them in different places.

Markers are viewed in the Edit window, in the Markers ruler.

Memory locations are viewed by opening the Memory Location window from the Window menu. Memory Locations have some other useful features that Markers don't, but we won't be using most of them in this book.

1]
Create a marker at Bar 2. In Grid mode, using the Selector, click at Bar 2 and press the Enter key *on the numeric keypad.* (Not Return.) The New Memory Location window opens.

Under General Properties in the Name field, type "Do Re." Make sure none of the boxes in this section are checked. In the Time Properties section, make sure that Marker, not Selection, is selected. Click OK.

➤ **MARKERS:** *Reference Guide, p. 382*

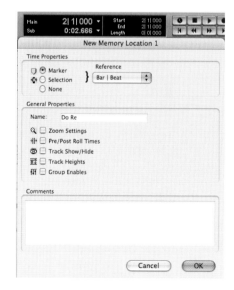

2] **Observe the Markers ruler.** Notice on the Markers ruler in the Edit window that you now have a yellow triangle showing Do Re.

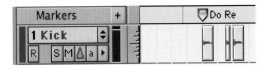

3] **Create a marker at Bar 4.** Click at Bar 4 and press Enter again. Do exactly as you did for Bar 2 in step 1, and name this new memory location "Mi Fa."

4] **Create a marker at Bar 6.** Click at Bar 6 and press Enter. Name this new memory location "So La."

5] **Create a marker at Bar 8.** Click at Bar 8 and press Enter, and name this last memory location "Ti Do."

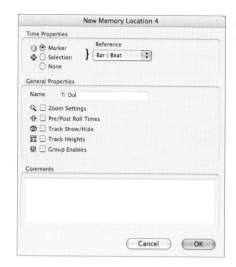

6] **Observe the Markers ruler.** Notice on your Markers ruler now, the four markers clearly demonstrate the location of each syllable. Usually, for music, markers would say "Verse 1," "Verse 2," and so on.

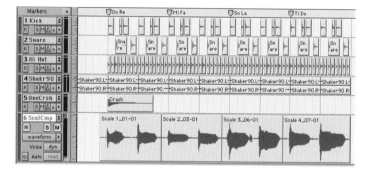

7] **Click on a marker.** Move your cursor on top of one of the markers in the Markers ruler. Notice that the cursor changes into a hand with a pointing finger.

You can click on markers during a song's playback, as well. Press Return to go back to the beginning of the song. Press spacebar to play, and try clicking on various markers while the song is playing back.

8] **Open the Memory Locations window.** Choose Memory Locations in the Window menu.

9] **Use the memory locations.** Instead of clicking in the marker track, you can work with memory locations in the Memory Locations window.

10] **Use a memory "shortcut."** See how each marker is numbered? You can use these numbers as shortcuts to your markers. You can quickly go to any of these by pressing the period key *on the numeric keypad*, followed by the number of the memory location.

11] **Delete a marker or memory location.** To delete a marker or memory location, hold down Option/Alt and click on either a marker in the Markers ruler, or a memory location in the Window > Memory Locations window.

12] **Move a marker.** To move a marker, simply click and drag.

The Secret to Doubling

So many people think you should double a part by listening to what you're doubling and playing or singing along with it. I find that to be completely inefficient, not to mention difficult for even an expert to do.

Some think "making a double" is using the same exact track on another track. Try it for yourself. In reality, it actually only makes the same track louder.

Some try using the same track and nudging it a tiny bit forward or back, but you may as well use a chorus effect—that's not a double, either.

For me, the best approach to doubling is to concentrate on singing or playing the exact same part while you're recording your original track and then simply record more playlists than you need. Then you create a double with the parts of your playlists that you're not using in your main track.

EXERCISE 6:
Try Out Doubling

In this exercise we're going to create a double with the leftover and unused parts of our scale. Keep in mind that this is just an exercise to teach you the concept of creating doubles. By all means, if you want to pick up your guitar or sing a few more playlists and create your own composite, feel free to work with something other than these slightly boring scales.

1] **Make a new track.** Make a new track, size it medium, and name it "Scale Dbl."

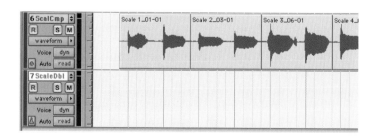

2] **Go to the Playlist menu and select Scale 4.**
Since we've recorded nothing in this track,
there are no playlists; however, go to the
Playlist menu and you'll see an option for
Other Playlists. In that submenu, you can see
all the playlists you made in earlier exercises.
Choose Scale 4.

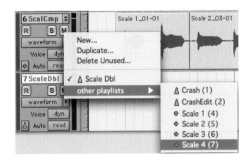

3] **Copy the first two syllables.** With the
Selector, highlight the first two syllables and
use ⌘+C/Ctrl+C to copy.

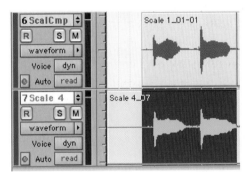

Note

*It's not really important to be in Grid mode for what we're doing at this point. If you find Grid
mode limiting, go ahead and change to Slip mode to highlight your syllables. Grid mode is
mostly used when you're pasting something to a new place and you want to make sure it's on the
beat. Since we're copying and pasting from the same location in the session, Slip mode is fine.*

4] **Change the playlist and paste.** Change to the Scale Dbl playlist and paste the copied syllables (⌘+V/Ctrl+V).

Notice that on both the Scale Comp track and the Scale Dbl track you can clearly see which playlist each part is from. Scale Comp is from Scale 1, and the Scale Dbl track uses Scale 4. This demonstrates once again how important it is to name your playlists and number them correctly.

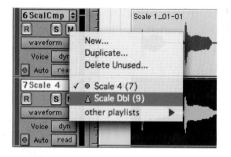

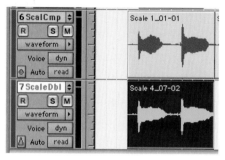

5] **Change playlists again.** Go to the Playlist menu's Other Playlists option again and choose Scale 3.

Now copy the third and fourth syllables of Scale 3.

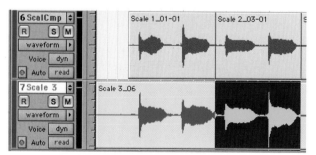

6] **Go to Scale Dbl and paste.** Change back to the Scale Dbl playlist and paste the copy.

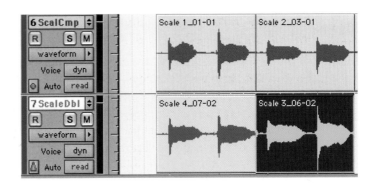

7] **Change playlists again.** Return to Other Playlists and choose Scale 2. Now copy the third and fourth syllables of Scale 2.

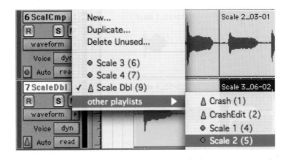

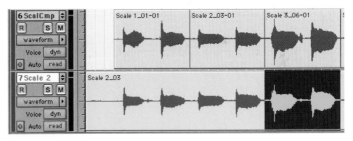

8] **Go to Scale Dbl and paste.** Change back to the Scale Dbl playlist and paste the copy.

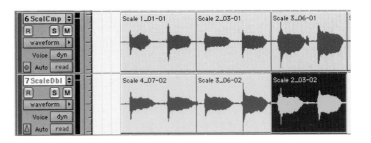

9] **Change playlists again.** From Other Playlists, choose Scale 1. Copy the third and fourth syllables of Scale 1.

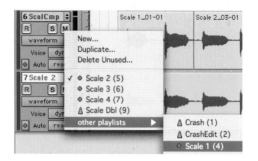

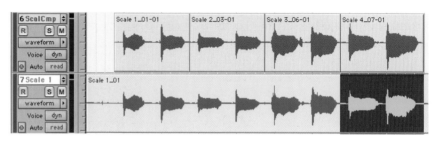

10] **Go to Scale Dbl and paste.** Change back to the Scale Dbl playlist and paste.

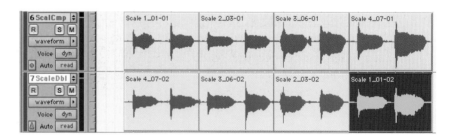

Remember, this is just an exercise to teach you how to take the best of your performances and edit them together. The result probably won't sound like a perfect double—which is okay, as long as you understand how to create one.

VocALign: The Ultimate Secret to Doubling

If you feel brave and daring, go to www.synchroarts.com/downloads and download and install the demo of the amazing plug-in, VocALign. You will want to download the VocALign Project for Pro Tools.

VocALign is one of my favorite plug-ins and I can't teach a lesson on doubling without mentioning it. It retails for $375, but you can try the demo version free for a limited number of days. If you're serious about doubling parts, whether guitars or vocals, VocALign is a must-have plug-in. Here's how it works.

After installing, you'll find VocALign installed under the AudioSuite menu in the Other category. From there, you first highlight the track from which you want to create a double—this is known as the Guide track. So for our purposes here, you would highlight the Scale Comp track, then click Guide, and then click Capture. The Scale Comp track waveform would show up in the Guide section of the plug-in.

Your next step will be to highlight, from the exact same bars as the previous selection, the track you want to double. *But hold on—* before you do this, duplicate the playlist, so that you can always go back to what you had previously, in case the doubling doesn't

work as you want it to. Name the duplicated playlist "Aligned," and with that track highlighted, click Dub and then Capture.

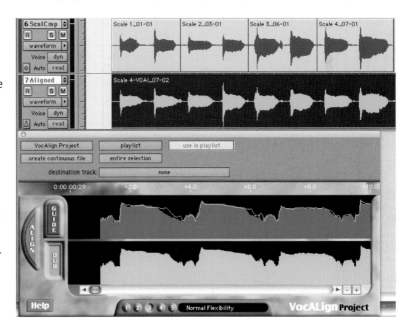

Now you have both waveforms in the VocALign window. Just click Process, and VocALign will line up your Dub track with your Guide track and create an almost perfect double.

A couple of tips for using VocALign:

◆ Only use VocALign a few lines at a time. For some reason, it works much better on small sections.

◆ Highlight your Guide track, hit Capture, and then use the shortcut Ctrl+; (Mac) or Start+; (Windows) to keep the same highlight boundaries while moving the highlight down to the next track. Use Ctrl/Start+P to move the highlight up.

Wrap Up

You're making excellent progress. In the next chapter, we're going to move on to using some EQ plug-ins and learn about using plug-ins as inserts. So take a break now, if you want, or record some of your own playlists. When you're ready, we'll pick it up again in Chapter 5.

USING PLUG-INS

At this point you should understand how to create tracks, record, and do some basic editing in Pro Tools. Now it's time to start learning how to give your songs a more professional sound. This is accomplished with plug-in effects such as EQ, compression, reverbs, and delays.

There is no question that many plug-ins are very intimidating at first glance. I'm going to tell you what most engineers won't: It's not so important that you understand the ins and outs of every plug-in and what every knob and button does, or the exact frequency you're working with. Spend your time and skill on what you do best, whether that's songwriting or performing. When you encounter an intimidating plug-in or any other strange window, simply turn the knobs, listen to what happens, and trust your own ears.

Two Types of Plug-Ins

So let's talk about plug-ins in Pro Tools. You used a plug-in for the first time in Chapter 1, when you created a Click track and inserted a Click instrument.

There are two types of plug-ins in Pro Tools LE: AudioSuite plug-ins and Real-Time AudioSuite (RTAS) plug-ins. The difference is easy. AudioSuite plug-ins actually process the effect into a new audio file—making the effect permanent when you save your changes. RTAS plug-ins, on the other hand, are used as real-time effects. It's like when you add reverb in a studio. You're not actually recording reverb onto the sound; you're simply listening to the sound with reverb on it.

You might think of an AudioSuite plug-in as a real tattoo, and an RTAS plug-in as a temporary one that you can wash off later. Consider the RTAS plug-in exactly the same thing as, say, an outboard reverb, or a delay effect that you would use in a studio.

RTAS plug-ins are what you'll mostly be using throughout this book and what we'll concentrate on in this chapter.

There are two ways that you will use an RTAS plug-in; as an Insert, or on an Aux track as a Send. We covered Inserts and Sends briefly in Chapter 2, and here we'll review both and learn more about them.

In the Mix window, at the top of each track are three sections with tiny up-and-down arrows. The first section is called Inserts. There are five Inserts, A through E, from top to bottom. The two sections below are called Sends, containing Sends A through E and then F through J.

When you use an Insert, you are inserting an effect—such as an EQ or a compressor—to that track only. When you use a Send, you are sending a sound somewhere else. (We'll get to Sends in Chapter 6; for now, let's just concentrate on Inserts.)

An example of a common Insert is a *de-esser.* As you may know, a de-esser takes the high-sibilance sounds such as *s* or *t* and makes them less prominent in a vocal track. You wouldn't really use a de-esser on multiple tracks of vocals. Rather, you'd assign or insert one de-esser to one vocal at a time.

When to Use an AudioSuite Plug-in

I very rarely use AudioSuite plug-ins, but I don't have any tattoos, either. When I do use an AudioSuite plug-in, it's for something like a reverse effect, or to add gain to a track with low level, or when using VocALign. Often when I'm editing a radio commercial that has to be exactly 60 seconds, I'll use the Time Compression/Expansion AudioSuite plug-in.

I have a personal rule to steer clear of processing my effects into audio files unless it's absolutely unavoidable. And if and when I do use an AudioSuite plug-in, I *always* duplicate my playlist before I add the plug-in to a track. I like to be able to change my mind. You can't take reverb off an audio file, just as you can't remove a real tattoo without a major ordeal.

The Anatomy of an EQ

Another good example of a typical insert is an EQ. You can EQ multiple tracks such as background vocals, but more typically you would EQ one track at a time. Think of a typical mixing board. If the vocal is too bright, you'd reach for the EQ section on that channel only and bring down the high EQ.

What Exactly Is an EQ?

EQ means *equalizer*, and the EQ's function is to change (equalize) the frequencies of a sound.

The frequency of a sound is how low-pitched or high-pitched it is. Frequency is measured in hertz (Hz), which is a measurement of vibrations per second. The lower the number of a frequency, the lower the sound. The higher the frequency number, the higher the sound. So a 100 Hz sound is much lower in pitch than a 2000 Hz sound. High frequencies are usually given in thousands of hertz, or kilohertz (kHz). 1000 Hz = 1 kHz.

An EQ plug-in allows you to zero in on specific frequencies and raise or lower their level in order to increase desirable frequencies and/or decrease the unwanted frequencies of a sound.

The human ear can generally hear between 20 Hz and 20 kHz. All acoustic instruments produce sounds that are composites of many different frequencies (overtones), but each note produced by an instrument will have a fundamental frequency, which is its lowest or most prominent tone. Here are the fundamental frequencies produced by a few important musical instruments:

Kick drum	40 to 150 Hz
Bass	40 to 300 Hz
Guitar	80 to 700 Hz
Voice	75 to 900 Hz
Piano	25 Hz to 4 kHz

In this chart of piano notes and the frequencies of each note, take note of A4, which is 440 Hz. This is the most important frequency in all of modern music because practically every instrument is tuned to this one single note. It's typically referred to as *A-440*—meaning that this specific note vibrates 440 times a second.

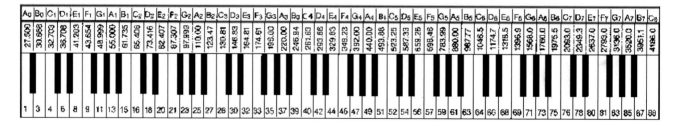

EXERCISE 1:
Add a 1-Band EQ

The cool thing about using an RTAS plug-in is that you can always change your mind. No matter which knob or button you turn, you're not going to mess anything up—so go for it; experiment all you want. Don't worry for now about what you're doing, and don't stress about the technical fine points. If the technical stuff bores you to tears, you can skip it and come back later. For those of you who want to push through now, I'll try to make it as painless as possible.

You have many, many choices among today's plug-ins. Pro Tools comes with a nice collection of Digidesign plug-ins, called the DigiRack plug-ins. I could devote an entire book to third-party plug-ins, and we will look at a few, including VocALign (which you read about in Chapter 4) and the Waves Musicians II bundle, as well as IK Multimedia SampleTank Free. But we'll mostly be using DigiRack plug-ins.

To begin, we're going to take a close look at the DigiRack 1-Band EQ II. This plug-in may look complicated at first, but just think of it—and any EQ—as being exactly the same thing as the treble and bass controls on your car stereo, with perhaps a bit more functionality. If you know how to turn up the bass and turn down the treble in your car, you can easily figure out the 1-Band EQ II.

1] **Start a new session.** With Chapter4Tutorial open, use File > Save As and rename your session "Chapter5Tutorial." Make sure to save this session in the same folder as the Chapter4Tutorial. You'll use this new session to insert some EQ and compressor plug-ins to get a better idea of how they work in Pro Tools.

Note

We used Save As in step 1 because, for the next two chapters, we'll be using/sharing the same audio files while learning how to work with plug-ins. Also, I want you to be able to open each Pro Tools session from the chapter so that you can go back and review your work. So, since we won't be recording anything new or deleting any audio files, it's OK for us to use Save As.

2] **Change all track sizes.** Hold Option/Alt and click any track's Track Height selector, and set the size to small.

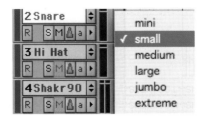

3] **Highlight the snare.** Zoom in a bit. Then use the Selector tool in Grid mode, and highlight your Snare track from 2/1/000 to 4/1/000.

4] **Turn on Loop Playback.** Go to the Options menu and turn on Loop Playback. Now whatever is highlighted will loop continuously. Using Loop Playback while editing plug-ins allows you to hear your changes continually in real time, without your having to stop and rewind the song over and over.

5] **Solo the snare.** Go to the Mix window and solo your Snare track. Ordinarily it's better to apply EQ while listening to your entire mix rather than while soloing a track, but right now I want you to learn to hear exactly what an EQ does.

6] **Insert an EQ.** At the top of the Snare channel strip, click one of the Insert arrows. From the pop-up menu, select Plug-in > EQ > 1-Band EQ II (mono).

Note

Pro Tools applies any plug-ins in order from A to E. If you like your effects in a particular order, pay attention to which Insert you're using. Fortunately, you can change a plug-in's Insert later.

The plug-in window for your EQ opens. For this and any other DigiRack plug-in, just position your mouse above any button to get a tool tip telling you what the function is.

The top section of the plug-in window is where you choose the track this plug-in is being used on, the Insert (A through E) being used, and the preset that's in effect. You can use the Bypass button to disable the plug-in temporarily. The Auto, Safe, and target-like buttons are used for automating functions, which we'll get to in Chapter 11.

The rest of the window contains the actual EQ controls, so let's try 'em out.

7] **EQ the snare with Peak.** The five somewhat-arcane buttons to the right of Type control what kind of EQ you're choosing. The default type for this plug-in is Peak. Leave that as is, and play your snare. (It should play in a non-stop loop.)

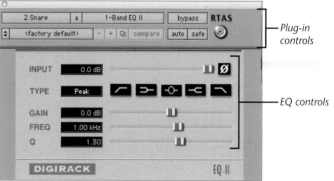

Plug-in controls

EQ controls

Note

The five Type buttons represent these types of EQ, from left to right: High-Pass, Low-Shelf, Peak, High-Shelf, and Low-Pass. Peak EQ is your basic, generic use of an EQ.

8] **Change the frequency and gain.** Use the
Freq slider to find a frequency that sounds
weak or needs boosting. Then move the Gain
slider to the right, bringing the frequency up
or down in level. For my ears, around 200 Hz
feels weak. So I set the Freq slider to 200 Hz
and move the Gain slider up to 7 dB (*decibels,
which is a measurement of volume or loudness*).

Other controls in the plug-in window include
the Input slider, which allows you to raise or
lower the signal of the sound coming into your
EQ. The Phase switch to the right of the Input
slider is used to invert the signal polarity to
compensate for microphone mistakes.

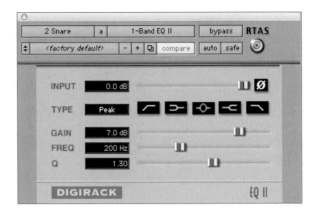

Note

*EQ is completely subjective. I find that sometimes the easiest and most efficient way to EQ
something is to move the Gain slider all the way to the left and right in each frequency band,
and then move the frequency slider up and down (from left to right) and listen for frequencies
I want to increase or decrease.*

9] **Compare settings.** Use the Bypass button at
the top of the plug-in window to turn the EQ
on and off while the snare plays. Listen to the
difference between the snare with and without
EQ. It's very subtle, but with EQ the snare has
a slightly deeper sound.

10] **Change the Q.** Peak EQ includes a slider to change the Q, or range of frequencies affected. Lower Q means a wider range; higher means a narrower range. Move the Q slider all the way to the right. The snare sounds thinner, right? Because you're raising the Q, you're focusing almost exclusively on 200 Hz and no longer boosting other frequencies around 200 Hz.

Now drag the Q slider to the left, maybe around 0.50. Sounds a bit better, right? You have told the EQ, "Hey, I think 200 Hz is low, but I want to play it safe and boost the frequencies around 200 Hz, as well."

More About Q

The Q of an EQ is a measurement of the range of frequencies that you want to affect outside your chosen amount. For example, if an acoustic guitar is very boomy, you may decide that the EQ problem is somewhere around 150 Hz—but you don't want to select only 150 Hz specifically. You probably also want many of the frequencies above and below the problem frequency. In other words, you want all frequencies *surrounding* 150 Hz; therefore, you want a wider Q. So you select 150 Hz as your frequency, bring the Gain slider down a few dB, and then take the Q slider to the left.

The smaller the Q number, the larger the range of frequencies (or bandwidth) you're choosing. You'd use a high Q when you do want to target a specific frequency, as when you're removing a hum or white noise.

The Q slider allows you to create a frequency response curve that has a wider, bell-like shape rather than zeroing in on just one specific frequency number. On the Q "bell," the smaller the number, the wider the bell; the larger the number, the narrower the bell. (That has confused me for years, always seeming the opposite of what it should be....)

11] **Save and name the setting.** At the top of the plug-in window, click the Settings menu (it currently shows <factory default>), and choose Save Settings. In the window that opens, name your setting "Beefy Snare" and click Save.

12] **Save the session.** As always, save your session before moving on.

EXERCISE 2:
Repair the Snare

I want you to get used to mixing and editing at the same time. Sometimes when you're mixing and adding plug-ins, you'll hear parts of the song that need a little fixing or editing. It's good to be able to smoothly switch gears and move to editing, and then resume mixing. You may have noticed while soloing the snare using the EQ, that some snares are missing their decay. This is easy to fix, so let's do that real quick.

1] **Use the Trimmer.** Click and hold on the Trimmer tool and choose Standard.

Make the Snare track medium-sized. Then go back to Grid mode, and with the Trimmer tool click and hold at the end of the first short snare and pull it to the right.

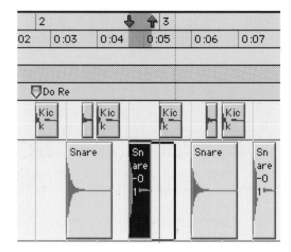

2] **Trim another snare.** Grab the next short snare and pull to the right.

You should now have four snares of the same size.

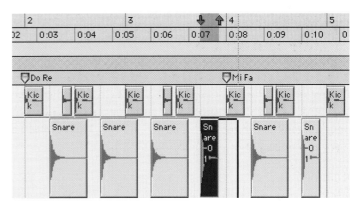

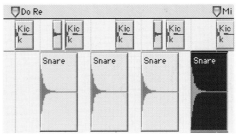

3] **Highlight the snares.** You could keep using the Trimmer for a few more bars—but we can make this an easier task by duplicating these first bars a few times. However, we want to make sure first that what we are duplicating does *not* edit the snare again. Notice that if we highlighted exactly from Bar 2 to Bar 4 and duplicated this, we'd be chopping off the decay of the last snare once again.

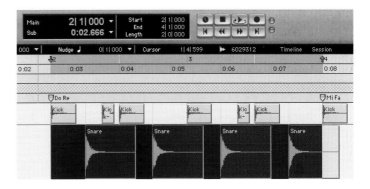

4] **Highlight again.** So now highlight from 2/2/000 to 4/2/000, making sure that your highlight is two bars in length.

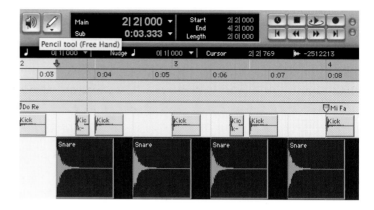

5] **Now duplicate.** Use Command+D/Ctrl+D and duplicate the highlighted segment three times. Now you have a repaired Snare track.

6] **Save.**

EXERCISE 3:
Add More EQ

The EQ we used previously, 1-Band EQ II, has been around for many years in Pro Tools. Digidesign's new EQ III plug-in interface is a lot more visually satisfying, with a sonic improvement over the EQ II as well. We'll use the EQ III this time.

1] **Solo and highlight the vocal.** Make everything small-sized again, and turn off Solo on the Snare track. Now solo one of your Vocal Scale tracks. Zoom out to see the full eight bars, and highlight from Bar 2/1/000 to 10/1/000.

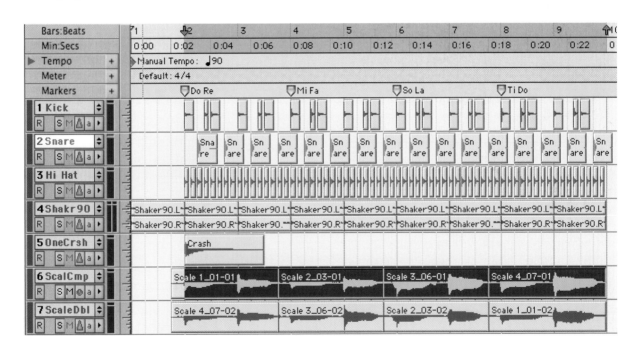

2] **Add a new EQ.** Go to the Mix window and, in the first Insert position of the Scale track, add a 1-Band EQ III plug-in.

This EQ III may look a little different from the 1-Band EQ II used previously, but it's exactly the same thing. It just has a slightly different interface.

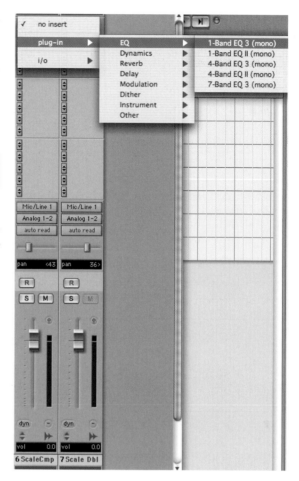

Note

For a vocal track, you'd most likely use a 4-Band EQ, which gives you individual controls on four different frequencies from Low to High. However, to facilitate learning and avoid overwhelming you, we'll use another 1-Band EQ in this exercise.

Those icons at the bottom-left of the plug-in window represent the EQ types: They're the same Shelves, Peaks, and Filters you saw before. To enable any of them, simply click an icon and you'll see the Type change. The default is always Peak—that generic EQ we used in Exercise 1.

Let's start with the icon on the far left, the High-Pass Filter.

Tip

The best way to learn anything in audio work is to simply start pushing buttons and listening. Listen to the difference made by one knob or button and then another until you get an idea of what each one is doing. Using plug-ins, it's also helpful to use the Bypass switch in the plug-in window so that you can listen to how something sounds with and without an effect.

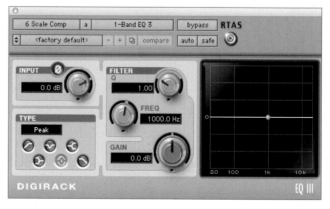

3] **Turn on High-Pass.** Click the top-left Type icon to turn on the High-Pass filter. Play the vocal. If you're in Loop Playback, you'll hear your scale over and over. This is the best way to EQ anything: Solo it and loop it.

Notice that the High-Pass filter gives you a very hip, old-fashioned-radio voice. High-Pass only passes high frequencies. This one is set to 1000 Hz, or 1 kHz, and so you're saying, "Only pass frequencies of 1 kHz and higher; filter out any lower frequencies."

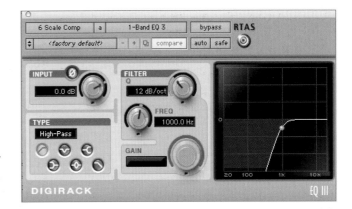

4] **Try a Low-Pass filter.** Now click the far-right Type icon, the Low-Pass filter. It only allows low frequencies in.

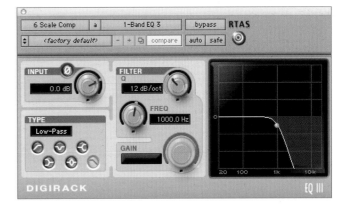

About Those High-Pass and Low-Pass Filters

Think of the High- and Low-Pass filters as big, muscular guys standing at the front door of a happening bar in New York City. The High-Pass filter dude lets in the tall people only, and the Low-Pass dude lets in only the short people. The owner of the bar tells Mr. High-Pass, "Let only people 5'2" and taller come in." Then he tells Mr. Low-Pass, "Let only people 6' and shorter come in."

In audio, you are the club owner, and you can tell your High- and Low-Pass filters what frequencies you want allowed into your sound. The High-Pass filter can be used to get that very hip telephone-voice effect by letting in only high frequencies. High-Pass is also commonly used to get rid of low hums by blocking those frequencies. The Low-Pass filter is commonly used on, for instance, a low-kick sound, to filter out any high-frequency attack.

It's pretty easy to remember: Mr. High-Pass only lets the high frequencies pass, and Mr. Low-Pass permits only the low frequencies.

5] **Choose a Low-Shelf filter.** The icon just below the High-Pass filter is the Low-Shelf filter. A Low-Shelf filter raises or lowers everything below the chosen frequency by an equal amount.

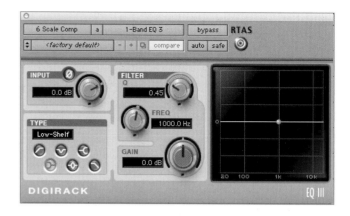

6] **Target the Low-Shelf at 450.** You can turn the Frequency knob until the display shows 450, or type "450" into the Frequency field (remember to press Enter after entering any number), or just click the little white control dot in the Frequency display and drag left and right until you find 450.

The cool thing about the EQ 3 plug-in is that the Frequency graph shows you what you are doing to the frequency. See the little white control dot in the center? That shows your target frequency. You move it left or right to choose low or high frequencies. You move it up or down to turn frequencies up or down.

7] **Boost the low frequencies.** Turn the Gain knob to 10 dB, or type "10" in the Gain field, or drag the control dot upward to around 10 dB.

So now, every frequency 450 Hz and lower is 10 dB louder.

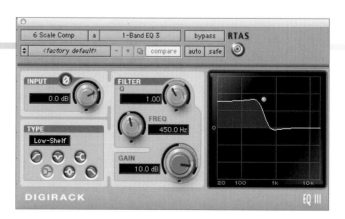

8] **Change the Q.** Notice that shelving types also have a Q knob. Play with the knob with Low-Shelf selected and see how it influences the sound. Remember, smaller Q numbers affect more of the area around a frequency; the larger numbers focus more on the actual selected frequencies rather than the surrounding areas. With a shelf, a Q of 1 works well.

9] **Use a High-Shelf.** See the icon that looks like a mirror image of the Low-Shelf? Click that, and the plug-in will do exactly opposite of what the Low-Shelf was doing. Now we're telling the plug-in to "take all frequencies from 450 Hz and up and raise them exactly 10dB." (10 dB is a pretty substantial amount, but using large numbers in the exercise makes the sound difference more obvious while you're learning.)

"When should I use shelving?"

Well, if you've ever turned up the bass or treble on your car's sound system, you've already use shelving. It simply turns up or down all frequencies that you choose. If you move the bass knob to the left in the car, you hear less bass, and when you turn it to the right you hear more bass. Low-Shelf is the bass knob, and High-Shelf is the treble knob—it's up to you to decide whether you want more or less of each.

A typical use of shelving in mixing would be to put High-Shelf on a cymbal because you want to boost that high sizzle sound. You might use Low-Shelf to lower the bass decay of a boomy kick drum. Again, it's all subjective; there's no wrong or right setting. If it sounds good to you, then it's right, and don't worry about what anyone else says.

10] **Use Notch EQ.** The top-center icon is the Notch EQ, sometimes called a Notch filter. This is used to select and cut (or "notch out") specific frequencies. Where Peak gives you a nice, round bell-like bandwidth, Notch EQ is very specific. It's used to target and remove things like a guitar buzz or a low room noise.

Notice that with the Notch EQ, you have no Gain control. The Gain for Notch EQ is automatically turned all the way down.

11] **Go back to Peak.** Put the familiar Peak to work again, allowing you to choose your frequency and the bandwidth (Q) around your frequency. The Peak type in EQ III is just the same as what we used in Exercise 1. Notice that because our Q is turned down low, bandwidth is very large—which makes this EQ resemble something we used to draw and giggle at in grade school.

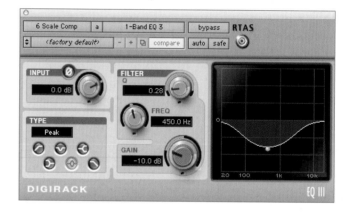

12] **Change to a 4-Band EQ.** Click in the field at the top of the plug-in window and change the selected plug-in from 1-Band EQ 3 (mono) to 4-Band EQ 3 (mono). (Notice that there's a 7-Band EQ available, as well.)

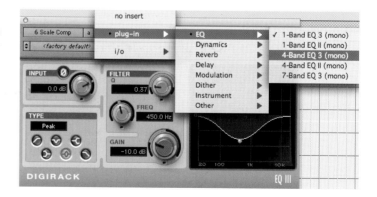

13] **Don't freak out.** I know—this expanded window looks a little scary. It's not. Let's take it from the top, where in this case you have both input *and* output levels.

Below that are LPF and HPF—the Low-Pass and High-Pass filters.

Next is a row of five Frequency sections: LF (Low Frequency), LMF (Low-Mid Frequency), MF (Mid Frequency), HMF (High-Mid Frequency), and HF (High Frequency). The three Mid Frequency sections are disabled in the 4-Band EQ but would be enabled for 7-Band EQ.

This 4-Band EQ works just as you've already learned, but instead of one band, you have four. (Back in your car, LF would be bass, HF would be treble, and LMF and HMF would be two knobs between bass and treble.)

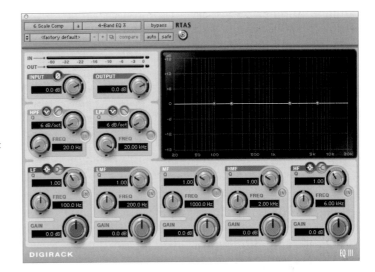

14] **EQ your own voice.** Try dragging the various colored control dots representing each frequency band in the Frequency graph. Experiment until you find an EQ setting you like for your own voice.

Tip

If you drag a control dot and then want to reset it to 0, hold the Option/Alt key and click the control dot; this resets it to the default. It will work with any knob and button, on any plug-in.

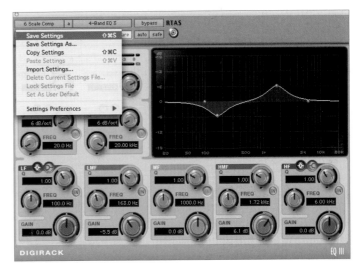

15] **Name and save your EQ setting.** Click in the Settings menu and choose Save Settings. The EQ setting is set to go into the correct folder automatically. Name your EQ setting as you like. Now, in any song, you can use this same EQ setting over and over.

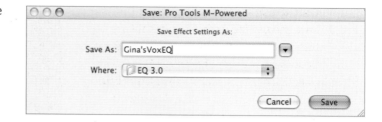

If You Know One EQ, You Know Them All

The DigiRack plug-ins included with Pro Tools are a good place to start learning the lingo of specific plug-in categories, such as EQ and compression, before buying more. When you *are* ready to take the plunge and buy more plug-ins, rest easy and know that it doesn't matter if you're using a Sony Oxford EQ or a DigiRack EQ—every EQ uses the same exact functions. Whether they have sliders or knobs, they all do pretty much the same as what the DigiRack EQ does, but each product has its own special sound.

EXERCISE 4:

Copy, Mute, and Move Plug-ins

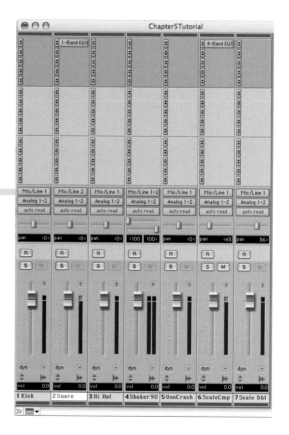

1] **Close the plug-in window.** Close the plug-in window you have open and go to the Mix window. You should have two plug-ins active now, one on the Snare track and one on the Scale Comp.

2] **Copy a plug-in.** To copy a plug-in to another track and use the same settings, hold Option/Alt and drag the plug-in to another track. Try it with your new vocal EQ plug-in: Hold Option/Alt; then click the plug-in and drag it to the Scale Dbl track. You'll see a ghost outline image of the plug-in, indicating that you're copying it.

3] **Bypass a plug-in.** The easiest way to bypass a plug-in is to hold down the Command/Ctrl key and just click the plug-in. Do that to the EQ plug-in you've copied to the Scale Dbl track. Notice it turns a darker color, indicating that it is bypassed.

4] **Move a plug-in.** In the next exercise, in Chapter 6, we're going to play with compression. Usually, a compressor comes before an EQ, so we need to move our EQ plug-ins down one place in order to put the compressor in. To move a plug-in, click it with your mouse and drag it to the Insert slot below.

Tip

You can also change a plug-in's slot in the plug-in window. Click the lettered button next to the track name at the top of the window, and select a different Insert slot.

5] **Move and mute.** Let's move both EQ plug-ins to Insert slot B, and mute them (Command-click/Ctrl-click).

6] **Save.** Don't forget to save your session.

Wrap Up

The more you can practice working with EQ, the better. Try to EQ your Kick or Hat tracks. Be adventurous and try some other plug-ins. In the Pro Tools Help menu, you'll find the DigiRack Plug-ins Guide, which is quite helpful in teaching you more about plug-ins.

In Chapter 6, we're going to work with Sends, as promised earlier. And we'll also learn about bussing—that's the really fun stuff using reverbs and delays.

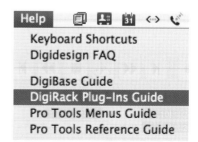

INSERTS & BUSSES

6

In this chapter we're going to get more familiar with the use of plug-ins, focusing on reverbs, delays, and compression.

Keep in mind that in this book we're using the DigiRack plug-ins that come with Pro Tools because I know everyone reading this book will have them. These plug-ins are very useful, but there are some other exceptional reverb, delay, and compression plug-ins made by other companies, too. Once you get a basic understanding of how to use the DigiRack plug-ins, you'll want to start investing in a palette of other effects. Do you cook? Well, even if you don't, you can think of the DigiRack plug-ins as your basic salt and pepper. The third-party plug-ins are like your garlic, saffron, and lemongrass—you might not combine them in the same dish, but they're great ingredients to have in your spice rack.

Before we get started, use Save As *one last time* and name the new copy "Chapter6Tutorial." Be sure to save it into the same folder as Chapter4Tutorial and Chapter5Tutorial.

I promise that this is the last chapter in which we'll reuse this session. And if you have other sessions of your own, by all means, use those—you don't *have* to keep using this same session. For these exercises, we need tracks to apply our effects to, so we may as well use our existing session rather than starting from scratch. But if you feel inspired to record more parts or apply what you're learning to something else you've been working on, I encourage you to go off and be independent.

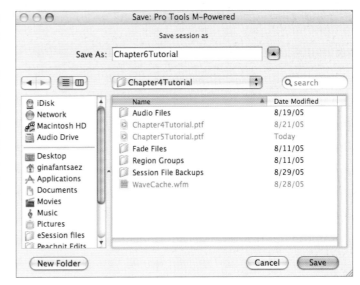

EXERCISE 1:

Use a Reverb as an Insert (the Wrong Way)

In this exercise I'm going to show you the wrong way to use a reverb. Why? Because I want you to understand *why* it's wrong so that you won't make the mistake of using a reverb like this. In Exercise 2, I'll teach you the right way.

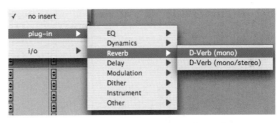

1] **Insert D-Verb.** In the Mix window, on the Scale Comp track, click an Insert slot and select Plug-in > Reverb > D-Verb (mono).

The plug-in window opens, with the usual plug-in controls at the top, and the controls for this specific plug-in below them.

➤ **INSERTS:** *Reference Guide, p. 482*

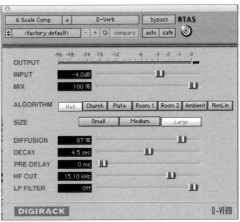

D-Verb Overview

Here's a brief rundown of the D-Verb sliders and buttons and what they do:

◆ **Output:** This meter shows you the output level of the effected sound.

◆ **Input:** Use the slider to adjust incoming level to the effect.

◆ **Mix:** When set to 100%, you'll hear 100% of the effect: 0% is with no effect at all.

◆ **Algorithm:** What kind of room or space do you want to sound like you're in?

◆ **Size:** How large a space do you want to sound like you're in?

◆ **Diffusion:** If you want the reverb to get bigger over time, turn this up. For more natural-sounding reverb, stay with a low level.

◆ **Decay:** This is how long the reverb continues after the original sound is over. It's directly affected by the Algorithm and Size settings.

◆ **Pre-Delay:** This is the time between the original sound and the first reverb that you hear.

◆ **HF Cut:** (High-frequency cut) This is where you EQ the sound of the decay.

◆ **LP Filter:** (Low-Pass filter) Use this to EQ the overall reverb sound. As explained in Chapter 5, you tell it the maximum frequency, and it lets in only frequencies below that.

2] **Open DigiRack Plug-Ins Guide.** Go to the Help menu and choose DigiRack Plug-Ins Guide. Scroll down the Table of Contents on the left until you see the D-Verb plug-in, and click it.

This Guide can be extremely helpful at times but is also somewhat technical. If you do feel overwhelmed, skip the technicalities and just turn the knobs (or move the sliders) until you like the way it sounds.

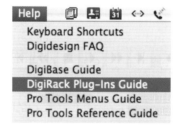

Note

I could explain every parameter of every plug-in (as I did with EQ), but I'd run out of room for the other lessons. So I won't be able to tell you all the ins and outs of reverbs—just a few pointers. For those who want to learn more about using reverbs, the DigiRack Plug-Ins Guide available from the Help menu is a good place to start.

3] **Change the D-Verb Mix level.** Solo your vocal track and play. Too much reverb, right? Notice that the default Mix level is 100%. The Mix level lets you determine what percentage of reverb you want. So, bring down the Mix level until you hear maybe 90 percent of your voice and 10 percent reverb.

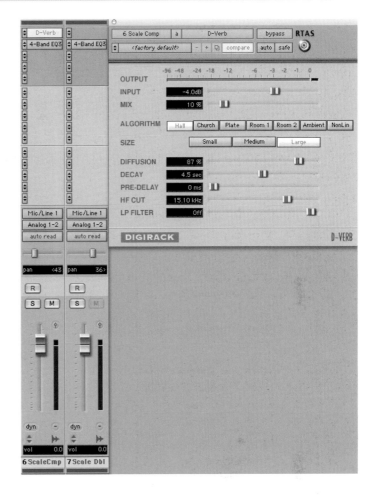

So now you've used a reverb as an Insert. What's the big deal—why is it a bad thing to do? You'll understand very clearly after the next exercise, but the main reason is this: One song may have many tracks that need reverb, and if you get into the habit of using reverbs as Inserts, you're going to run out of processing power very quickly. On the other hand, when you put a reverb on a send bus, you can share one reverb among many tracks and send each individual track to that one reverb plug-in. Let's move on to bussing, and it'll all start making sense.

Bussing confuses a lot of new users. It took me a long time before I really understood how simple bussing actually is. I think a good way to discuss it is actually with two explanations: one explanation for those with some previous audio experience, and another for those with little to no audio experience.

Bussing for Those with Some Audio Experience

Most of you have used a mixer before, right? Here is a very common Mackie mixer.

See your row of Aux knobs? Let's say Aux 1 adds reverb to a channel, and we'll look at the conventional way in which a reverb box is hooked up in the back.

If the Aux 1 knob sends reverb to a track, then Aux Send 1 is connected with a cable to the input of a hardware reverb box. So, that also means that Aux Return 1 left and right on the back of the Mixer are connected to the outputs of the reverb.

Many years ago when I was learning all this stuff for the first time, an engineer told me to memorize "Send In/Return Out," meaning that Sends are always connected to Inputs, and Returns are always connected to Outputs. Whenever I get confused, I just remember that. Sometimes I'm still confused, but at least my gear is hooked up correctly.

On the center section of the mixer are the Stereo Aux Return knobs. That's where you turn up the volume of the entire reverb module. So the Aux knob on the channel sends that track to the reverb, and the Aux Return is the amount of reverb you hear. With me so far?

Front

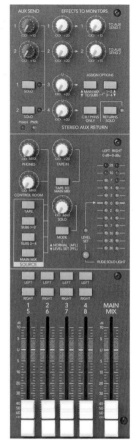

Center

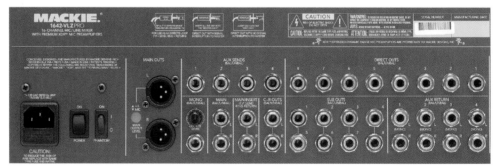

Back

Since the Mackie is hardware, your knobs and buttons are all created for you. But Pro Tools is software, and you have to create your own Aux Sends and Aux Returns. If you try to look at Pro Tools as being exactly like a mixer onscreen, it'll make perfect sense. You create a new track exactly as we have many times before, but instead of an audio track, you create a mono or stereo Aux Input. This is exactly the same thing as creating an Aux Return on a mixer.

On a Pro Tools channel, the Sends section is right below the Inserts. So Send A in Pro Tools is, in a sense, Aux Send 1 on the Mackie mixer.

On the Mackie mixer, you have four Aux knobs to use for effects; in Pro Tools, you have 32 mono busses, any pair of which can be combined as a single stereo bus. Click on Send A, and you'll see them.

I promise that this will make much more sense after you do Exercise 2.

Bussing for Those with No Audio Experience

Think of an audio bus as an actual vehicle bus with wheels, and it makes the whole concept a lot simpler. Like a bunch of travelers being picked up by the bus at various stops and being taken to the bus station, which is their chosen destination, it's a bunch of instruments taking a bus to a chosen effect such as a reverb or delay. The main difference is that no one can get off the bus until it reaches the station.

If the instruments are the travelers and the effect is the destination, then the bus station is what Pro Tools calls an Aux Input.

The reason a city has a main bus station is so that travelers have a place to be dropped off. The reason an audio bus needs an Aux Input is so that the sound has somewhere to go. You can't just buy a bus ticket to nowhere, and you can't bus a sound without having someplace to send it.

Pro Tools gives you 32 busses to drive anywhere you want. You can drop a single passenger off at 32 different destinations, pick up everyone at Reverb City and take them to Delay Town, and send them to any effect metropolis on the planet.

EXERCISE 2:

Use Reverb on a Bus (the Right Way)

In this exercise we'll create an Aux Input track, which is almost exactly like an audio track. We'll insert a reverb effect onto the Aux Input track, and then bus (send) our instruments to that effect.

1] **Create an Aux Input track.** Use ⌘+Shift+N/ Ctrl+Shift+N to create a new track. This time in the New Tracks window, select Mono and Aux Input.

Notice that your new Aux Input channel looks almost exactly like an audio track, only without the Record button.

2] **Name your Aux Input.** Name your Aux Input "Verb 1," by double-clicking its name in either the Mix or Edit window and typing the new name.

➤ **AUX INPUTS:** *Reference Guide, p. 479*

3] **Insert D-Verb.** On the new Verb 1 Aux Input, insert D-Verb by clicking the top Insert A and choosing Reverb > D-Verb (mono).

This time, when your plug-in window opens, leave the Mix set to 100%.

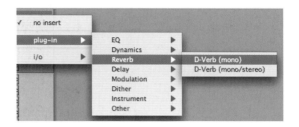

4] **Change the input.** You need to tell the sound where to go, which means setting the input of this channel. On your new Verb 1 Aux Input, change the input to Bus 1 (Mono).

Note

Remember: On a Pro Tools channel strip, the output is where it says Analog 1-2. Directly above that—where it says something like Mic/Line 1—is where you set the Input (or, what's going into a channel).

5] **Bus a track.** In the Sends section of whichever track you want to bus (I'm going to use the Scale Dbl track), click the top Send selector, A. Choose Bus 1 (Mono).

You'll now see a Send fader on the screen in the top-left corner.

At the top of the fader, the Track Selector lets you change which track you're bussing. The Output View tells you which Send is being shown on this fader, and the Pre/Post toggle lets you pick whether to send the effect before the volume level or after. The Audio Output Path shows what bus you're using. (The Target and Safe buttons are used for automation, and we'll cover those in Chapter 9.)

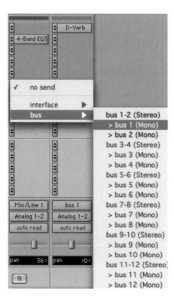

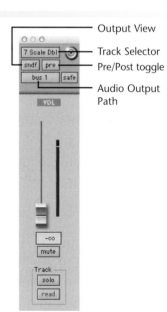

Output View

Track Selector

Pre/Post toggle

Audio Output Path

Tip

If you rest your cursor on an Insert or Send, a tool tip will tell you which one you're using.

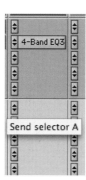

6] **Solo the Scale Dbl and Verb 1 tracks.**
So that you can hear what you're doing, solo both the track you're bussing from, and the track you're bussing to—in this case, Scale Dbl (the track you are bussing from) and Verb 1 (the track you are bussing to). Also, hold Option/Alt and click on the Volume slider of Verb 1 to bring the level up to zero.

7] **Move the Send fader.** Find the Send fader on your screen and drag it to a position next to the Scale Dbl track.

Use the Send fader to control the amount of the track's level you're bussing into the reverb. In other words, how much of this Scale Dbl do you want to send to the reverb? Notice that the default level of a Send fader is all the way down. This is to avoid feedback.

8] **Bring up the bus.** Play your vocal in Loop Playback, and slowly bring up the Send fader level until you like the amount of reverb.

9] **Bus the Snare.** Solo the Snare track and click on Send A. Choose Bus 1 to send the Snare to Bus 1.

Notice that your previous Send fader has now turned into the Snare track's Send fader, with the level back down at zero. Pro Tools will only show one Send fader at a time.

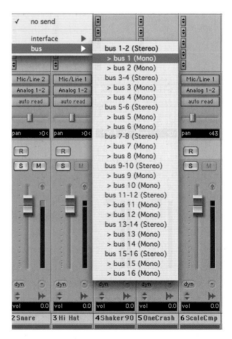

10] **Bring up the Bus again.** Play your Snare track and bring up its Send fader to bus as much reverb as you like. When you find a level you like, don't forget to save.

Now let's talk some more about the difference between the way we applied reverb in Exercise 1 and how we did it in Exercise 2.

In the first exercise, we used a reverb as an Insert—something you don't usually want to do. Inexperienced Pro Tools users make the mistake of using reverbs as Inserts simply because they don't understand bussing. Then they bring down the Reverb mix level, as we did in Exercise 1. That's a bad habit to get into, and here's why.

If you record a live drum kit with eight tracks and then use eight reverb plug-in as Inserts, you will run out of processing power very quickly. If you've ever worked in a studio, the studio probably has two or three different reverb modules, not ten or twelve. That's because one reverb module is used on many different tracks at the same time, and you simply turn up the Send level on those different instruments. Using a reverb as an Insert in Pro Tools would be like the studio's buying a new outboard reverb module every time you wanted to add reverb to a track!

In Exercise 2, we set up one reverb as an Aux Input and then we bussed to that reverb twice, once for the vocal and once for the snare. If our session were 24 tracks, we could've used that same Bus 1 as many times as we needed, without taking up precious processing power to add multiple reverb plug-ins. In short, bussing to one Aux Input 10 times, using only one reverb plug-in, makes much more sense than inserting 10 different Reverb Plug-ins as Inserts. It also makes sense for sonic reasons, because it puts all these affected signals into the same sonic space, giving your mixes a more cohesive sound.

EXERCISE 3:

Remove Inserts and Sends

So now let's turn off the reverb Insert on the Scale Comp track and bus it instead.

1] **Turn off the Insert.** On your Scale Comp track, click on the D-Verb plug-in Insert to open the window. Then click the Plug-in selector and choose No Insert.

You'll now see a window that says No Insert. You can close that.

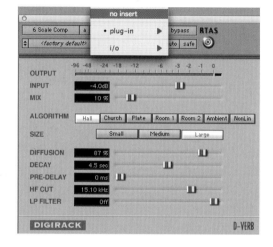

2] **Bus the Scale Comp.** On the Scale Comp channel strip's Send A, choose Bus 1 (Mono) again.

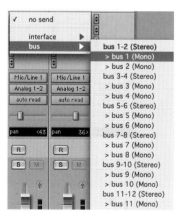

3] **Turn off the Send.** On the Scale Comp's Send fader, click on Bus 1 and choose No Send.

4] **Copy a Send.** Instead of creating a new bus and bringing up the level, let's use the same settings as the Scale Dbl bus we set earlier. Holding the Option/Alt key, click on Bus 1 of the Scale Dbl track and drag it to the same Send selector A slot on the Scale Comp track. Notice that Pro Tools shows you the outline of the Send as you drag it.

Now you have both vocal tracks bussed to the reverb.

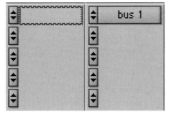

EXERCISE 4:

Name Your Busses

Sometimes when you're mixing a song, you'll have many busses and it will be difficult to keep track of them all. You'll be mixing and then wonder, "Was Bus 1 the reverb or the delay?" It's very easy to label your busses using a feature called I/O Setup (I/O meaning input/output). In this exercise, we're going to create another Aux Input—this time, a delay—and in the process learn how to name our busses.

Under Pro Tools's Setup menu, you'll see the I/O item. For large studios with lots of gear, the I/O settings come in very handy. They show how many inputs and outputs you have on your interface, and this is where you give them custom names. We're going to name our Bus 1 "Reverb 1," and our new Aux "Delay 1."

1] **Create a new Mono Aux Input.** Again, using your shortcut, create a new mono Aux Input and name it "Delay 1."

2] **Find your I/O labels.** Go to the Setup menu and choose I/O.

The I/O Setup window opens, showing your input and output labels. In this illustration, the bus labels are displayed. To see your Ins and Outs, click the tab at the top of the window.

➤ **I/O SETUP:** *Reference Guide, p. 72*

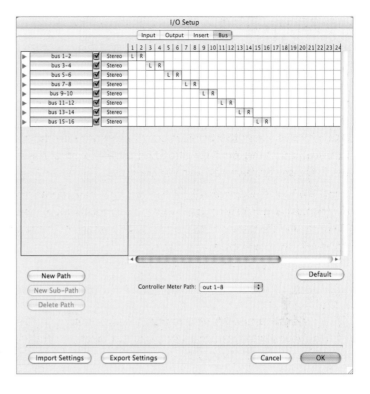

This window is a little different for each interface. Since I'm using the M-Audio FireWire Solo, the I/O Setup window only shows me two inputs and two outputs.

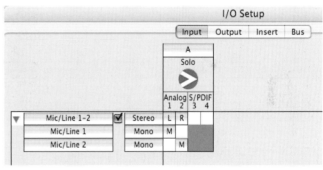

If you click the triangle next to the input or output name, the list will show you *both* ins and outs. Right now, my inputs say Mic/Line 1 and Mic/Line 2 and my outputs are labeled Analog 1 and 2.

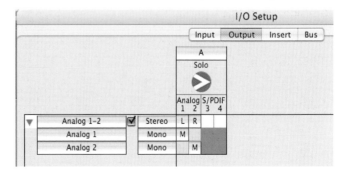

3] **Open the busses.** Click the Bus tab, and then click the Bus 1-2 triangle to expand it to show you Bus 1 and Bus 2.

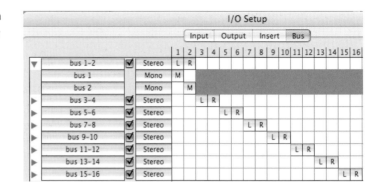

4] **Rename Bus 1.** Double-click Bus 1 and rename it "Reverb 1."

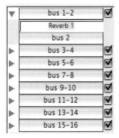

5] **Rename Bus 2.** Double-click Bus 2 and name it "Delay 1."

Close this window and look at your channels in the Mix window. Bus 1 is now labeled Reverb 1, and Bus 2 is Delay 1.

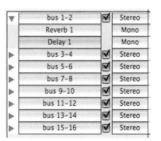

6] **Set the input of Delay Aux.** On the new Delay 1 Aux Input you created in step 1, set the input to our newly renamed Delay 1 (which used to be named Bus 2).

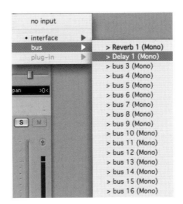

7] **Insert a delay plug-in.** On the Delay 1 Aux Input, insert the Medium Delay II plug-in. This time, choose the mono/stereo version.

When the plug-in window opens, you'll notice that it has two sets of identical controls. That's because it's a stereo plug-in and you can set different parameters for the left and right channels. We'll go over some of the parameters in the next exercise.

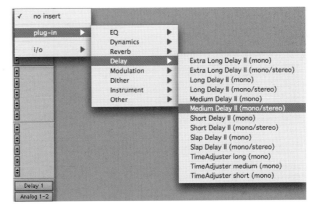

Plug-in controls ——

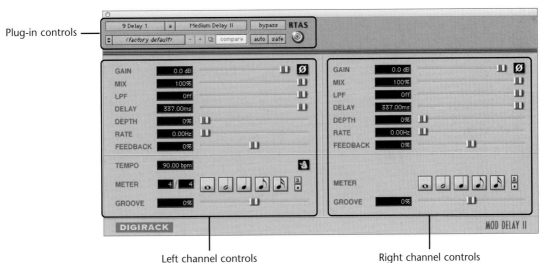

Left channel controls   Right channel controls

Why did we choose mono/stereo? And what does that mean, anyway? As a rule, if the source you're bussing from is mono (like a vocal), then you create a Mono Aux. But just because you're sending from a mono source doesn't mean that you can't use a stereo plug-in. Pro Tools's mono/stereo plug-ins mean Mono source in/Stereo output.

Earlier, we used a mono reverb to make things simple and easy for your first bussing experience. While mixing in the real world, though, I would have probably chosen a stereo reverb. As you may know and will definitely hear, stereo plug-ins are much richer and more interesting than mono. For most effects, two sides are better than one. It really depends on what type of music you're doing and how much space you want the effects to add.

EXERCISE 5:

Use a Delay

What's great about using a stereo delay is that you can put an eighth-note delay on one side and a sixteenth-note delay on the other. Using delays like this on anything such as vocals or even a static hi-hat part can give a song a completely different feel. Let's play with some delays and give our snare a different feel using a delay.

1] **Solo the Kick and Snare.** Solo the Kick and Snare tracks.

2] **Move the Delay Aux.** Move the Delay Aux to the right of the Snare track by clicking the track name and dragging it.

3] **Bus to the Delay.** On the Snare track, click Send B (below the Reverb bus) and choose the Delay bus.

The Delay Send fader will now show Snare.

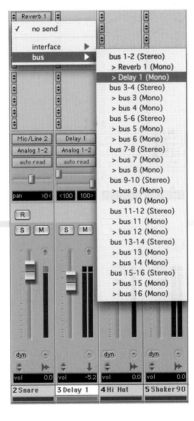

4] **Move the Send Fader.** Drag the Snare's Send fader next to the tracks you're working with.

5] **Loop the Kick and Snare.** In the Edit window, highlight four bars and set to Loop Playback.

6] **Change the left Delay settings.** In the Mix window Delay 1 channel, click the Medium Delay Insert to open the window. (Notice that a stereo plug-in gives you a mirror image of the settings on the left and right sides, allowing you to make one side's settings a bit different from the other side's.)

Now let's change some settings.

Note

Short Delay provides up to 43 ms of delay time. Slap Delay: up to 171 ms of delay time. Medium Delay: up to 341 ms. Long Delay: up to 683 ms, and Extra Long Delay: up to 2.73 seconds. We're using a Medium Delay.

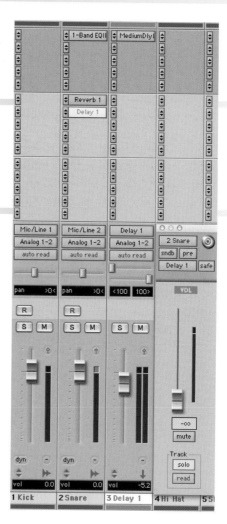

On the left side of the plug-in window, bring the Feedback up to around 20%. Now enable Tempo Sync by clicking the Metronome icon (which will turn orange) and then click the button for eighth-note duration value.

The Feedback slider controls how many times your sound delays. When you click the Metronome to enable Tempo Sync, the Tempo slider disappears, and the delay takes the tempo of your session.

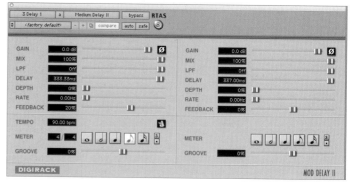

Try to click on the quarter-note duration; you can't, right? That's because we're using a Medium Delay. You can keep the same settings and change to the Long Delay, which will give you larger note values for longer delays.

About Delay Times and Reverbs

Experiment with the delay times and reverb sounds. Listen to some older music and study the use of effects then as compared with current music. You'll hear things such as the short/slap delays that were very common in the late 1950s, on guitar sounds and on Elvis's vocal of "Heartbreak Hotel." Long delays were very common in the power ballads of the 1980s—also the era of big reverbs, which saturated the huge background vocals and snare drums on most every pop song.

These days, reverb tends to make things sound dated, so be careful not to use too much of it. My personal philosophy is that if your voice always needs a lot of reverb to sound good, then maybe you should reconsider being a singer. It really depends on the song—but listen to artists with diverse bodies of work, like Sting or Peter Gabriel, and notice that they can sound just as great with no reverb as they do with it. For both delays and reverbs, sometimes less is more.

I've found that new Pro Tools users can be like young girls discovering how to use make-up; their mixes can sound quite effect-heavy. Inexperienced users want to make lots of "radio" voices and delays and reverbs because Pro Tools is a new toy and they love the diversity of the effects. Just be careful; first, be true to the song, and don't overuse effects simply because you know how.

7] **Bring up the bus.** While playing the loop, click on the Snare Send B, which is our delay send, and bring up the level on the Send fader until you like the delay sound.

You may notice some red clip indicators at the top of volume sliders in the Mix window. Although in general you want to avoid clipping, sometimes having a few red marks (on playback, not recording) is OK, as long as you can't hear distortion. You might want to bring down the level of the Snare Send fader if it's bothering you.

8] **Change the settings on the right.** While the loop is playing, adjust the right side of the Delay plug-in. Make the Feedback 30% and click on the sixteenth-note duration value.

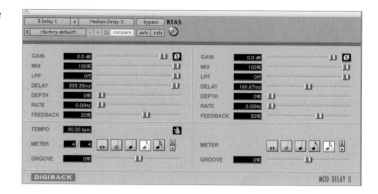

9] **Add the Reverb Aux.** Add the Reverb Aux by soloing it, as well. Now, with both delay and reverb, it sounds like too much reverb.

10] **Lower the Reverb.** Click on Send A of the Snare to bring up the Reverb Send fader and bring the level down to where it sounds good to your ears.

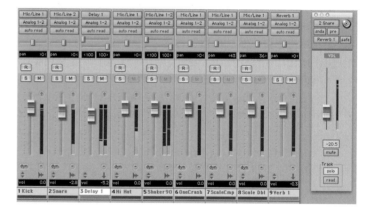

Warning

Be careful that you never bring the Reverb Aux's Send fader level down in order to lower the reverb on one track. Since other instruments are also using this Reverb Aux, that would lower the reverb level on every instrument using it. So, be sure to raise and lower reverb levels from the Send of the track you are adjusting—unless you want to adjust the reverb level in the whole song.

Delay Times and How to Find Them

The most crucial setting of a delay effect is the delay time. The delay time must work with the tempo of your song, or everything will start sounding off beat (in a bad way). I love using delays—but I make sure that my delays work in time with the tempo of my song.

For example, a very hip thing to do these days is to play a piano or guitar chord on the quarter note of a song and then bus that to an eighth-note delay. You then turn the delay's feedback up a bit so that you get more than one repeat of the chord—and then your effected track sounds like someone is playing chords on the eighth note. Yet as each chord repeats, the sound fades more and more as the delay repeats. It can give your part rhythm and depth. If you're working with drums or a loop and this delay does not work with your tempo, it's going to sound like your chords are being played to the wrong song. Most delay plug-ins these days give you simple icons of note values that you click to choose your delay times. The Pro Tools DigiRack Delay plug-in provides this feature and makes it easy to match your delay times with your song's tempo.

Look above the note values on the Delay plug-in, and you'll see that the delay time for an eighth note at our song's tempo is 333.33 ms, and the delay time for a sixteenth note is exactly half that at 166.67 ms. Rather than boring you with an explanation of the math, I'll tell you about getting one of the free applications that help you find delay times. Just google "Delay Calculator"; or go to VersionTracker.com (my favorite place to find software), and type "Delay Calculator" in the search field. My new favorite is a Widget for the Mac called Delay Finder.

Back in the days of tape machines and outboard delay boxes, every studio had a delay chart on the wall to figure out the correct delay times. I still have mine taped on the side of a rack, because sometimes it's just faster. Also, I've posted an Excel file of a delay chart on the protoolsformusicians.com site, in the Bonus Files pulldown menu.

	A	B	C	D	E	F	G	H
1	Tempo	Whole	1/2	1/4	1/8	1/16	1/32	1/64
2	60	1000.00	500.00	250.00	125.00	62.50	31.25	15.63
3	61	1016.67	508.33	254.17	127.08	63.54	31.77	15.89
4	62	1033.33	516.67	258.33	129.17	64.58	32.29	16.15
5	63	1050.00	525.00	262.50	131.25	65.63	32.81	16.41
6	64	1066.67	533.33	266.67	133.33	66.67	33.33	16.67
7	65	1083.33	541.67	270.83	135.42	67.71	33.85	16.93
8	66	1100.00	550.00	275.00	137.50	68.75	34.38	17.19
9	67	1116.67	558.33	279.17	139.58	69.79	34.90	17.45
10	68	1133.33	566.67	283.33	141.67	70.83	35.42	17.71
11	69	1150.00	575.00	287.50	143.75	71.88	35.94	17.97
12	70	1166.67	583.33	291.67	145.83	72.92	36.46	18.23
13	71	1183.33	591.67	295.83	147.92	73.96	36.98	18.49
14	72	1200.00	600.00	300.00	150.00	75.00	37.50	18.75
15	73	1216.67	608.33	304.17	152.08	76.04	38.02	19.01
16	74	1233.33	616.67	308.33	154.17	77.08	38.54	19.27
17	75	1250.00	625.00	312.50	156.25	78.13	39.06	19.53
18	76	1266.67	633.33	316.67	158.33	79.17	39.58	19.79
19	77	1283.33	641.67	320.83	160.42	80.21	40.10	20.05
20	78	1300.00	650.00	325.00	162.50	81.25	40.63	20.31
21	79	1316.67	658.33	329.17	164.58	82.29	41.15	20.57
22	80	1333.33	666.67	333.33	166.67	83.33	41.67	20.83
23	81	1350.00	675.00	337.50	168.75	84.38	42.19	21.09
24	82	1366.67	683.33	341.67	170.83	85.42	42.71	21.35
25	83	1383.33	691.67	345.83	172.92	86.46	43.23	21.61
26	84	1400.00	700.00	350.00	175.00	87.50	43.75	21.88
27	85	1416.67	708.33	354.17	177.08	88.54	44.27	22.14
28	86	1433.33	716.67	358.33	179.17	89.58	44.79	22.40
29	87	1450.00	725.00	362.50	181.25	90.63	45.31	22.66
30	88	1466.67	733.33	366.67	183.33	91.67	45.83	22.92
31	89	1483.33	741.67	370.83	185.42	92.71	46.35	23.18
32	90	1500.00	750.00	375.00	187.50	93.75	46.88	23.44
33	91	1516.67	758.33	379.17	189.58	94.79	47.40	23.70
34	92	1533.33	766.67	383.33	191.67	95.83	47.92	23.96
35	93	1550.00	775.00	387.50	193.75	96.88	48.44	24.22
36	94	1566.67	783.33	391.67	195.83	97.92	48.96	24.48
37	95	1583.33	791.67	395.83	197.92	98.96	49.48	24.74

EXERCISE 6:
Use Solo Safe

When you solo something, every other track mutes, right? Well, usually when you're mixing and you solo your vocal, for example, you don't want your effects to mute. So you put the effects track in what's called Solo Safe— meaning that when you solo anything, this effects track will not mute but will continue to pass signal.

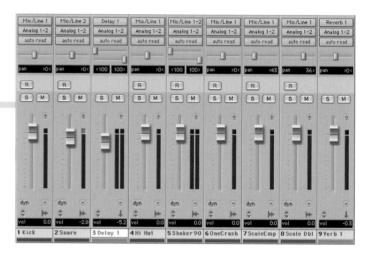

1] **Unsolo everything.** Always remember that holding down the Option (Mac) or Alt (Win) key will make your setting happen on all tracks. Now, rather than clicking Solo on each Soloed track to turn the Solo off, hold Option or Alt and just click on one active Solo button.

2] **Solo Safe the reverb.** Hold the ⌘/Ctrl key and click on the Verb 1 channel's Solo button. It will turn gray—what many computer users call "grayed out"—telling you that you can't use it now.

3] **Move the Delay track.** Get used to dragging plug-ins around! Drag the Delay track over next to the Reverb.

Tip

I try to keep all like tracks together. Usually my sessions are, from left to right in the Mix window, Drums, Percussion, Bass, Keys, Guitars, Misc. Instruments; and then last in each session is where I keep the Vocals. So when I'm editing an entire album of 10 different songs, I can move from song to song very quickly because I have an established method of working. I know where to find the drums and vocals and everything else quickly, because I organize my tracks and move them around as I work.

For global effects such as reverbs that are shared by many instruments, I use a position at the very end of the session after the vocals. If one Aux Input effect is just for the drums, then I will place that track after all the drums and make sure it's named "Drum Delay," so its role is clear. Try to come up with your own method of organization to keep things easy to find.

4] **Solo Safe the Delay track.** Hold down ⌘/Ctrl and click on the Solo button of the Delay track.

5] **Test it.** Solo your vocal or snare and play the song. Now you hear the effects with the soloed track. To turn off Solo Safe, do the same thing you did to turn it on—hold down ⌘/Ctrl and click on the Solo button.

6] **Save!**

A Shortcut Recipe for Bussing

1. Create a stereo or mono Aux Input.

2. Insert the plug-in onto the Aux Input.

3. Set the bus input of the Aux Input.

4. Choose that bus for the track to which you want to add the effect.

5. Bring up the level of the Send fader you're using.

6. Bring up the level of the Aux Input fader.

Compression

Compression is one of the most complicated things in the audio world. The difference between the softest part and the loudest part of a track is called the dynamic range. A compressor is used to limit the dynamic range or to smooth it out. A compressor usually consists of both a compressor and expander.

Think of a compressor/expander as a sort of antidepressant or a mood stabilizer. When a person's mental and emotional state gets consistently too high or too low, a doctor might prescribe a mood stabilizer. A compressor/expander does the same thing to audio: Something too loud gets brought down, and something too soft is brought up.

Compression can also be used as an effect. You may have seen some common outboard compressors, including Urei LA2A or 1176. These compressors over the years have become as much or more about the effect they apply to the sound as about the actual compression.

We're going to start here with the DigiRack Compressor plug-in.

EXERCISE 7:

Tackle the Compression Plug-in

You may have noticed that on the vocal tracks, I left Insert position A open for the compressor. Some engineers will apply compression after using EQ first. Some engineers say that compression before EQ is the best way to go. Let the engineers argue—I will move them around until it sounds right to my ears. You won't be sent to Pro Tools Prison for doing it wrong. I personally don't believe in rules—but I got kicked out of Girl Scouts and two summer camps, so maybe you shouldn't listen to me. What you *should* do is try it both ways and choose what you like. Find your own way, trust your own ears, and you just might be proclaimed a genius.

1] **Insert the Compressor.** On the Scale Comp track, go to the top Insert slot A that we left blank, above our EQ plug-in, and choose Compressor from the Dynamics category.

The Compressor window opens, with the familiar controls at the top, and the Compressor's controls under that.

The Input meter shows the level of your sound coming into the Compressor before it gets compressed. The Output meter shows the level of sound coming out of the Compressor, including any adjustments to the Gain value. The Reduction meter shows you how many dB (decibels) you are reducing your sound.

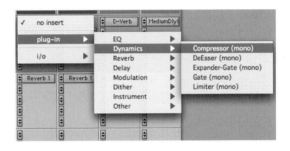

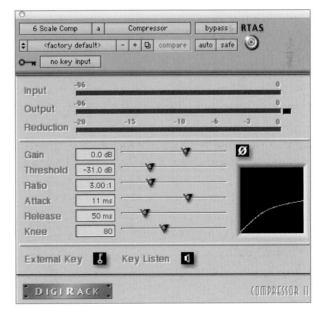

2] **Play with the Compressor.** Solo your Scale Comp track and adjust the Compressor plug-in settings. Move each slider all the way left and right to get a grasp of the effect these elements have. Compression is difficult to understand and to do. It definitely takes a trained ear to hear the very subtle differences in various settings, including changes in Attack and Release and Knee. These are the settings I chose for my voice.

In each of the next steps, move each slider until you have some understanding of its purpose. Then choose whatever sounds best for you.

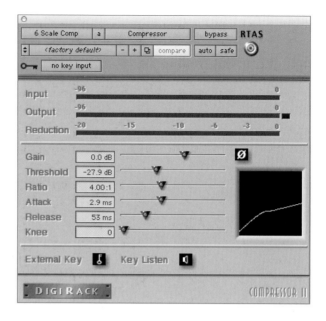

3] **Adjust the Gain.** This allows you to bring the overall level back up after compressing a sound, or bring it down if it's still too loud. The Gain allows you to change the level of your compressed sound globally as you need to.

4] **Change the Threshold.** This is the most important setting on a compressor: It's the level at which the compressor starts compressing. If Threshold is set to 0 dB, anything *below* 0 dB is unaffected, but anything 0 dB and *above* is compressed by the amount of your specification for the *compression ratio*.

5] **Set the Ratio.** The compression Ratio determines how much you want to compress something and is measured in decibels. If the Ratio is set at 2:1, that means for every 2 dB above the Threshold, the Compressor will increase it by 1 dB. At a compression ratio of 9:1, you would need 9 dB of level coming into the Compressor in order for the output to increase by 1 dB.

Lower settings for Ratio have less effect on the sound. Anything above a 10:1 Ratio, however, is often referred to as a *limiter*, because you are limiting the dynamic range. With high Ratios, you are telling the Compressor, "I pretty much want everything, loud or soft, to be the same level."

6] **Set the Attack.** This is measured in milliseconds (ms), and it tells the Compressor how quickly to react to the compression after it reaches the Threshold level. Once a signal reaches your Threshold value, the Attack time is the amount of time it takes your sound to decrease by the Ratio you have chosen. Short Attack times can cut off some sounds, such as the end of a sung word or the decay of a snare drum.

7] **Set the Release.** Like Attack, Release is measured in ms. The Release is how long it takes for the sound to return to normal, or how long it takes for the Compressor to stop compressing. In technical terms, the Release represents the amount of time the Compressor takes to return to zero.

If a Release time is too long, the Compressor may be decreasing a loud part that suddenly moves into a soft part and, due to the long release, the soft part may not be increased soon enough to be heard. If a Release time is too short, you may have too much background noise, depending on your compression level.

8] **Change the Knee.** The Knee setting is almost like the Q of compression. Knee determines whether the compressor kicks in *exactly* at the Threshold level or whether it's more gradual and starts taking effect *around* the Threshold level. There are settings known as "soft Knee" —the more gradual setting—and "hard Knee," when the compression starts only when it reaches the Threshold.

Side Chain Processing and Key Inputs

The Key Input selector. Using a Key Input is something we won't be tackling in this book because it's quite an advanced concept. Essentially, a Key Input works a lot like the plot in *Cyrano de Bergerac*. Remember how Cyrano gave his friend Christian the words to woo Roxanne? OK—the compressor is Christian, and the Key Input is Cyrano telling the compressor what to do and when. The Key Input is some other signal telling the compressor when to compress. In engineering terms, this is called *side chain processing*.

An example of when side chain processing might be used is when you have a kick drum and bass track working together, and you want them to be very tight. You might compress the kick and the bass separately, but set the Key Input of the bass compressor to be the kick drum. So the kick controls when the bass is compressed, and they both compress at the same time.

The **External Key** turns on side chain processing.

When **Key Listen** is on, you can hear the source of the sound you're using to open and close the compressor. If the kick drum is the source, you would hear that. Using the above analogy, this is the "eavesdropping button" that lets you hear exactly what Cyrano is saying, rather than Christian.

9] **Move the EQ first.** Drag the Compressor plug-in to Insert slot C below the EQ, to hear the difference between compression before EQ, and EQ before compression.

10] **Mute each plug-in.** Hold ⌘/Ctrl and click the plug-in in the Mix window. Mute the EQ now and listen to the Compressor without it.

11] **Save.**

Helpful Hints for Compression

Confused about compression? I don't blame you. My head spins every time I think about it.

While writing this chapter, I called my friend and brilliant engineer Kevin Killen and asked, "What should I tell new users about compression?" Here are some tips he gave me:

1. If you don't know what you're doing, lower your Input and Ratio so that you're not overcompressing.

2. If you hear the singer's breath louder than the word that follows it, you're overcompressing.

3. If you can hear the compression, you're probably using too much. You can always add more later.

Kevin also gave me these pointers as an overall guide to instrument compression:

◆ **Vocals:** Adjust your Threshold so that there's between 3 and 6 dB of Gain reduction (look at the Reduction meter). Use a Ratio between 2:1 and 4:1. Use a slow to medium Attack, a medium Release, and a soft Knee. A shorter Attack and a short Release will give you that "in your face" vocal sound.

◆ **Kick Drum:** Adjust your Threshold to have between 6 and 10 dB of Gain reduction. Use a 4:1 or 5:1 Ratio, a fast Attack, fast Release, and soft Knee.

◆ **Rock Snare:** Adjust Threshold to have between 4 and 8 dB of Gain reduction. Use a Ratio of between 4:1 and 8:1, depending on how hard the drummer is hitting the snare. Use a fast Attack, fast Release, and soft Knee.

◆ **Softer Snare:** For brushes or rods, use a Ratio from 2:1 to 3:1. Use a slow Attack for brushes, a medium Attack for rods. Set a medium or fast Release and a soft Knee.

◆ **Toms:** Use the same settings as for the kick drum.

◆ **Room (Drums):** For a pumped-up U2-like Room sound, adjust Threshold so there's between 8 and 12 dB of Gain reduction, between 10:1 and 20:1 Ratio, slow Attack, fast Release, and soft Knee. This setup may bring up cymbals and hi-hats, depending on where the room mics are placed.

◆ **Piano:** Adjust Threshold to have between 2 and 5 dB of Gain reduction, depending on how loud the player is playing. Set Ratio between 3:1 and 6:1, a medium Attack, a medium to long Release, and a soft Knee.

◆ **Acoustic Guitar:** Adjust threshold to have 2–3 dB of Gain reduction. Use a low Ratio such as 1:5:1 or 2:1, a medium-fast Attack, medium Release, and soft Knee. If the player is strumming more aggressively, raise the Ratio to 4:1.

◆ **Rock Guitar:** Give Threshold between 6 and 10 dB of Gain reduction. Use a high Ratio such as 8:1 to 12:1. Give it a fast Attack, medium to slow Release and soft Knee. For more atmospheric guitars, lower the compression ratio.

◆ **Bass:** If the bass is played aggressively, use higher Ratios such as 8:1 or 10:1. Set a medium Attack, fast Release, and soft Knee. For more melodic bass parts, use a Ratio between 3:1 and 4:1.

Keep in mind that these settings won't work for every track. It depends greatly on the type of song, the player, how hard or soft they play, their skill, and their instrument's setup. Typically, the better the player and the better the instrument, the less compression you need.

Wrap Up

I don't know about you, but this chapter has been a tough one for me. Spend as much time as you can applying EQ, as you learned in Chapter 5, and compression, and creating Aux Inputs.

For your homework, create a stereo Aux Input and add a stereo Reverb plug-in. See if you can tell the difference between the mono one we created in the exercises, and the stereo version. The more you do it, the easier it will become.

Be sure to go through the DigiRack Plug-Ins Guide and teach yourself about the other DigiRack plug-ins. We'll be covering a few more of these in later chapters, but the more you can discover on your own, the faster you'll become a Pro Tools aficionado.

MIDI TRACKS

7

In this chapter we're going to take our first steps toward learning and using MIDI. For some reason, MIDI intimidates a lot of people. If it intimidates you, forget everything you've learned or heard about MIDI up until now. Let's wipe the slate clean.

What is MIDI? It's an acronym for Musical Instrument Digital Interface, but don't let that scare you. If you think of MIDI as a translator, it will make more sense. Imagine that your computer speaks Spanish and your MIDI keyboard speaks German. MIDI is the guy between them, translating back and forth so they understand each other. MIDI simply allows your keyboard or any other MIDI device to talk to your computer, that's all.

You've seen that when you record an audio track in Pro Tools, an audio waveform is drawn on the screen, and whatever you record is created as a separate file and placed in your Audio Files folder within the Pro Tools Session folder. MIDI is not audio; it's computer information. So MIDI doesn't take up much disk space at all, and recording MIDI doesn't create separate files on your drive. When you record MIDI in Pro Tools, you'll see the actual notes you played on the screen, not an audio waveform. This is why MIDI is so efficient, especially for writing. If you record five tracks of piano as audio files, you could use over 200 MB of disk space. If you record ten piano tracks using MIDI, or twenty tracks, you'll take up almost no space whatsoever, because the MIDI tracks record performance information rather than audio. This difference will make much more sense when we actually use it, so hang in there.

Using MIDI gives you the extra advantage of being able to move each note, edit each note, delete one note at a time, transpose the track to a new key, and even quantize what you play. *Quantizing* simply means that you tell the computer, "Hey, I know my timing was a little sloppy. Please move my notes to the closest beats and make me sound better." You'll learn more about quantizing later in this chapter.

A few years ago, MIDI was primarily used to record tracks that would be played by external hardware keyboards and MIDI outboard gear. But these days you can use a software instrument that's installed in your computer, playing it in real time from an external keyboard controller. Your external keyboard is not used to generate its own sound but simply to trigger the sounds built into your software. In this chapter we'll use a free software instrument (SampleTank Free) that you can download. Even if you own other hardware or software instruments, I suggest you work through the exercises using SampleTank Free. MIDI offers so many options that if you're not completely familiar with how it works, it's easy to get off on the wrong track.

➤ **MIDI:** *Reference Guide, pp. 19-20*

Note

As this book was in its final stages of production, Digidesign unexpectedly released Xpand!, a great-sounding and versatile RTAS synthesizer that will be provided free to all new purchasers of Pro Tools. Existing owners of Pro Tools can receive a copy of Xpand! for a nominal fee to cover the cost of duplicating and mailing the CD. (Xpand! has hundreds of megabytes of sounds, so it's too big to download.) You'll find it easier to follow the examples in this book if you download SampleTank Free, but for your own productions Xpand! would be a better choice.

EXERCISE 1:
Download and Install SampleTank Free

Before we can start the exercises in this chapter, you need to make sure you have the correct software. In this chapter we'll be using IK Multimedia's software sample playback instrument SampleTank Free. If you have an Mbox or 002, you'll already have a copy of SampleTank SE 2, which you can use instead. In the next two Exercises, I'll tell you how to get SampleTank Free from the IK Multimedia website, but a more convenient download of the same software is available at www.protoolsformusicians.com.

Those of you who purchased Pro Tools M-Powered won't have SampleTank SE, so this chapter's exercises use the Free version. For best results with these exercises and the ones in Chapter 8, you'll need to download the Free software. Here's how:

1] **Go to Google.** Rather than clicking around IK Multimedia's website trying to find SampleTank Free, it's *much* easier to type what you want into Google. The more precise you are when using Google, the better. Go to Google and type "SampleTank Free Download."

2] **Click on the first link.** Notice that the very first link is exactly what we want. Click on that.

3] **Download SampleTank Free.** In the middle of the SampleTank Web page, you should see "Download SampleTank 2 Free." Choose either Mac or Windows. Make sure you take note of what the files are named and what folder on your machine they'll be downloaded to. You might want to create a folder on your hard drive called Downloaded SampleTank to store all the files you're about to download. (On a Windows computer, I recommend creating a folder called Downloads in the My Documents folder and putting all downloads there.)

4] **Open the download window.** If your download window doesn't open automatically, you'll need to open it yourself:

On a Mac using Safari, go to Window > Downloads. The Downloads window will show that something is actually downloading, how long it will take, and when it is finished. (You can also come back to this window anytime to download something again, should you ever need to.)

On a Windows PC using Internet Explorer, clicking on the SampleTank download link should open the File Download window. If it doesn't, right-click on the link and choose Save Target As. In Windows, you'll automatically see a download progress window. Each download process is separate, so you'll have to start over from your browser each time.

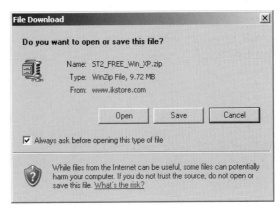

5] **Expand the file.** On a Mac, when the file download is almost done, Safari will give you this window: So you're in luck. The Mac will do the work for you. It will uncompress the file and get it ready for you to install by placing the uncompressed file on your desktop.

In Windows, you'll need to unzip the file. If you don't have the WinZip utility (not free, but cheap and useful), you can right-click on a zipped file in Windows Explorer and choose Explore. This will open up the .zip file as if it were a standard Windows folder.

6] **Locate the SampleTank Free installer.** Now that you have downloaded the file, you can install the software. Many users get confused about this. Think about downloading as going to the mailbox to get a letter—you still have to open the letter and read it.

On a Mac, the file should be on the desktop and look like this:

In Windows, the file should look like this in Windows Explorer:

7] **Install the software (Mac).** Double-click on the SampleTank Free installer. You'll be asked for your Mac's password to authenticate the install.

This is a fairly straightforward installation: accept the License and do an Easy Install. You'll see the installation progress, and finally a window will come up telling you that the software was installed correctly. Choose Quit.

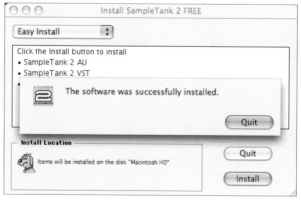

8] **Install the software (Windows).** When you double-click the installer, you'll see the Security Warning, which comes up whenever you install software that Microsoft hasn't authenticated. (Many software manufacturers don't bother with the authentication process, not because they don't care about compatibility but because it's expensive.) Click Run. The installer will recommend that you close all currently running programs, so do that.

9] **Choose the plug-in format.** Choose the plug-in formats you want to install. Be sure the RTAS option is checked.

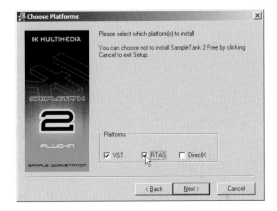

10] **Choose the RTAS folder.** Next, you'll need to tell the installer what folder your RTAS plug-ins are located in. The default on the Mac (Macintosh HD > Library > Application Support > Digidesign > Plug-ins) will almost certainly be correct, but the installer's default for Windows systems is wrong. The default is C:\Program Files\Digidesign\DAE\Plug-Ins. You need to change this manually to C:\ Program Files\Common Files\Digidesign\ DAE\Plug-Ins.

11]

Choose where the application is installed.
In Windows, the installer will want to put SampleTank itself into C:\Program Files\ SampleTank 2 Free. On the Mac it will go in Macintosh HD > Applications > SampleTank 2 Free. This is fine.

On the Mac: "What do I do with files after I install them?"

I like to keep my desktop clean and free of extraneous files. Nothing is worse than a messy desktop, and leaving files there makes it far more difficult to find things when you need them. I keep two folders on my hard drive, one called Installers and one called Downloads. When something lands on my desktop and I think I may need it again, I immediately put it into the appropriate folder. So on my machine, the SampleTank Free installer would go into my Installers folder (**A**).

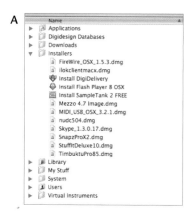

To make a new folder on a Mac, use the familiar command in the Finder, ⌘+Shift+N, or go to the File menu and choose New Folder. Be sure to name your folders appropriately.

You can tell Safari to download files to a particular place. In Safari, go to Preferences and click the General tab (**B**). See where it says "Save downloaded files to"? The current selection is probably Desktop. Click on that and change it to Other (**C**). Then select the Macintosh hard drive and choose your new Downloads folder (**D**). Now all downloads will go into this new folder rather than onto your desktop (**E**).

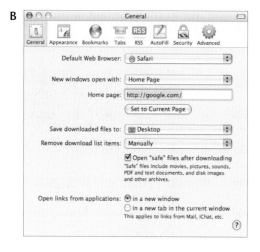

EXERCISE 2:
Download SampleTank Sounds

After all this, you'd think we'd be done, right? No. Unfortunately, we have two more steps. We need to download and install SampleTank Free's sounds, and then we need to authorize the software. Since we still have our Web browser open to the SampleTank page, let's download the sounds and put them in the right place. I'm going to show you how to do two of them, and then I'm going to let you download and place the rest on your own.

You may be wondering why you can't download just one file that contains the software and the sounds. Every other plug-in I've installed does just that, and it's straightforward and simple. I don't know why this installation process is so complex, especially since the purpose of SampleTank Free is to entice new customers to IK Multimedia. But never mind: Let's just finish it up so we can dive in and make some music.

1] **Download the first sound.** Go back to the same SampleTank page in your Web browser. Below the software download link, you'll see the sounds. Click on the first sound, 73 EPiano. This will start the file download and place the new file in your new Downloads folder (or wherever you have your browser set to download).

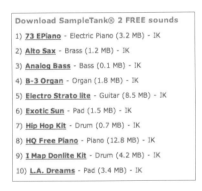

2] **Prepare to move files (Mac).** Find the 73 EPiano file you just downloaded. Mine is now inside my Downloads folder. Open another Finder window by holding the ⌘ key and clicking on your hard drive. In the new window go to Applications > SampleTank 2 Free and set the windows side by side.

3 **Move the 73 Epiano (Mac).** See the ST2FreeInstruments folder on the window to the right? This is where you will copy all of your downloaded Instruments. Drag the uncompressed 73 EPiano folder (not the contents of this folder) into the STFreeInstruments folder. It will disappear from your Downloads folder because it has been moved.

4 **Prepare to move files (Windows).** In Windows Explorer, find the "73 EPiano" folder you just downloaded. If you've been following the exercises, it will be in My Documents > Downloads. Unzip it using WinZip or Explorer the same way you unzipped the SampleTank installer.

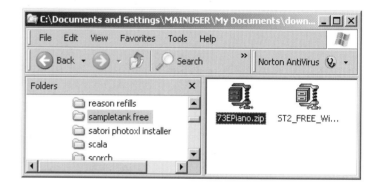

5 **Move the 73 EPiano (Windows).** Drag the EP folder into the folder C:\Program Files\SampleTank 2 Free\ST2FreeInstruments.

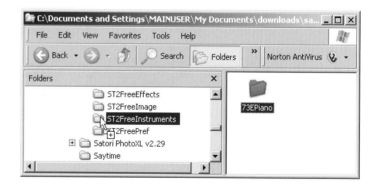

On the Mac: An Amazing New Shortcut for Switching Applications

Since we're going to be going back and forth between our Web browser and the Finder, let me teach you a great Mac shortcut for that. In any application, press ⌘+Tab. A giant, transparent Application Switcher will appear in the middle of the screen. By pressing Tab repeatedly without releasing the ⌘ key, you can change from one application to the next.

Notice that I have Pro Tools, FreeSnap (a screen capture program), iChat, Safari, Microsoft Entourage (my email program), and Microsoft Word all open at the same time. This Application Switcher is how I move among these applications quickly and easily. Also in the Switcher is the Mac Finder. By going from Safari to the Finder, I can move downloaded sounds immediately after I download them.

6] **Download the Alto Sax.** Go back to your Web browser and click on the second sound, which is Alto Sax. Go ahead and download all the sounds now, by clicking them one at a time. Make sure all folders are uncompressed and ready to be moved into the ST2FreeInstruments folder.

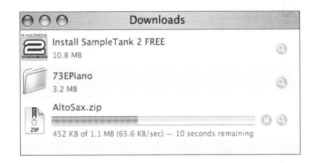

7] **Move all downloaded sounds.** Drag all of the instrument folders from your download location into the ST2FreeInstruments folder. There should be 13 sounds ins STFreeInstruments.

Why SampleTank?

I have to be honest. I'm not a huge fan of SampleTank. But because SampleTank Free is free, it's the most affordable way to get you guys started using MIDI. Please use it just to get a broad understanding of how to use MIDI, but don't base your opinion of software plug-ins on this particular one. Although IK Multimedia makes some great plug-ins, I don't find SampleTank to be particularly user-friendly compared with other software samplers I have used.

In an appendix that's downloadable from this book's companion web site (www.protoolsformusicians.com), you'll find a list of my favorite virtual instruments and plug-ins. When and if you're ready to invest in more toys, you can turn to this for some suggestions.

The obvious disadvantage to using only SampleTank Free or SampleTank SE is that they are minimized versions of IK Multimedia's professional software sampler, SampleTank XL, which costs $499. The version we will be using in this book gives you very limited sounds in the hope that you'll be enticed into buying the full version, which comes with 4.5 gigabytes of sounds and allows you to add your own sounds as well.

Before making a decision about whether to invest in SampleTank XL, look at other software samplers, too, such as Mark of the Unicorn's Mach 5 (for Mac only), or Kontakt from Native Instruments. I always tell people to talk to the people who are *using* the software, not the people *selling* it. You'll get a much better idea of what's popular among folks who make their living creating music.

What Is SampleTank?

SampleTank is a *virtual instrument.* More specifically, it's a *software-based sampler.*

What is a virtual instrument? In the old days, you had to have a real piano or a real organ, or carry around these 50-pound MIDI samplers and hardware instruments and keyboards. I have had big trucks deliver Hammond B-3 organs to my studio over the years.

But today you can find a software version of every instrument you can think of. Instead of hiring roadies to lug it into the studio, you simply access it as a plug-in and the instrument shows up on your screen. You'll see a graphical representation of the instrument, and it will work and sound almost identical to the real thing, without all the physical hassle. There are software-based pianos that give you recordings of actual Steinways, Yamahas, and Bösendorfers, and there are virtual B-3 organs that allow you to use the drawbars and pedals and add rotary speaker effects (Leslies) just like the real thing.

B4 from Native Instruments

About Virtual Instruments

From my perspective, there are three types of virtual instruments: software samplers, software synths, and sample playback synths.

A *software sampler* plays back and records sounds based on real audio files and usually real instruments. A software sampler typically comes with a large library of its own sounds, and allows you to expand this library either by creating your own sounds or by purchasing and importing sample libraries (such as the ones found at SoundsOnline.com). If you have a large library of sounds for your sampler, you'll need lots of disk space.

A *software synth* creates artificial and electronic sounds. A synth uses an *oscillator*, which is a device that plays a simple waveform at a specific frequency. You then alter the frequency and the waveform to create synthesizer sounds. Examples of software synths would be the Absynth and FM7 from Native Instruments, and Arturia's Minimoog. Software synths usually don't take up much space on the hard drive, because they are using the computer to generate sounds rather than requiring a library of audio files.

A *sample playback synth* is a combination of a sampler and a synth, and usually gives you a nonexpandable library of sampled sounds. Examples include Synthogy Ivory, my favorite piano plug-in, and Spectrasonics Atmosphere, my favorite pad plug-in. Both of these plug-ins give you a huge multigigabyte library of sounds. Though you can edit the sounds and create your own sounds based on them, the libraries themselves are not expandable.

SampleTank Free is a sample playback synth. The full version of SampleTank is a sampler.

EXERCISE 3:
Testing MIDI, 1 2 3...

Using a software instrument without a MIDI keyboard is possible, but difficult. Most of you will have a MIDI keyboard with a USB connection that plugs into your computer. Some of you will have a MIDI keyboard that plugs into a MIDI interface, which is then plugged into your computer. Make sure that you have installed the software drivers that came with your USB keyboard or MIDI interface. If you can't find the product's CD or are worried that the drivers are out of date, go to the manufacturer's Web site and download and install the latest drivers. (In Windows, you may need to restart the computer after installing a driver.)

Before we start using SampleTank to explore the MIDI features in Pro Tools, let's do a quick test to make sure that your MIDI keyboard is working.

1] **Make a new session.** Save whatever you're working on and close the session. Press ⌘/Ctrl+N or go to the File menu and select New Session. Name the new session "MIDI Chapter" and, as always, be sure to save this new session to your Audio drive.

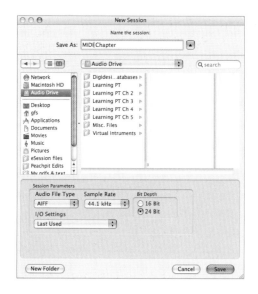

2] **Make a new track.** Use ⌘/Ctrl+Shift+N to create a new track. This time we're going to create a MIDI track.

3] **Put the track in Record.** With the track in record, play your MIDI keyboard. You shouldn't hear anything, but you should see level on this meter as you play. The level is not audio level but rather MIDI input level. This is telling you that the computer sees your MIDI keyboard and that your MIDI is set up and ready to go.

4] **Delete this track.** We're not going to use the MIDI track now, so highlight the track name, go to the Track menu, and choose Delete.

"What if I don't have MIDI level?"

If you don't see MIDI level, here is a checklist of ways to troubleshoot the problem:

1. Unplug and replug your USB cable.

2. Make sure your MIDI track is set to play the correct MIDI device and channel.

3. Make sure you've installed the latest driver software for your MIDI keyboard.

4. Go to the Setup menu, choose MIDI, and then choose Input Devices (**A**). Make sure your device is selected as an Input Device (**B, C**).

 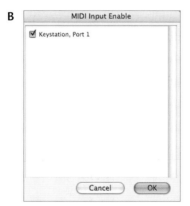 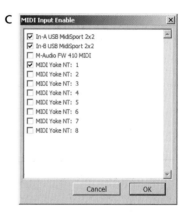

5. On a Mac, go to Applications > Utilities > Audio MIDI Setup and click on MIDI Devices. You should see your MIDI keyboard or interface in this window. If you do not, then you need to reinstall your drivers and restart the computer (**D**).

(continues on next page)

6. In Windows, go to the Start menu and choose Settings > Control Panel > System. Click the Hardware tab and then the Device Manager button (**E**). In the Device Manager window, click the plus sign beside Sound, Video and Game Controllers to expand it (**F**).

E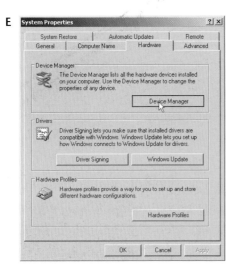

F

If your hardware is not listed here, the driver has not been installed properly. If it's listed but you see a red X through the speaker icon, try double-clicking the item in the list and take a look at the Properties dialog box for the driver. If you're unable to figure out what to do in Properties, contact the MIDI hardware manufacturer for support.

EXERCISE 4:
Authorize SampleTank

Most of you already understand the concept of *authorizing software.* Basically, you're telling the manufacturer, "I downloaded your software. Now will you unlock it so it'll work for me?" The company gives you permission via a file or serial number. Following their instructions will turn on the software for you.

There are many different ways to authorize software. What we're going to do now with SampleTank is just one of many of the procedures you may be using at one time or another. After you start buying and using more third-party plug-ins in Pro Tools, you'll get used to the various types of authorization.

In our Pro Tools session, we're going to create a new feature called an *instrument track.* We'll insert SampleTank on this track so that we can authorize the software via the Internet. Then in the following exercise we'll learn about working with instrument tracks as we begin to learn how to use SampleTank.

1] **Create a new track.** Press ⌘/Ctrl+Shift+N to create a new track, and choose Stereo Instrument Track from the New Tracks pull-down menu.

2] **Insert SampleTank Free.** On Insert A of the instrument track, choose Instrument > SampleTank 2 Free.

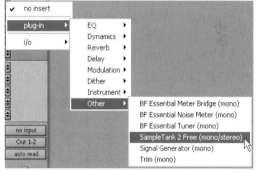

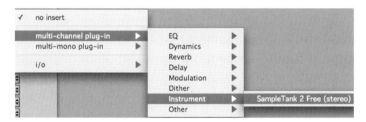

3] **Authorization, step 1.** A window will open asking you to authorize this software. Click Next.

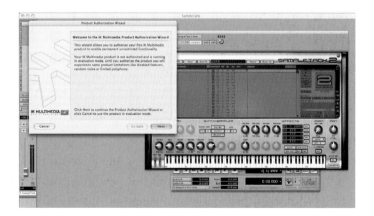

4] **Authorization, step 2.** The next window asks if you can connect to the Internet with the computer you're using. Assuming you're able to do so, choose the first selection, which is to connect to the Internet now.

5] **Authorization, step 3.** The next window gives you a serial number and a digital ID. If you're registering online, you don't need to worry about writing these down; click Register On Line.

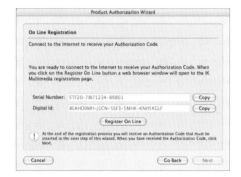

6] **Authorization, step 4.** Your Web browser will start up, and you'll see a Welcome page where you have to fill in some personal information. Do this, and click Submit.

7] **Authorization, step 5.** After you click submit, an email will be sent to you with an authorization code. Get this email and copy or write down the number. Now go back to Pro Tools and click Next in the authorization window. This will open a window that requires the authorization code. Paste or type in the code that was emailed to you.

8] **Authorization, last step.** The last authorization window tells you that you have successfully authorized the software. Click the Finish button. You should now see the SampleTank plug-in window. Finally, it's time to play some music!

EXERCISE 5:
SampleTank and Instrument Tracks

The SampleTank plug-in may look scary at first glance, but don't worry about it—just follow the instructions and you'll learn about it as you go.

1] **Choose a sound.** On the top-right of the plug-in interface is the Browser, where you'll see a list of sounds. To the left of each name is a white arrow that you can click to open subfolders. Click the arrows next to 73EPiano and its subfolders until you see the three electric piano presets. Double-click on Ballad EP.

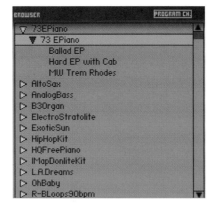

2] **Play the electric piano.** On the left side of the interface, your piano is loaded into the first slot, called a part. Put the instrument track in Record and bring up the fader. Play your keyboard and hear the electric piano sound. You should see level in the Level column at the right end of the Part 1 line, and the keys you play will be highlighted on the keyboard.

3] **Load another sound.** Open another instrument folder in the Browser. In our example, I'm trying out the B3Organ. Double-click one of the two organ sounds and try them out.

Notice that you have 16 parts in the Parts list. That means you can have 16 different sounds loaded and play them on 16 different MIDI channels, all at once. You could have a piano on channel 1, a bass on channel 2, etc. Think of MIDI channels as being a lot like TV channels. *Wheel of Fortune* might be on Channel 5 and Oprah on Channel 7, so you simply change channels to watch you want. Same thing with MIDI: You change channels to play different sounds.

Part 1 in SampleTank is set to play MIDI channel 1, Part 2 is set to play MIDI channel 2, and so on. So how do we add a sound to Part 2? Let's do that now.

4] **Load a sound into Part 2.** Click on the Part 2 line in the SampleTank window. Notice that the selector box moves down to this part. Now choose a new sound in the Browser and double-click it. It will load into Part 2. I used the Analog Bass sound. So now we have two parts loaded in SampleTank.

5] **Activate Instrument view.** With the track still in Record, play the MIDI keyboard. You still hear Part 1, right? Why? Because MIDI messages are still reaching SampleTank on MIDI channel 1. You need to tell the track that you want to play channel 2 now. To do this, you have to change a View setting in Pro Tools to view the instrument track's MIDI channels. So go to View > Mix Window and check the Instruments selection. Notice in the Mix window that you have some new settings up on top.

➤ **MIDI TRACK OUTPUT:** *Reference Guide, pp. 105–106*

Don't be intimidated by what you see in the Mix window. Remember to use the tool tips: Simply hold your mouse over a selection, and Pro Tools will tell you what it is. The top selection is your MIDI Input Selector. Notice it is set to All. This is the default and probably the best selection 99 percent of the time. (The only reason you'd ever need to change this is if you have multiple MIDI controllers. In that situation, you might want one controller to play the piano parts while another, which might be a pad controller, plays drum parts.) As a rule, leave the MIDI Input Selector set to All.

6] **Change the output channel.** In the Mix window, the setting below the MIDI Input Selector is the MIDI Output Selector. This is where you choose the MIDI channel on which you want to play SampleTank. Think of a MIDI output like this: What device or instrument do I want to hear going *out* of this track, and what channel should it be on? Click on the MIDI Output Selector tab and you'll see a list of available channels. Choose channel 2. Now play your keyboard, and you should hear the sound you chose for Part 2.

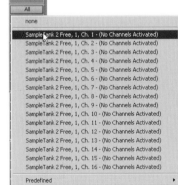

7] **Load a sound into Part 3.** I like to reinforce what you learn by having you do things twice. So let's click on Part 3 in the SampleTank Free interface and add another sound from the Browser. I'm choosing Electro Strato lite.

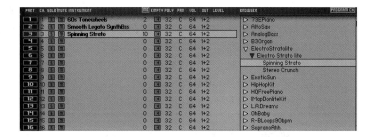

8] **Change the instrument channel.** Go to the MIDI Output Selector and change the channel to 3. Play your keyboard. You should now hear the Strat guitar sound.

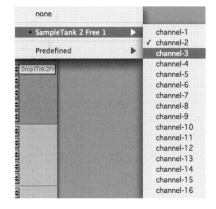

9] **Delete the instrument track.** In the next exercise you're going to learn how to record multiple tracks at once, so highlight the instrument track, go the Track menu, and delete this track. We now have a clean slate to start from again.

EXERCISE 6:
Record Multiple MIDI Tracks

Remember how we learned that SampleTank is capable of playing 16 parts at once? This is because it's a *multi-timbral* plug-in. (Incidentally, *timbre* is pronounced "tam-br," so *timbral* is pronounced "tam-brl.") Multi-timbral simply means "many sounds." Not all MIDI plug-ins are multi-timbral, however. Spectrasonics Trilogy and Native Instruments Elektric Piano, for instance, play only one sound at a time on one channel only. Instrument tracks are perfect when you're not using a multi-timbral plug-in. With SampleTank, we can take advantage of another way of using MIDI in Pro Tools.

Note

If you're using Digidesign's new Xpand! synth instead of SampleTank (as suggested at the beginning of this chapter), you need to know that Xpand! is not multi-timbral. Each Xpand! sound that you use will need a separate instance of Xpand! The best way to do this is by creating as many instrument tracks as you need and inserting Xpand! on each of them.

As you noticed in Exercise 5, we had to keep changing the MIDI channel to hear different sounds on different channels. When we get to producing a song, however, we want to be able to have several MIDI tracks, each playing one of these sounds, right? If we used instrument tracks, we'd have to insert the SampleTank plug-in onto each instrument track for each MIDI instrument we wanted to use. While this will work, it's not convenient (and in any case you can't do it with SampleTank Free because only one instance of this plug-in can be used at a time). There's a much faster, better way to do exactly what we want.

In Chapter 6 we shared a reverb among multiple tracks using aux inputs. Now we're going to do the same thing with MIDI. We're going to create a stereo aux track, insert SampleTank on that track, and then create multiple MIDI tracks that share the one plug-in. Then we can start creating an entire song.

1] **Create a new track.** Create a stereo aux track, name it "SampleTank," and bring the volume up by Option/Alt-clicking the volume slider. (This is a handy shortcut for setting a channel to unity gain.)

2] **Insert SampleTank.** On Insert A, insert SampleTank 2 Free.

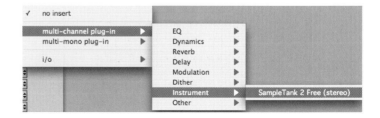

3] **Put a loop on Part 1.** In Part 1, choose R&BLoops 90 BPM, and choose the sound 33RPM. You will hear a record scratch sound running continuously.

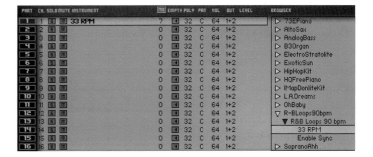

4] **Create a MIDI track.** Create a MIDI track and name it "Drum Loop."

5] **Set the output instrument.** Remember the MIDI settings for an instrument track that were at the top of the channel strip? Well, with MIDI tracks, they're down below where the audio input and output usually are. In MIDI tracks, these selectors are for the MIDI input and output. See where it says None? (Or you may see a MIDI hardware output listed.) This is where you need to select SampleTank channel 1 as the output device.

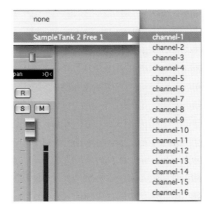

6] **Play the loops.** Put the MIDI track in record and start playing keys. You'll hear different drum loops on various keys. (Not all of the keys have loops.) Choose one you like.

7] **Put SampleTank in Sync.** What if you want to change the tempo of this loop? Near the bottom-right corner of the SampleTank interface is a button called Sync. Click it to turn it on, and play the loops again.

If you're using a Mac, you'll notice that the loops play faster now. This is because the default tempo of Pro Tools is 120 BPM, and these loops are now syncing to the Pro Tools tempo.

If you're using Windows, unfortunately, you're out of luck, because the Windows RTAS version of SampleTank Free doesn't sync. (This problem may be fixed by the time you read this. Let's hope so.) To do the rest of the exercises, Windows users will need to set Pro Tools' tempo to 90 BPM.

Mac users, let's change the tempo.

8] **Change the tempo (Mac).** Open the Transport window and turn off the Conductor so you'll be in manual tempo mode. Now, while playing a drum loop on the keyboard, drag your tempo slider up or down and play a new note. Your loop will also change tempo.

9] **Choose a tempo and a loop (Mac).** Find a loop and a tempo that you like. Notice that if you play two (or more) notes starting at the exact same time, you can layer loops and parts together.

Once you have chosen a loop, take note of which key(s) you're playing.

Below each track in the Mix window is a small Comments field. To type in it, just click and type. I leave notes and reminders for myself in sessions all the time, such as "edit vocals" or "re-cut bass." For MIDI tracks, often I will note a preset and/or the note I'm playing. In this case, I wrote "33RPM – F2," which means I'm using the 33RPM sound and playing the F2 key.

10] **Turn on Wait for Note.** In the Transport window, the top-left button to the right of the counters is the Wait for Note button. When this is turned on, you can put Pro Tools in Record, but until you play a MIDI note, it won't begin recording.

11] **Record the loop.** Put Pro Tools in Record by pressing ⌘/Ctrl+spacebar. The Record button on the Transport and the Wait for Note button will flash. When you're ready, press the loop key(s) you have chosen and hold them for a few bars.

It's best to record MIDI-triggered loops in two- to four-bar lengths, because if you record one held note that sustains throughout the song, you'll have to start the song from the beginning every time in order to retrigger the drum part.

12] **Change the track size.** Open the Edit window. You should see your MIDI notes on the Drum Loop MIDI track. (You can always recognize a MIDI track in the Edit window by the tiny vertical keyboard.)

Your MIDI notes probably look very small to you. Let's make this track jumbo size.

The MIDI still looks small, right? Zoom horizontally with the ⌘/Ctrl+] shortcut until you can see the MIDI better. This still is too small, though. See the vertical keyboard on the right side of the track name? We're looking at almost five octaves, but we really only need one or two. So we need to use MIDI zoom.

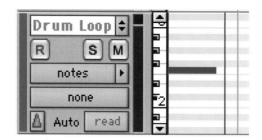

13] **Use MIDI zoom.** At the top of the Edit window, to the left of the editing tools, are the four rectangular buttons that control the zoom settings. The buttons at the far left and far right have only arrows on them, but the middle two buttons also have icons. The left icon is the audio waveform zoom, and the right icon is the MIDI zoom. Above and below both of these icons are an up arrow and a down arrow. Clicking the up arrow zooms in, and the down arrow zooms out.

Click on the up arrow of the MIDI zoom. Now look at your vertical MIDI keyboard in the Edit window. You should now have one less octave, making your MIDI notes thicker. Click to zoom in one more level. Now you can see your MIDI notes clearly, as well as what note on the keyboard they use. If you can't see the MIDI notes, it's because you've zoomed them up or down out of the track view area. Click the little arrow button at either the top or bottom of the keyboard strip to scroll the notes back into view.

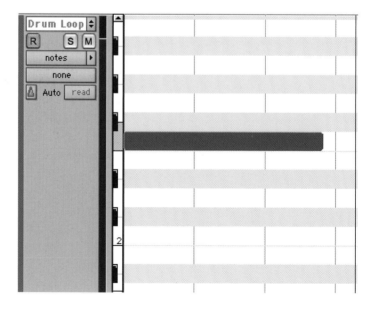

14] **Trim the MIDI note.** We want the drum loop to be exactly two bars, stopping precisely at the downbeat of bar 3. So go into Grid mode, make sure your grid is set to quarter notes, and select the Trim tool. Trimming MIDI works exactly like trimming audio. Click at the end of your drum loop MIDI note, pull it to the downbeat of the closest bar, and let go. The MIDI note should snap to this beat, giving you an exact number of bars.

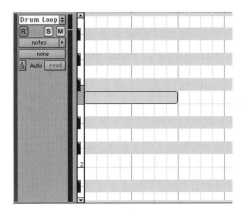

➤ **TRIM TOOL:**
  Reference Guide, pp. 254, 421

15] **Repeat the loops.** Grab the Selector tool and highlight from bar 1 to bar 3, or for as long as you held your loop. Then use Option+R (Alt+R in Windows) and repeat 25 times, or as many times as you want. You'll now have enough drum loop to play to.

16] **Prevent flams.** If you listen closely, you may hear that at the very end of one loop and the beginning of the next, the kick sound has a *flam* (two drum hits sounding at almost the same time). To prevent this, switch to Slip mode before using the Repeat command, and with the Trim tool drag the left end of the MIDI note just slightly to the left. Watch the Cursor or the End and Length fields at the top of the window to make sure the note ends before the bar line.

Now go back to Grid mode and use the Repeat command. One loop will shut off cleanly before the next one starts.

17 **Change the track size.** Change the SampleTank and the Drum Loop MIDI track size to small.

18 **Edit the SampleTank sound.** This book is not about sound programming in virtual instruments. But if you find you're getting tired of the "vinyl" noise that's part of SampleTank Free's drum loops, here's how to turn it off: Click on Part 1 in the SampleTank interface (the part that contains the 33 RPM drum preset). Then look for the Effects section, toward the right end of the panel under the Parts list. This is where SampleTank's effects are inserted. Next to the word PHONO is an On button, which is glowing red. Click the button. Ahh, that's better.

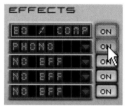

19 **Save.**

EXERCISE 7:
Record a Bass Line

1] **Add a new MIDI track.** Create a new MIDI track and name it "Bass."

2] **Change the MIDI output.** On the new MIDI track, change the MIDI Output Selector to SampleTank, channel 2. Put the new MIDI track in Record. You won't hear anything, because we haven't yet loaded a sound to play on channel 2.

3] **Add a bass sound to Part 2.** Click on the SampleTank plug-in to open the window, and click on the Part 2 line to create a box around Part 2. In the SampleTank Browser, choose Analog Bass, and double-click the SmoothAnalog SynthBss to load it into Part 2.

4] **Play along with your loop.** With the bass track in Record, press the spacebar to play the loop you just recorded. Play a bass line along with the loop until you're ready to record something.

5] **Record the bass.** Recording MIDI is exactly like recording audio. Just as with audio, you put a track in Record and then press ⌘/Ctrl+ spacebar to record. When in Record, let the first bar of the loop go by as a count-in and then start playing. If you make a mistake, press Return (the QWERTY keyboard Enter key on a PC) to go back to bar 1 and start over. This will record over your previous take. Record one take and keep it. Double-click on the Zoomer tool (*not* the zoom buttons discussed in Exercise 6) to see the entire song.

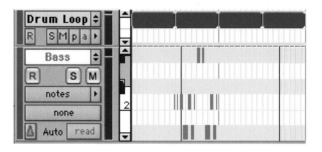

6] **Zoom in again.** Make your bass track jumbo-sized. Grab the Zoomer tool and draw a box around your bass notes. It should look something like this: You can see how I started recording at bar 3. And although my notes are close to the beat, they're not quite perfect. So let's quantize them.

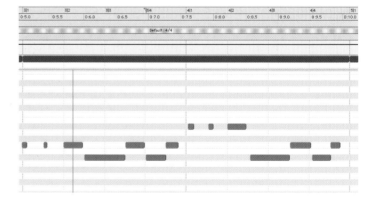

Quantizing: What Is It?

I'm sure you've heard the term before, and many of you know what it means. When you *quantize* a MIDI part, you're simply telling the MIDI notes to move to the closest beat. Before you quantize, you need to tell Pro Tools what note value you want to quantize your notes to. If it's a busy part, you may want to quantize to 16th or even 32nd notes. For a simpler part, you may want to quantize to eighth or quarter notes.

Nobody plays perfectly in time, and quantizing can help straighten out your MIDI parts to work better with your drum parts.

I think of quantizing MIDI notes as being like airbrushing photos. Everyone does it, so it's nothing to be ashamed of, and it sure can make you look better. These days, most airbrushing is done so skillfully, it looks completely natural. However, heavy-handed airbrushing can look artificial. Quantizing works the same way. You can quantize something to be 100% correct, which actually works well for some techno tracks but can make a flowing piano part sound stiff and robotic, or you can quantize your tracks around 80% or 90% to keep them sounding fluid and human, though a little better than you played them.

Remember to always duplicate your playlist if you're the least bit unsure about editing any track. MIDI playlists work exactly like audio playlists. The great thing about duplicating the playlist *before* you quantize is that you can always go back to your original part. No matter how badly I mess up a track by quantizing, I can go back and keep trying until I get it right!

➤ **DUPLICATING A PLAYLIST:** *Reference Guide, p. 237*

7] **Highlight the bass part.** Choose the Selector tool and highlight your bass MIDI notes.

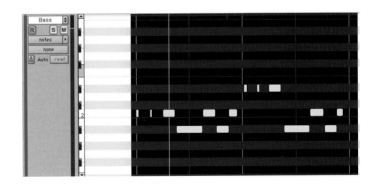

8] **Quantize.** Under the Event menu, go to MIDI and then choose Grid/Groove Quantize.

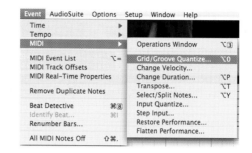

The Quantize Window

When you choose Grid/Groove Quantize in the Event > MIDI menu, the MIDI Operations window opens directly to the Grid/Groove Quantize window. The first choices at the top of the window ask, "What do you want to quantize?" The default setting is fine for Exercise 7. We want to quantize the attack (start time) of each note, and we want the durations of the notes to stay the same.

The center section of the window is called the Quantize Grid. This is where you choose what note value to quantize your MIDI part to. Use the menu to choose the smallest note value that you played in your bass part.

Below the Quantize Grid is where you can choose to quantize to triplets. You can also offset the grid (an advanced option we're not going to worry about for now), and randomize your quantization so that it sounds more human (or at least less perfect).

The Options section at the bottom is the one you'll be most concerned with. The first option is swing, which is most useful for tracks such as hi-hats, shakers, and bass lines. As always, the best way to learn anything in Pro Tools is to turn the knobs, move the sliders, apply the changes, and then listen. If you don't like it, undo it with ⌘/Ctrl+Z. For light swing, add maybe 10–15%.

The next two options, Include Within and Exclude Within, allow you to tell the quantization, "Hey, if I was way off, fix it; but if I was within 80%, don't fix it." Or "If I was close to the beat, make it even closer; otherwise, leave my playing alone."

The main slider you'll be concerned with is Strength. How much do you want to quantize something? I usually set this between 80 and 90%. Again, it depends on the song and the part I played.

Remember, you always have the Undo command. And if worse comes to worst, you can always return to your original, unquantized MIDI playlist. Always better safe than sorry.

▶ **QUANTIZING:** *Reference Guide, pp. 438–443*

9] **Quantize the bass.** For this example, set the Quantize Grid to 16th notes, the swing to 15%, and the strength to 90%. Hit Apply, and you should see your notes move a little.

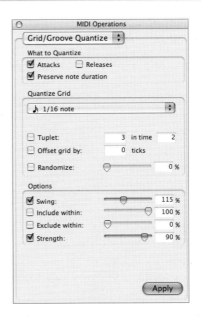

10] **Rewind and listen.** If you're overdubbing a MIDI bass part with an audio drum loop, you can start playback anywhere and hear what you've done. But with the SampleTank Free MIDI drum loop, playback has to start at a bar line; otherwise, the drums won't line up with the beat. When you select a bunch of MIDI notes, Pro Tools moves the Transport's start time to the beginning of the first note. If the note doesn't happen to start on a bar line, you'll need to click the Return to Zero button before starting playback.

11] **Undo the quantization.** Get used to using ⌘/Ctrl+Z to undo the quantization if you don't like the changes. Tweak the options in the Quantize window until you like your settings. Experiment and learn how different settings change the way you played your part.

12] **Edit your note.** Hold the Grabber tool over a MIDI note. Notice how it becomes a pointing finger? Click on a note to play it. Click and drag a note to move it. Move notes up and down to change pitch, and move notes left or right to change the start time of the note. If you're in Grid mode, notes will only be moved left or right so that they snap to the grid value you have selected. You can shorten or extend notes using the Trim tool. As I mentioned earlier, editing MIDI works just like editing audio regions.

13] **Punch into the bass part.** If you need to punch in on your bass line to record a new note or phrase, you can do this just the way you do with audio tracks. In Grid mode, choose the Selector tool. If you want Pro Tools to punch in and then punch out, click and drag across the bars where you want to punch into and out from. If you want to punch in and play to the end of the song, or stop anywhere at any time, click with the Selector where you want to punch in, but don't drag to highlight an out point. Pro Tools will punch in at the point where your cursor is placed and will keep recording until you stop it.

Now set the number of bars of pre-roll that you want in the Transport window, and turn on pre- and post-roll. With your cursor at the bar you want to punch into, press ⌘/Ctrl+spacebar.

Recording MIDI with Loop Playback

If Loop Playback is enabled in the Options menu and you have pre-roll turned on, you'll hear your pre-roll before your first take only. When the punch-out point is reached, Pro Tools will loop the region back to where you're punching in and you will no longer hear your pre-roll. This way, you can do several takes in a row—but each time the section loops, the preceding take will be erased. So if you like a particular take, you need to be careful to stop recording *before* the next loop starts.

Recording audio does not work the same way at all. If you want to loop-record audio, you'll need to use a feature called Loop Recording, which we'll cover in a later chapter.

14] **Duplicate the bass.** Create a 4-, 8-, or 16-bar bass line that you like. Then use Grid mode with the Selector tool to highlight the exact number of bars that you created, and duplicate or repeat as many times as you need.

15] **Save.**

Wrap Up

You should now have a good grasp of how virtual instruments work, and knowhow to load sounds into SampleTank parts. You should know how to create an aux track, insert an instrument plug-in, create a MIDI track, and play that instrument. You should be comfortable with basic MIDI recording and editing and should understand the concept of quantizing MIDI tracks. In the next chapter, we'll venture deeper into the world of recording and editing MIDI.

MORE ON MIDI

8

In the last chapter, we barely scratched the surface of what you can do with MIDI. In the exercises in this chapter we'll continue using the same Pro Tools MIDI session that we started in Chapter 7. We'll add some more tracks and begin using more advanced MIDI functions.

You'll learn how to change your song's start time so that the bars are always numbered correctly. You'll see how to use the MIDI Real-Time Properties to experiment with the way your MIDI tracks play back without altering the track data itself. Then you'll learn how to perform those real-time alterations manually, so that you have complete control over your MIDI tracks.

You'll also start getting acquainted with the different types of groups in Pro Tools, and learn how creating groups of regions and tracks can make music production faster and more efficient.

Pro Tools 7 introduces a new feature called *mirrored MIDI editing*, which allows you to edit one MIDI region and have any of your edits in this region also be applied to any copies of the region used in your song. You will see how to use this new feature as well.

This chapter also introduces you to the Pencil tool and teaches you how to use it to insert MIDI notes. We'll use the Pencil to create a shaker track within your song, and then again to alter the velocities of the shaker notes. Then we will re-create the same musical effect using *step recording*.

Chapter 8 ends with a lesson about MIDI Merge mode, in which you can record a cymbal crash into the shaker track without recording over what's already there.

We've got a lot of ground to cover, so let's get started.

Note

As I mentioned at the start of Chapter 7, Digidesign released a new RTAS synthesizer called Xpand! after this chapter was written. I suggest that you use Xpand! rather than SampleTank. Because Xpand! is not multi-timbral, each instrument sound you want to use should be set up in Pro Tools as a separate instrument track, with its own instance of Xpand!

EXERCISE 1:
Set Up a Keyboard Track

1] **Load Part 3.** In SampleTank, click Part 3. In the Browser area, open the folder for the 73 EPiano and double-click Ballad EP. This will load Ballad EP into Part 3 of SampleTank.

2] **Add a MIDI track.** Add a MIDI track and name it "ElecPiano."

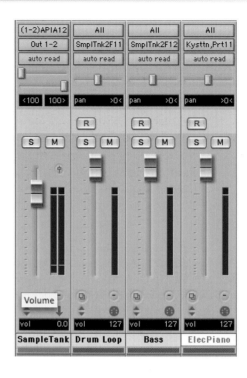

3] **Change the MIDI output.** Change the MIDI output selector of the new track to SampleTank channel 3.

4] **Put the track in Record.** Put the ElecPiano track in Record, and play along with your loop and bass line—but don't record anything yet.

EXERCISE 2:

Change the Song Start Time and Create a Count-Off

I want you to understand how to move your song's start time so that your bars are never misnumbered. Many times you'll create a session and start recording right away. You'll usually start recording at bar 2 or 3 because you need the first few bars as a count-off, which is what we did in the preceding chapter. Sometimes your song will require a pick-up beat before the first downbeat. Whatever the case, bar 1 should always be the actual starting bar of your song. Let's learn a few different ways to move the start time, and when (or when not) to use each one.

➤ **MOVE SONG START:** *Reference Guide, p. 381*

To make sure we're all on the same page, be sure your bass track begins at bar 3. If it doesn't, create a new playlist on your Bass MIDI track, let the drum loop play for two bars as a count-off, and record your bass track beginning at bar 3. You can also cut and paste your previous bass part so that it starts at bar 3.

A simple way to move the song start is to click the red diamond in the Tempo ruler of the Edit window and drag the diamond forward. But when you do this, the MIDI tracks will also move, as will any audio tracks that are set to ticks rather than samples. Try it now. As you'll see, this is not what we want, because it moves the count-off track as well, so we have the same problem as before. Dragging the diamond in the Tempo ruler is a good method to use *before* you start recording, but not after. Avoid moving your start time in this way unless you do it before you record your first MIDI track for a song.

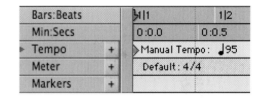

Use ⌘/Ctrl+Z now to undo the start time change if you made one. There are two easier ways to make this change.

1] **Choose Move Song Start.** Go to the Event menu, choose Time, and then choose Move Song Start.

2] **Enter the new start time.** A window called Time Operations will open. In the Timebase pull-down menu, choose Bars. We want to move our song start to bar 3, so enter "3" in the Move Start To field. We also want to renumber the bars so that bar 3 becomes bar 1, so check the Renumber Song Start box and leave this set to 1. We don't want to move the tracks along with the start time, so under Move, select Song Start Only. Then click Apply.

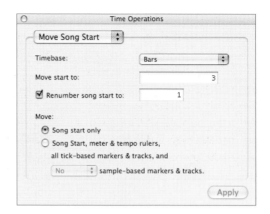

3] **Zoom in.** Zoom in on the first few bars. You'll notice on the Time ruler that you now have two bars of count-off before bar 1. There's bar –1, bar 0, and then bar 1 exactly where it should be.

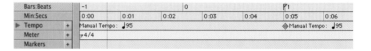

4] **Undo.** Press ⌘/Ctrl+Z to undo the Move Song Start change. Let's learn another way to do the same thing.

5] **Renumber the bars.** The simplest solution that does what we want is simply to renumber the bars. Go to the Event menu and choose Renumber Bars. A small window pops up asking you to "Renumber bars so that…". We want bar 3 to become bar 1, so enter that and then click Renumber.

6] **Change the count-off.** Now we have our two-bar count-off from bar −1, and bar 1 is where the music comes in. What if we want the count-off to be a different sound than our loop? Make the drum loop track jumbo, and zoom into the first bar. Choose the Grabber and move the drum loop's first MIDI note to a different note that that plays a different loop. Now you can tell the count-off from the song's loop.

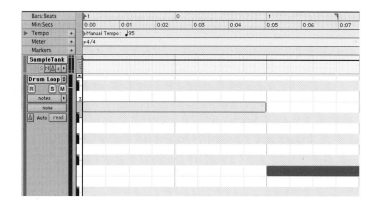

7] **Save.**

Solo Safe and When to Use It

Usually when you're mixing, it helps to solo the instrument you're working with. Try soloing the Bass MIDI track in the song you're currently working with, and press play. You don't hear anything, right? When you solo MIDI, you also need to solo the instrument that the MIDI track is playing; otherwise, you won't hear anything. In order to hear the bass track soloed, you need the SampleTank track to solo as well, because that's where the bass sound is coming from.

Here's a great feature that I use all the time: In the Mix window, press and hold the ⌘/Ctrl key and then click the Solo button of the SampleTank Aux track. See how Solo becomes grayed out? This is called Solo Safe mode. Now this track is safe from being soloed. When you solo one track, it mutes all the other tracks, right? When a track is in Solo Safe mode, it won't be muted when you solo anything else. Now, when you solo your bass, you'll hear only the bass. (⌘/Ctrl-click again to turn off Solo Safe mode.)

I usually always solo-safe my MIDI instruments and my effect returns.

EXERCISE 3:

Adjust Real-Time Properties

1] **Record a keyboard.** Put your ElecPiano track in Record and record something for a few bars.

2] **Size and zoom.** Make the ElecPiano track jumbo-sized, and use the Zoomer tool and your MIDI zoom settings to get a zoom that allows you to see what you've recorded. At the top and bottom of the vertical keyboard of this track in the Edit window are tiny up and down arrows. You can use these to make sure you're seeing all the notes you need to see.

3] **Turn on Real-Time Properties.** Pro Tools 7 has a feature in the Edit window called Real-Time Properties. Go to View > Edit Window > Real-Time Properties.

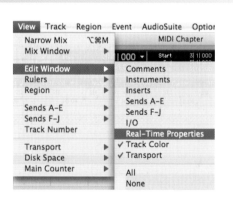

Remember in Chapter 7 when we quantized our bass track and actually physically affected the notes on screen? Well, Real-Time Properties allow you to change what you hear, not what you played. These properties are a bit like audio insert effects. Look at the buttons to the left of the vertical keyboard. These are the five real-time properties that you can use for MIDI tracks: Quantize, Duration, Delay, Velocity, and Transpose. Let's try each one.

➤ **REAL-TIME PROPERTIES:** *Reference Guide, p. 460*

4] **Turn on loop playback.** Under Options, make sure Loop Playback is checked. In Grid mode, highlight what you played, from downbeat to downbeat, using the Selector tool.

5] **Change the Quantize option.** Click the QUA button to turn on the Quantize real-time property, and then click the correct note value for what you played. Again, this does not affect what you actually recorded, so feel free to experiment.

To look at a pop-up menu of quantization options, click the button that shows a note icon. Try some of the built-in groove templates and see what they do. The only way you learn is to try things. Add some swing. Notice that nothing you do affects the notes on the screen. Turn Quantize off and on, and listen to the difference while the part loops. If you're an accomplished keyboardist, the differences may be small, but you should still be able to hear them.

Input Quantize

Using Real-Time Properties, you're only changing what you hear, not what you played. In Chapter 7, we quantized our track after we played it. But there is one more way to quantize a track—with Input Quantize. Some people like to quantize a track at the same time that they record it. (Be careful, though: If you do it this way, you won't be able to switch the quantization on and off, as you can do with Real-Time Properties.)

To turn on Input Quantize, go to Event > MIDI > Input Quantize. This opens the MIDI Operations window. Check the top box to enable Input Quantize and set your Quantize settings. Now whatever you record will be quantized on input. Input Quantize comes in handy when you program drum tracks one note at a time. I don't use it when I'm playing an instrument, because I like my tracks to feel more natural.

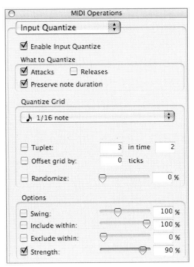

Turn Duration on and off. Turn on the Duration real-time property. As most of you know, duration is how long a note lasts. What if you want everything to be legato—to make the part smooth from one note to the next? Click the button to the right of the Duration button and you'll see a menu of options. Go down to the Legato/Gap option. Now start playback. Hear the difference? Turn Duration on and off while the music loops, and try various settings.

7] **Experiment with Delay.** Turn on the Delay real-time property. The Delay property makes what you played happen later or earlier in time. This could be helpful if you programmed a snare track and you want it to be a bit more laid-back. If so, turn on Delay, set the delay units to ms (milliseconds), and tell the snare track to advance by 20 or 30 milliseconds.

"What's the difference between volume and velocity?"

Velocity is how hard you play the keyboard. If you play this electric piano preset very hard or very soft, it completely changes the character of the sound. (This is because SampleTank will choose a different sample based on your key velocity.) If you play any instrument with more force, whether it be a drum or a trumpet, it sounds different, right? That's velocity.

Volume is simply how loud the sound is, regardless of how hard or soft you played it. Often, MIDI velocity is used to control volume, which is why the two are sometimes confused.

8] **Adjust Velocity.** Turn on the Velocity real-time property. Notice that you have a Dynamics percentage field and, next to it, what's called a Velocity Offset field. The first field is asking, "Do you want to expand or shrink the velocity differences in this track?" If you want more aggressive velocity accents, make the percentage over 100%; if you want the track to be smoother, make it under 100%. I set mine to 50%, and it makes a dramatic difference in the sound of the electric piano: Not only is there less difference in the velocities, but all of the velocities are lower (because each note velocity is in effect being multiplied by 1/2).

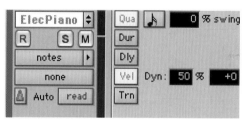

MIDI velocity ranges from 1 to 127, from softest to hardest. The Velocity Offset field allows you to use the chosen percentage to smooth out the sound, and then add or subtract a few more numbers to help boost the MIDI instrument back into the desired velocity range for your song.

9] **Try using Transpose.** Turn on the Transpose real-time property. This one is a bit obvious, right? The first field allows you to transpose by octaves. The second field allows you to transpose by semitones (half-steps). You can also transpose all of the notes to a single pitch by changing the By to a To and choosing a different key. This is useful mainly when you've recorded a single MIDI key to a track by itself in order to play a single drum sound: Using Transpose To, you can switch to a different snare sound, for instance.

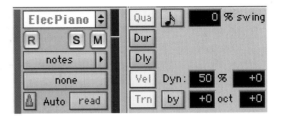

In this exercise, transposing probably won't sound right no matter what you do, because your bass will be playing in one key and the electric piano another. So turn this property off for now.

10] Save.

EXERCISE 4:
Edit MIDI Properties Manually

I'm not a huge fan of the Pro Tools Real-Time Properties, because it makes more sense to me to actually make up my mind and edit a track permanently. If I use Real-Time Properties at all, it's for quantizing; everything else I do manually. But that's just me. Let's learn how to manually edit a track, and then you can make your own decision about how to work. You know how to quantize a track permanently because we did that in the preceding chapter. In this exercise, let's work with the same MIDI edits as in Exercise 3, but we'll make the edits manually.

1] **Make a new playlist.** Make a new playlist on the electric piano track and name it "Staccato."

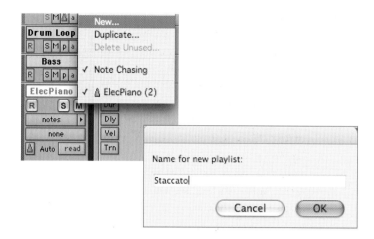

2] **Record a track.** Record a very staccato part for four bars. Here is my four-bar part.

3] **Duplicate the playlist.** Duplicate the Staccato playlist and name it "Legato."

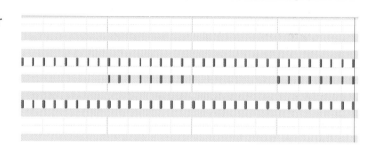

Note

It's interesting to note that playlists retain their individual real-time properties. One playlist can have Quantize only enabled, while another playlist on the same track has both Quantize and Velocity properties enabled.

4] **Highlight and zoom.** Highlight your entire staccato keyboard part with the Selector tool (or select all the notes with the Grabber tool). Then, with the part still highlighted, zoom into the first bar.

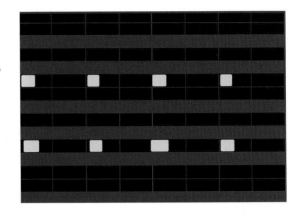

5] **Manual duration editing, take 1.** Select Grid mode and a sixteenth-note grid value, and choose the Trim tool. Grab the first keyboard note until the Trimmer looks like this:] Pull the first note to the right until it meets the next note, and let go. Your notes should look something like this: You've just changed the durations of the notes in the entire keyboard track. You can change one note at a time with the Trim tool or only highlight certain sections of a song.

Undo this using ⌘/Ctrl+Z, and you should see the staccato notes reappear.

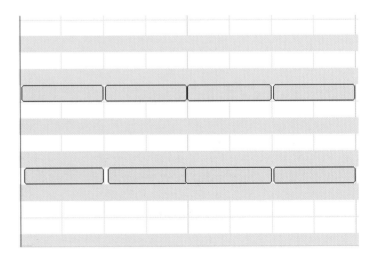

6] **Manual duration editing, take 2.** There are many ways to perform the same function in Pro Tools, and as you learn the program you can choose what works best for you. Here's another way to edit a track's durations: Highlight the entire track. Remember, you can select all the notes in the track using the Select All command (⌘/Ctrl+A). If the Grabber tool is active, click one note and then use ⌘/Ctrl+A. If the Selector tool is active, click anywhere in the track and then give the same command.

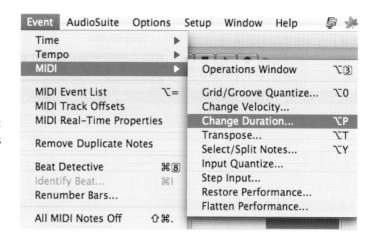

With the track highlighted, go to Event > MIDI > Change Duration. The MIDI Operations window opens, showing you the Duration settings. This window has much more powerful functionality than Real-Time Properties or manual editing. To make this track legato, select the Legato option and rather than Gap, choose Overlap, which makes each note last until the start of the next one. Click Apply and listen to the results. The settings in this window are pretty deep, so we won't go into them here, but they're worth exploring when you have a little time.

➤ **CHANGE DURATION WINDOW:**
  Reference Guide, p. 452

7] **Change Track View to Velocity.** Choose whichever playlist you prefer (your original ElecPiano, the Staccato playlist, or the new Legato playlist). With the track still set to jumbo size in the Edit window, click below the R, S, and M (Record, Solo, and Mute) buttons where it now says Notes. This is called the Track View selector. Instead of viewing notes, we want to view velocity, so click on the word Notes and select Velocity from the drop-down menu.

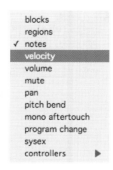

8] **Manual velocity editing, take 1.** Now each note has a velocity stem, which shows how hard each note was played. You can edit velocity one note a time with the Grabber tool. Or you can Select All using the Selector tool and ⌘/Ctrl+A to highlight the entire track, and then use the Grabber to move any one velocity stem up or down. When you've used Select All, editing one velocity changes the velocity globally across the whole track.

Undo what you did and let's learn another way to edit velocity.

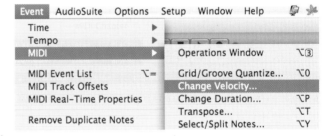

9] **Manual velocity editing 2.** With the track still highlighted, go to Event > MIDI > Change Velocity. The MIDI Operations window opens, showing you all the ways you can edit a track's velocity. I commonly use Scale By and enter the percentage by which I want to scale the velocity. This gives the same result as in Step 8.

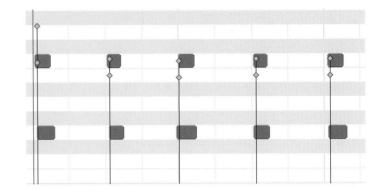

Tip

Notice that the MIDI Operations window has a pull-down menu at the top. You can switch MIDI functions from this window. A shortcut to the MIDI Operations window is Option/Alt+numeric keypad 3.

➤ **CHANGE VELOCITY WINDOW:** *Reference Guide, p. 450*

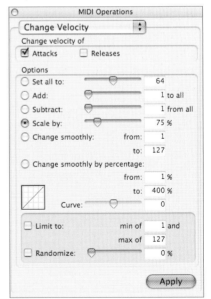

10] **Change the track view.** Change the track view back to Notes.

11] **Save.**

EXERCISE 5:

Work with Region Groups and Transposing

There are three types of groups in Pro Tools: Mix Groups, Edit Groups, and Region Groups. We'll cover Mix and Edit Groups in Exercise 6.

Region Groups allow you to combine audio and MIDI regions to create one cohesive region. Imagine that the chorus of a song is eight bars long, and imagine that this chorus is made up of eight different tracks, some audio and some MIDI, all of them being tracks with many edits. You can highlight all eight tracks for all eight bars and create one cohesive Region Group, making the entire chorus one big region on the screen that you can move around or copy and paste easily. You no longer see all of your edits, but rather one giant region that you can rename "Chorus." (Regions can always be ungrouped later, if you should need to.)

To make things easy for me in this example, I edited my original bass track into a simple four-bar loop so that it matched the length of my keyboard part. Feel free to make a playlist of your bass track and then either copy and paste a four-bar loop into a new playlist, or record a new four-bar bass line.

➤ **REGION GROUPS:** *Reference Guide, p. 321.*

1] **Highlight the bass and keyboards.** Using the Selector tool in Grid mode, with a quarter-note grid resolution, highlight a loopable section of your bass and keyboard tracks together. Press the Shift key to select multiple tracks. Make sure you've selected an even number of bars. I'm going to use bars 1 through 5, an even four bars.

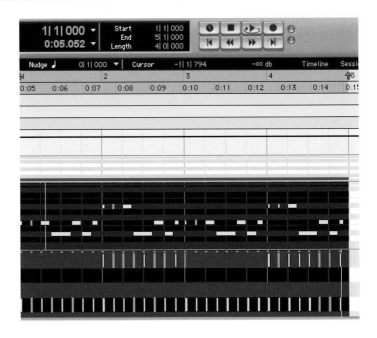

Tip

I cannot emphasize enough how important it is to keep an eye on the Event Edit area and make sure that whatever you are editing is at the correct start and end places.

Start	1| 1| 000
End	5| 1| 000
Length	4| 0| 000

2] **Create a Region Group.** Go to Region > Group (the shortcut is ⌘+Option+G or Ctrl+Alt+G). Notice in the Edit window that your tracks look completely different now. Both the bass and keyboard tracks are now one big region. Looking at the Track View selectors for these tracks, you'll see that both tracks have switched automatically to view Regions.

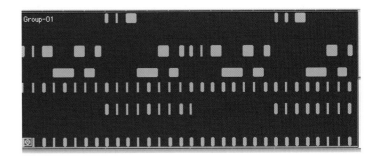

To ungroup a Region Group, highlight the group in the Regions List on the right side of the Edit window, and choose Ungroup from the Region menu.

3] **Rename the Region Group.** Look in the Regions List and see your new Region Group. To rename this group, select it and go to the drop-down Regions menu at the top of the Regions List (not to be confused with the Region menu in the main menu bar). Choose Rename, or use ⌘/Ctrl+Shift+R. Name this group "Bass/Keys."

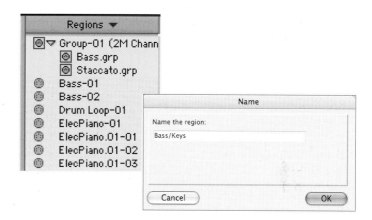

If you don't see your Regions List, click the arrow icon at the bottom-right corner of the Edit window.

I will always remind you to develop good habits such as renaming Region Groups. When you have a song with many tracks and many sections, it will help you out so much to be able to look at anything on the screen and know exactly what it is, without having to play it. So develop these good habits now, and memorize the keyboard shortcuts.

4] **Delete other regions.** Notice that I have two regions on my bass track that are outside of my new Region Group. There are no notes in the old regions, so I can delete them. Click them with the Grabber and hit the Delete key. Now the track looks nice and neat.

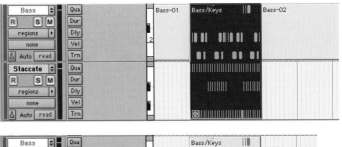

5] **Duplicate the Region.** Use the Grabber to select the Region Group, and press ⌘/Ctrl+D to duplicate this Region once.

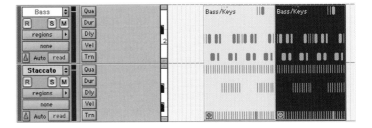

6] **Transpose the Region Group.** Click one of the Region Groups and press Option/Alt+T to bring up the Transpose window. (You can also go to Event > MIDI > Transpose.) Choose to transpose in octaves or semitones. Click Apply.

▶ **TRANSPOSING:** *Reference Guide, p. 453*

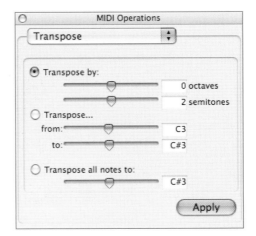

7] **Listen to both regions.** Listen to your song and notice that any changes made to the Region Group affect all tracks. Use Undo if you don't want to keep your transposition.

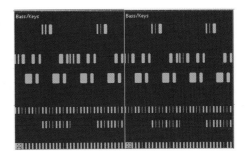

EXERCISE 6:

Work with Mix and Edit Groups

Mix and Edit Groups, which include Mix Groups, Edit Groups, and Edit-and-Mix Groups, are different from Region Groups. Let me show you the difference.

➤ **MIX AND EDIT GROUPS:** *Reference Guide, p. 117*

1] **Move the volume sliders.** Go to the Mix window and move the bass and electric piano tracks' volume sliders up or down. They work independentlyof one another, right?

2] **Highlight the bass region.** In the Edit window, use the Selector tool in Grid mode and highlight the bass track from bar 0 to bar 2. Notice how this only highlights the bass region. This is because you started selecting a region in an empty part of the track. Now highlight bars 2 and 3, and you'll see both the bass and the keyboard track highlighted. So you can see that only if you click within a Region Group will it select both tracks.

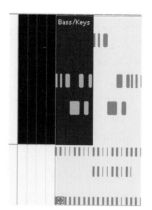 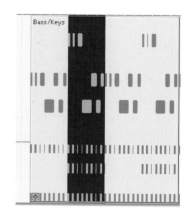

3] **Highlight the track names.** In either the Mix or Edit window, highlight the track names for the bass track and the electric piano track. Hold the Shift key to select multiple tracks.

4] **Create an Edit-And-Mix Group.** Press ⌘/Ctrl+G. The New Group window opens, prompting you to choose a type and name for this group. When creating groups, I typically make Edit-And-Mix Groups, so for this exercise I've chosen the last option. Name the group "Bass/Keys."

"When would I create just a Mix Group or just an Edit Group?"

Imagine you are mixing a song and have 10 tracks of drums. You have the balance and panning of each drum exactly the way you want it. Now you want to ride the level of the drums as a group in the Mix window, but you also want the freedom to edit the noise out of the tom tracks within the Edit window.

If you highlighted all 10 drum track names, created an Edit-and-Mix Group, and named it "Drums," then when you edited the tom track in the Edit window your cursor would high-light all 10 tracks. However, if you had created a Mix Group only of the drums, your group would work only within the Mix window.

That said, you'll want to use combined Edit-and-Mix groups 90 percent of the time.

5] **Move the volume sliders again.** Go to the Mix window and move either the bass or keyboard volume slider. They move together now, right?

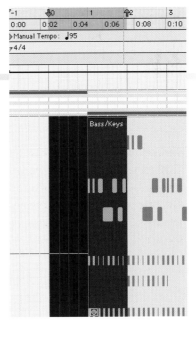

6] **Highlight the bass region again.** Go to the Edit window and highlight from bar 0 to bar 2. Now whatever track you edit, it's part of this group, so the whole thing will be edited, regardless of whether it's part of a Region Group.

I hope this system is starting to make sense. Creating an Edit-and-Mix Group will make both of these tracks mute and solo together, as well as change track size together. Next, let me show you some tricks using Edit-and-Mix Groups with playlists, and how to combine all of this with your new MIDI skills to get you thinking like a real Pro Tools editor.

7] **Duplicate the bass playlist.** Go to the Edit window and duplicate the bass playlist. Notice that Pro Tools didn't ask you to name it. Now notice that because these tracks two tracks are grouped, the Duplicate command made two new playlists, one for each track. Pro Tools chose its own names for the playlists.

8] **Rename both new playlists.** It's very important that you rename these new tracks according to what kind of edit you're doing. Double-click the bass track name to rename it "Bass TP-C#." Rename the keyboard track "EP-TP-C#."

9] **Transpose these tracks.** Highlight the Bass/Keys Region Group and press Option/Alt+T to transpose it. I played my original part in C. Now I'm going to transpose this Region Group up one semitone to C#. Listen to the playback to hear the difference.

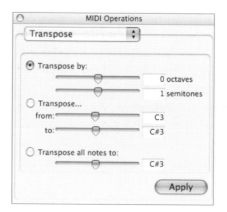

Rename your own playlists to the appropriate key according to what you played.

10] **Change playlists.** Click the track name of your bass playlist and change to the original bass track. Notice that the tracks both went back to original playlists in the original key. Now you can easily go back and forth between two keys by changing playlists.

```
New...
Duplicate...
Delete Unused...

✓  Note Chasing

   ♪ Bass (6)
✓  ♪ Bass-TP-C# (8)
   other playlists          ▶
```

So imagine this: You can't decide whether a song should be a step up or a step down. Here is exactly what you should do: You create a Region Group of all the tracks to be transposed. Then you create an Edit-and-Mix Group of all of the tracks. Duplicate the playlists of all tracks, renaming the playlists to include the name of the new key. Then transpose the duplicated playlists. Now you have two playlists, one in the original key and one in the new key. You can easily go back and forth among many tracks all at once, and choose whatever you want.

Think of using playlists in this way for many functions, not just for transposing. One playlist could be edited to be more funky, one playlist could be quantized differently, one playlist could have the vocals in a different language. The possibilities of using playlists with groups are endless.

Changing Pitch and Tempo for Audio Tracks

I've had clients come into my studio with a multi-track song and say, "I want this song to be one step up and I want it to be a little slower in tempo." Though it's fast and easy to transpose and change tempo with MIDI, keep in mind that it's not that easy to transpose audio files and change the tempo of entire songs. It's possible to transpose using the AudioSuite pitch-shift plug-in that's built into Pro Tools, but 80 percent of the time a transposed guitar or a vocal will not sound natural. It really depends on two things: What the instrument is, and how far you're transposing it.

The same limitation applies to changing the tempo of entire tracks. Sometimes it works and sounds fine; sometimes it doesn't. Again, it depends on what the instrument is and how far you're stretching it.

EXERCISE 7:

Use Mirror MIDI Editing

In Pro Tools, the Mirror MIDI Editing option ("mirrored editing") allows you to edit one MIDI region and have your edits automatically mirrored in any copy of that region used in the song. Let's go back to our transposed playlist so we don't mess up our original tracks.

Note

Duplicating playlists is a great way to experiment with different functions without destroying your original performance. It's another good habit to develop.

➤ **MIRRORED MIDI EDITING:** *Reference Guide, p. 415*

1] **Change track size.** Make the EP track large. Notice that the bass track also changes size because the two are joined in an Edit-And-Mix Group (Bass/Keys).

2] **Turn off the Bass/Keys group.** On the left side of the Edit window, you'll see your Mix and Edit Groups listed. To temporarily disable the Bass/Keys group, click its name in this list.

Tip

A command I use all the time is ⌘/Ctrl+Shift+G. This turns all Mix and Edit Groups on and off.

3] **Turn on Mirror MIDI Editing.** To turn on mirrored editing, go to the Options menu and make sure the Mirror MIDI Editing option is checked. An easier way to enable mirrored editing is by clicking on the icon to the left of the Grid Note Value selector.

4] **Change EP View.** In the Edit window, on the Track View selector of the electric piano track, deselect Regions and select Velocity.

5] **Edit the velocities.** Now let's see how mirrored editing works. Zoom in to the EP track so that you have both Region Groups visible right next to each other. Keeping in mind that we all played different things in these exercises, choose the Grabber tool and edit the velocity of one note in the first Region Group. While you're moving the velocity stem up or down, look at the duplicated Region Group on the right. Notice that the same velocity stem in the same place in the duplicated Region Group is moving as well. See the large stem in my track?

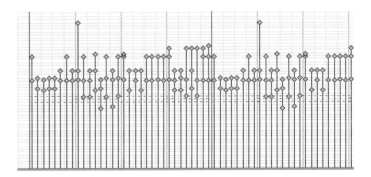

6] **Change track heights and zooms.** Now let's move some notes in our bass track. Click the bass track's Track View selector and change it to Notes. Your bass MIDI notes might appear very small and be difficult to edit, so make the bass track size jumbo. Then use the MIDI zoom buttons to zoom in so that you can see the notes but also see both regions. You may also need to use the up and down arrows on the vertical keyboard at the left end of the track.

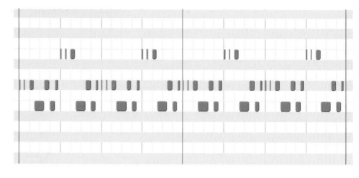

7] **Edit some notes.** With the Grabber, click one bass note and press Delete. The note disappears from both regions. Now move a note or two with the Grabber. The note moves in both regions.

Tip

Notice how the Grabber tool becomes a pointing finger when it's placed directly on a note, and a crosshairs cursor when it's in a MIDI track but not specifically on a note. This allows you to draw a box with the crosshairs cursor around a group of notes. The box selects those notes, after which you can move or delete them as a selection. Try highlighting a group of notes and moving or deleting them.

See how cool mirrored editing is? There are times you'll want it on, and times when you won't. For example, you may want the intro of a song to sound a little different from the verse. Maybe it's using the same bass region as the verse, though, so in this case you would turn off Mirror MIDI Editing and edit the bass region in the intro only. However, when you decide you want to change the pitch of a note in all of the choruses, obviously that's a good time to turn on mirrored editing. If two regions start out identical and you then edit one of them with mirrored editing turned off, they won't be identical anymore, so mirrored editing won't work with them. So be careful that you know when Mirror MIDI Editing is on and when it's off. When it's off, all of your editing will be done to individual regions; when it's on, all regions with the same name will be edited globally.

EXERCISE 8:

Create a Shaker Track with the Pencil Tool

Earlier I told you that the Pencil tool comes in handy for working with MIDI tracks. Now I'm going to show you how.

➤ **PENCIL TOOL:** *Reference Guide, p. 418*

1] **Load a drum kit into SampleTank.** Click the SampleTank plug-in in the Mix window. Click Part 4, which is empty, to select it. Then in SampleTank's Browser choose HipHopKit, and load the preset called Slam HipHop.

2] **Create a new MIDI track.** Create a MIDI track and name it "Percussion."

3] **Set the output channel.** On the Percussion MIDI track, set the output channel to SampleTank channel 4.

4] **Play the kit.** Put the track in Record and play some notes on the keyboard. Notice that A2 (the A below middle C) is a shaker. We're going to use that sound.

5] **Change the track height.** Hold the Option/Alt key and make one track small. All the tracks become small. Now make the Percussion track jumbo. Make sure that the vertical keyboard of the Percussion track clearly shows the keys around and below C3. Use the keyboard's up and down arrows if necessary to show the correct octave.

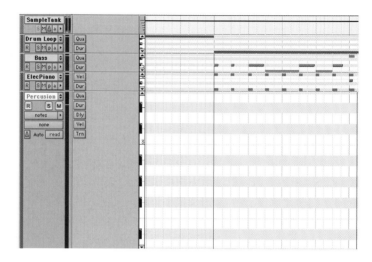

6] **Change the Grid value.** Change the Grid value to sixteenth notes.

7] **View Notes.** Make sure the Track View selector is set to Notes.

8] **Click and hold the Pencil tool.** You'll see a long list of choices. Choose the Square.

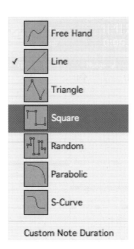

The Pencil Tool: Our New Friend

The Pencil tool performs various functions, which are used for different purposes. For example, we're using it in Exercise 8 to create shaker notes, but we could change the Track View to Pan and use the Pencil to create a rhythmic panning effect. Or we could assign a track to use MIDI data to control the filter of a synth sound, and make the synth sound change texture in time with the beat of the song.

Each Pencil tool shape performs a different function:

Free Hand allows you to draw single notes. The further you drag with this tool, the longer the note.

The next four Pencil shapes allow you to draw notes based on your grid value setting. With the grid set to sixteenth notes, for example, dragging with the Pencil creates sixteenth notes. The Line tool creates notes with identical velocities; the Triangle tool creates notes with velocities that ramp up and down; the Square tool creates notes with alternating velocities from loud to soft: and the Random tool creates notes with random velocities.

The last two shapes, Parabolic and S-Curve, don't work with MIDI notes.

9] **Find the right note.** This step is a bit tricky. With your Pencil tool in the Percussion track in the Edit window, look at the vertical keyboard. The notes on the keyboard will change as you move the Pencil up and down. The note you want to find is A2. You should see A2 in two places: highlighted on the vertical keyboard and displayed as the MIDI note below the Transport Control at the top of the Edit window.

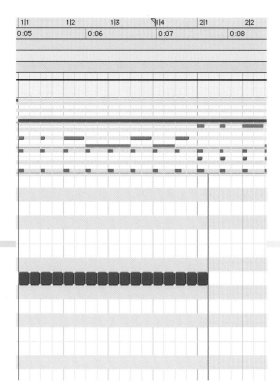

10] **Drag the Pencil.** This step is tricky, too. Move your cursor as close to the downbeat of bar 1 as you can while keeping the note at A2. When you get there, click and drag from left to right for one full bar. You should hear the first shaker sound and see your notes drawn across the screen. Your track should look like this:

11] **Play it back.** Choose the Selector tool and click at the beginning of bar 1; then hit Play to play the new shaker track. You should be able to solo your shaker track and hear sixteenth-note shakers in your session.

If you messed something up in the exercise so far and your notes went someplace else, start using your new MIDI editing skills to fix it. Use the Grabber to highlight the wrong notes and drag them to the right place.

12] **Create a Region Group.** With the Selector tool, highlight from the beginning of bar 1 to the beginning of bar 2 and go to Region > Group. Your shaker track will turn into a Region Group.

Region	Event	AudioSuite
Mute/Unmute		⌘M
Lock/Unlock		⌘L
Send to Back		⌥⇧B
Bring to Front		⌥⇧F
Group		⌥⌘G
Ungroup		⌥⌘U

13] **Create a Region Loop.** Now choose Region > Loop. In the Region Looping window that opens, set the region to loop eight times.

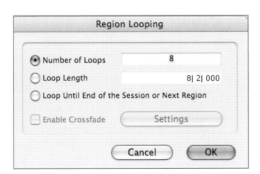

Region	Event	AudioSuite
Mute/Unmute		⌘M
Lock/Unlock		⌘L
Send to Back		⌥⇧B
Bring to Front		⌥⇧F
Group		⌥⌘G
Ungroup		⌥⌘U
Ungroup All		
Regroup		⌥⌘R
Loop...		⌥⌘L

14] Play it back and save.

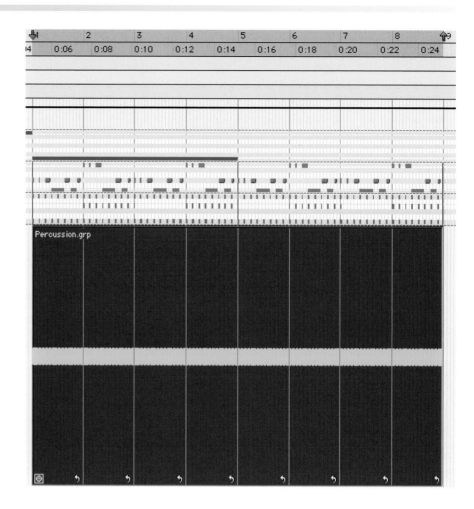

Use Step Recording

With *step recording,* you use your MIDI keyboard to enter one note a time while specifying the duration and note values you want to use. Many people use step recording as a way to enter parts that are difficult to play. Let's use it to create the same shaker track in a new way.

➤ **STEP RECORDING:** *Reference Guide, p. 200*

1] **Create a new playlist.** On your Percussion track, create a new playlist and name it "Percussion 2." While you're at it, switch the Track View selector from Regions to Notes.

2] **Find the shaker note.** Find A2 again on your keyboard, so you know what note to play.

3] **Open Step Input.** Go to Event > MIDI > Step Input. The Step Input window opens. Make sure the Enable box is checked. Set the note value to sixteenth notes. Under Options, tell Pro Tools to use input velocity. This means the Percussion 2 track will get its velocity data from the way you play the keyboard.

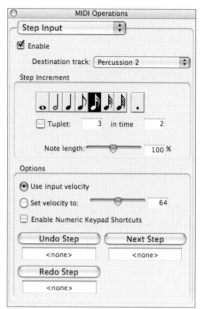

4] **Place your cursor.** With the Selector tool in Grid mode, click at the downbeat of bar 1.

5] **Play A2.** Play A2 on the keyboard and watch the Edit window as you do. Pro Tools will input each note that you play, one at a time. Keep playing until you've filled up an entire bar.

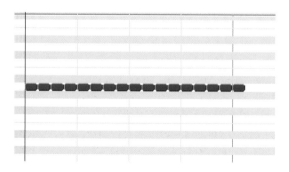

6] **Fix the track.** As you can see in my track shown in Step 5, I played one too many shakers. So I chose the Grabber tool, clicked on that one shaker, and deleted it.

7] **View velocity.** Change the Track View selector from Notes to Velocity. You can see on my track that my velocities are not very consistent.

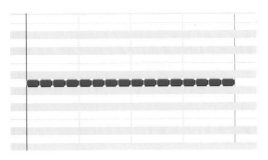

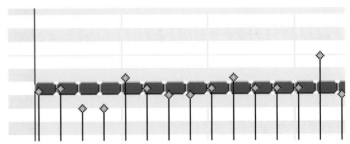

8] **Fix the velocities.** Choose the Pencil tool and, again, the Square shape. (If you're following the exercises, it will still be selected.) Change your grid value to sixteenth notes. Then with the Pencil tool, drag from left to right while also dragging up and down to choose your velocities. The lower you drag down or the higher you drag up, the more drastic the change between alternate notes' velocities. Listen to the playback, and if you don't like what you hear, draw it again.

9] **Create a Region Group and loop it.** Looking back at steps 12 and 13 of Exercise 8, do the same thing with this playlist.

Tip

If you have any extraneous regions outside your Percussion region, use the Grabber and delete them.

10] Save.

Now you have two Percussion playlists, each eight bars long, one created with the Pencil tool and one created using Step Record.

MIDI Event List

When MIDI sequencers first came into being, the only way to edit notes was through a feature called *event list editing.* Back in the early days of MIDI, there was no graphical editing and you never saw your notes on the screen as you do now. Everything was done by twiddling the numerical values in a list of MIDI notes. Some people still prefer to edit MIDI this way. Why? I have no idea. But if the idea intrigues you, go to Event > MIDI Event List. You'll see a list of all your notes in this format.

➤ **MIDI EVENT LIST:** *Reference Guide, p. 467*

EXERCISE 10:

Record in MIDI Merge Mode

Our last task in this chapter is to learn about the final button on the Transport window—the MIDI Merge button. You can also think of this as the "MIDI overdub" button. The MIDI Merge button allows you to record more notes into a MIDI track without erasing or overwriting what's already there.

➤ **MIDI MERGE:** *Reference Guide, p. 191*

1] **Turn on MIDI Merge mode.** Open the Transport window and click the top-right button.

2] **Turn on Notes view.** Switch from Regions view to Notes view on the Percussion track.

3] **Turn off Mirrored MIDI Editing.** I found that there was funkiness, and not the good kind, when I recorded with mirrored editing turned on, so you'll want to turn it off in the Options menu before starting to record.

4] **Put the Percussion track in Record.** Play notes on the keyboard, and find the crash cymbal on C♯2. Press Return/Enter and then the spacebar to play the song from the beginning. Press ⌘/Ctrl+spacebar to record. At the downbeat of bar 1, play a crash cymbal. Stop after you record it. If you made a mistake, hit Undo and record again. You should see one crash cymbal somewhere close to the downbeat of bar 1.

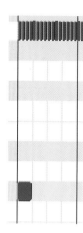

5] **Change the grid value.** Change the grid value to quarter notes.

6] **Quantize the note.** To quantize one note, choose the Grabber in Grid mode and move the note to the closest beat. Do that to the cymbal note now.

Absolute vs. Relative Grid

If you're in Relative Grid mode rather than Absolute Grid mode, dragging a note will move it *by* a quarter-note value rather than *to* a quarter-note value. Both modes are useful. Absolute Grid mode will snap loosely played notes to a precise rhythmic grid. But sometimes you might play a great lick with a loose feel, and you might want to move it to a different beat or a different bar. In this case you would choose Relative Grid mode, so that when you select and drag the MIDI notes they'll still have the same rhythmic relationship to the beat that they started out with.

7] **Place the cymbals.** Hold the Option/Alt key and, with the Grabber, click on the one cymbal note and drag to the right to make a copy of it. Drag the copied note to bar 3. Click Option/Alt again to make another copy, and drag to bar 5; and again to bar 7.

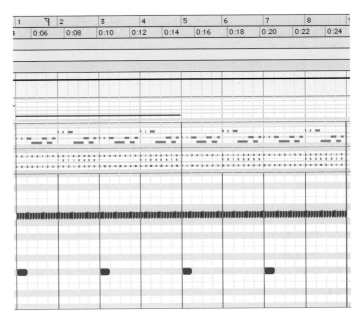

Tip

Option/Alt-dragging works with MIDI notes and audio regions and is an efficient way to make quick copies. I use it a lot with MIDI. For example, suppose I've played two notes on a piano part but after listening, I think it would sound better with a full four-note chord. I can Option/Alt-click one of the two notes and drag that note up or down in pitch to make a copy, adding it to my two-note chord.

8] Save.

Wrap Up

I'm sure your brain is a bit fried after going through all this new material. I know mine is. But hopefully, MIDI is now no longer a scary mysterious place. Try creating more MIDI tracks and more MIDI parts using SampleTank. Repetition is the best teacher. Continue recording and editing, and eventually all of this will become second nature. Before long, you'll be able to spend your time being creative rather than learning how to work the controls.

Hang in there—in the next chapter, we'll take on a real song that combines audio and MIDI. Now, go take a break.

ARRANGING A SONG

9

Now we're going to sit down and construct an entire song. We'll actually be working with a new song of mine so we'll have some MIDI and audio to work with. We'll be combining MIDI and prerecorded audio elements that I created, which will help me teach you how to create a whole song arrangement. In your own process, feel free to destroy my song, enhance it, rewrite it—but please do not release your own version of it, because it's copyrighted.

We're going to start with a very lame-sounding MIDI version of the song, to help you understand the writing process and how MIDI comes in very handy when sketching out an idea for a song. With SampleTank Free we are limited to 12 basic sounds, so there was only so much I could do with this MIDI arrangement. Please refer to this book's companion web site (www.protoolsformusicians.com) when you're ready to start assembling a professional palette of software instruments. Often when you purchase software instruments, they come with many, many gigabytes of sounds and samples, so you'll never need to feel limited by your choices in sounds.

I'm going give you the very beginnings of this song as a Pro Tools session in MIDI format, to help you understand the evolution of a song demo as it transforms into a full song production. After the song is written, most of the MIDI tracks are replaced with real instruments. I hope you'll get some insight into the difference between a songwriting demo in Pro Tools and a full song production.

You'll be combining your MIDI and audio editing skills and starting to learn about editing and arranging whole songs, as opposed to the tiny eight-bar pieces we've been working with up to now. Again, feel free to mute or delete any of my tracks and play your own. This song is just to get you familiar with arranging audio in Pro Tools. By the end of Chapter 11, we should have a finished song, edited and ready to be mixed.

Before we begin, you'll need to get the file we'll be working with. Go to protoolsformusicians.com, click Chapter Downloads, and click Chapter 9 Download UnderwaterGFS.zip. You'll need to download the version of the file that's compatible with your Mac or Windows computer. (Pro Tools session files are generally cross-platform-compatible, but while writing this book I ran into some problems with a SampleTank session created on the Mac that wouldn't load correctly in Windows, and vice-versa. So I've created two versions of the file. They're musically identical.) Copy the archive to your audio drive and expand the archive.

Thi is a rather large file and may take 15 minutes or more to download, depending on your Internet connection speed. Depending on how you've organized your audio drive, you may want to expand the file to a directory specifically devoted to Pro Tools sessions.

EXERCISE 1:

Create the Song's Markers

After you've downloaded and expanded the song, you'll have a folder called UnderwaterGFS. In that folder is the Pro Tools session of the same name. Open UnderwaterGFS.

If you see a window with a warning about disk allocation, don't worry. All this window is saying is, "Hey, the last time you opened this session it was on another hard drive— is that cool? Do you want me to print up a report telling you about the last hard drive you used?" Click No. The song should open fine. Hit the spacebar or click Play, and listen to a very wimpy-sounding MIDI arrangement. Don't worry—by the time we get done, it won't sound like this at all, I promise.

We're going to use the audio files in UnderwaterGFS to put together a full song arrangement. But let's get organized first by creating markers throughout the song.

➤ **MARKERS:** *Reference Guide, pp. 382-389*

1] **Open SampleTank.** To make sure you have the correct sounds, go to the Mix window and click the SampleTank plug-in. If you're using SampleTank Free, you should have these six sounds, in exactly this order, loaded into the Part window. If you're using SampleTank SE, you'll have to load equivalent sounds yourself.

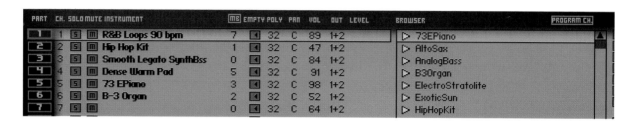

2] **Solo-safe SampleTank.** Look at the SampleTank channel in the Mix window. If the Solo button isn't already grayed out, press the ⌘/Ctrl key and click the Solo button so that it's grayed out. Now when you solo any MIDI tracks, you will hear them.

3] **Play the MIDI tracks.** Notice in the Mix and Edit windows that you have six MIDI tracks. Press the spacebar and make sure everything is playing back as it should. Solo each track to hear its part playing back.

4] **Move the song start.** Before we create markers, I want the first bar to be a bar of count-off and then I want the song to begin at bar 1. Right now the song starts at bar 2. I want you to get the hang of doing this, so let's move the song start one more time in order to reinforce how this works. Go the Event menu and choose Time > Move Song Start.

> ➤ **MOVE SONG START:**
> *Reference Guide, p. 381*

5] **Choose the correct settings.** Choose Bars as the timebase, enter "2" in the Move Start To field, check the box to renumber the bars starting at bar 1, and select the button to move the song start only. (We don't want to move the tracks—we just want to move the start time.) Click Apply.

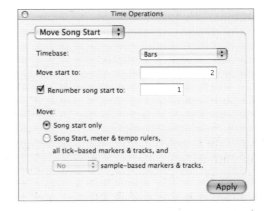

6] **Set your grid value.** In the indicator strip at the top of the Edit window, set your grid value to 1 Bar.

7] **Insert the vocal.** In the Region List, you'll see a list of audio files in alphabetical order. Choose Grid mode using the button in the upper-left corner of the Edit window. Then click the audio file called Vocals and drag it to bar 1 of the empty vocal track. Make the vocal track medium-sized so that you can see the waveform.

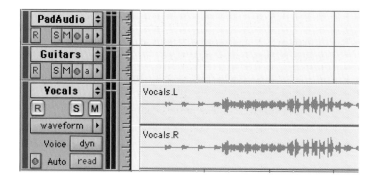

Tip

It's always helpful when working with other people to give them a vocal track so that they can tell where they are in a song. This is often called a "guide vocal."

Submixes and Stem Mixes

If you play "Underwater" and hear the vocals, you'll notice that there's more than one vocal track within this file. In order to minimize the download time, I didn't want to ask you to download six tracks of vocals. Instead, I created what's called a *submix,* also called a *stem mix* or *stem.* A stem mix is a stereo mix in which many edited tracks are mixed down into one cohesive track.

Stems are created for many purposes in professional music. Often when an album is being mixed in a commercial studio with a large console, an engineer will create stem mixes of each instrument category, such as vocals, drums, guitars, horns, and so on. In case some-one says, "I love the mix, but the drums are too loud," the engineer can use a small stem session. Instead of having to remix the entire song and, in a worst-case scenario, rerent the studio and turn all the knobs again, he or she can simply bring down the drum stem track.

Another convenient use of stems is for working with other musicians. It's obviously much faster to send someone a stem mix of drums or of many vocals, rather than many separate, edited, unmixed audio tracks.

8] **Create markers.** Now we're going to make markers throughout the song. Click bar 1 with the Selector tool in Grid mode, and press the Enter key *on the number keypad,* not the Return/Enter key on the QWERTY portion of the keyboard. The Memory Location/Marker window will open. Name this marker "Intro." Click OK.

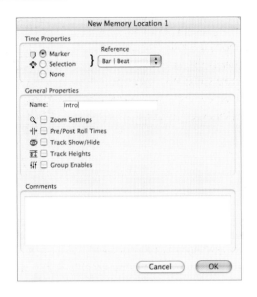

Tip

On my Apple PowerBook, since there is no numeric keypad, there is an Enter key to the right of the spacebar. This is what I use to create Markers.

Note

In this book, we'll treat memory locations and markers as being essentially the same thing.

9] **Create more markers.** Click bar 4, press Enter, and name this marker "VoxIntro1." Click bar 12, create a marker, and name it "Verse 1." Click bar 20, create a marker, and name it "Chorus 1." Your Timebase Rulers will now show you four markers, like this:

Bars:Beats	0		5		9		13		17		21	
Min:Secs	0:00	0:05	0:10	0:15	0:20	0:25	0:30	0:35	0:40	0:45	0:50	0:55	1:
▶ Tempo +	◆Manual Tempo : ♩90											
Meter +	▽4/4											
Markers +	▽Intro	▽VoxIntro1			▽Verse1					▽Chorus1		

If you mess up and create a marker incorrectly, you can use the Selector tool, drag across the marker to highlight it, and delete it with the Delete key. Here's another way to delete a marker: Notice that when you put your mouse over it, the mouse cursor turns into a pointing finger. At this point you can simply click on the marker and drag it off of the ruler.

If you click a marker and press the spacebar, the song will play from that location. You can also click markers while the song is playing to quickly change playback locations.

10] **Create the rest of the markers.** Let's finish the song's markers by adding them and giving them names as follows: bar 30, "VoxIntro2"; bar 38, "Verse 2"; bar 46, "Chorus 2"; bar 54, "Bridge"; bar 65, "VoxIntro3"; bar 73, Chorus 3"; bar 83, "Outro." Your marker timeline should now look like this:

| Markers + | Int VoxIntro1 | Verse 1 | Chorus 1 | VoxIntro2 | Verse 2 | Chorus 2 | Bridge | VoxIntro3 | Chorus 3 | Outro |

11] Save.

EXERCISE 2:

Create a Song Arrangement

Though we did not use SampleTank in writing this song, my cowriter Olly and I did use MIDI drums and loops with a plug-in called Spectrasonics Stylus RMX to create the preproduction drum tracks. After we had a good idea for the groove, I asked my friend Pat Mastelotto, the drummer for King Crimson, to perform live drums and create some percussion parts as well. Here is the original session of edited live drums:

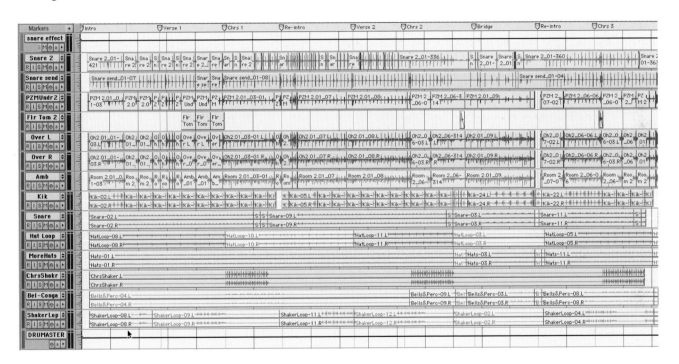

As you can see, recording and editing these tracks was no small job. Pat played five different takes of live drums. Each take was in a Grouped playlist like those we created in Chapter 8. I created an empty playlist and edited all of the live takes into one cohesive drum track, which as you know is called a *composite*. Pat then added percussion parts and I edited those tracks as well. After editing 14 tracks of drums and percussion to choose the bits we wanted to keep, we then had to mix them. Here is what our work looked like in the Mix window:

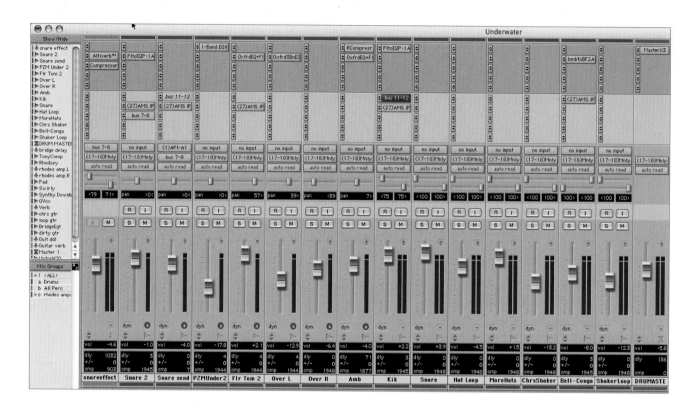

Because the drum files are in excess of 1 gigabyte and because my studio is using a Pro Tools HD system with plug-ins that aren't available for Pro Tools LE, I created a stem mix of these drum tracks to use in this exercise. We're going to place these edited drums and other live musical elements in the song.

➤ **SPOT MODE:** *Reference Guide, p. 301*

1] **Use Spot mode.** Let's learn a new way to place audio files in the Edit window. Choose Spot mode. Make the empty LiveDrums track medium-sized, and zoom in to where you can see the first verse and chorus. Now, from the Region List, drag the file IntroDrums to the LiveDrums track. You'll see a ghost image of the audio region as you drag the file to the Edit window. Drag the file anywhere within the LiveDrum track and let go of the mouse.

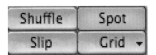

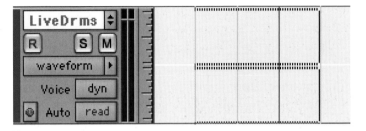

Tip

Get in the habit of using ⌘/Ctrl+] to zoom in quickly, and ⌘/Ctrl+[to zoom out.

2] **Set the start point.** At the top of the Spot Dialog window, below the Time Scale field (now showing Bars:Beats), is the start point. We want this region to start at bar 1. Enter "1" into the Start field and press OK. The audio region will now go to bar 1.

3] **Use Spot mode again.** This time, drag the file VsLoop to the LiveDrums track. In the Spot Dialog window, choose bar 4 as the start location. Click OK.

4] **Use Region Looping.** Make sure the VsLoop Region is highlighted. You already know how to duplicate a region using ⌘/Ctrl+D and how to repeat a region using Option/Alt+R. Now we're going to use a new feature in Pro Tools 7 called Region Looping. With the VsLoop highlighted, go to the Region menu and choose Loop. This menu will be grayed out unless a region is highlighted, but since we've just dragged the VsLoop region into the track, it should still be highlighted.

➤ **REGION LOOPING:**
 Reference Guide, pp. 328-332

5] **Choose the number of loops.** In the Region Looping window, click the Loop Length button and the make the loop 14 bars in length. Click OK. You now see three and a half loops after the Intro loop.

Notice that the three regions have little arrows at the bottom right-hand corner, showing you that they are a group of looped regions. Instead of three four-bar loops, you have created one cohesive 14-bar loop. So what is the advantage of Region Looping? Well, with Region Looping, when you're moving arrangements around, you only have to move one region instead of having to shift-click each four-bar region one by one in order to drag them as a unit. However, if you want to edit one of the regions within the new Looped Region, you'd want to use Duplicate rather than Region Looping. I suppose you could compare a Region Loop to a quilt. Each region is originally its own individual piece of fabric, but once they're sewn together, you have to take the whole quilt with you.

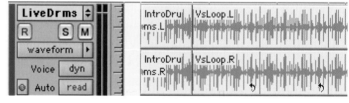

You may wonder why we didn't choose a number in the Number of Loops field that was evenly divisible by four, rather than choosing 14 bars in the Loop Length field. The vocal intro and verse are 8 bars each, so they total 16 bars, right? Well, I have a 2-bar fill that we're going to place at bar 18 before the first chorus. Since the VsLoop is 4 bars long, 3 loops would have been 12 bars, but 4 loops would have been too many. So we needed exactly 14 bars to save space for the 2-bar fill.

6] **Spot the first fill.** In Spot mode, drag the Fill1 region to the LiveDrums track and set the start point to bar 18.

7] **Spot the chorus drums.** Still in Spot mode, drag the file ChrsDrums to the LiveDrums track. Choose bar 20 as the start location.

8] **Spot the second fill.** In Spot mode, drag the Fill2 region to the LiveDrums track and set the start point to bar 28.

EXERCISE 2: CREATE A SONG ARRANGEMENT   **267**

9] **Mute the MIDI drums.** Mute the MIDI Loop track (not the SampleTank plug-in) and the MIDI Percussion track. You can mute the click track, too, if you want. Play back what we have created so far.

10] **Spot the bass.** Drag (in Spot mode) the file IntroBass to the LiveBass track and set bar 1 as the start point.

11] **Spot the verse bass.** Drag the file VsBass in Spot mode, and make bar 4 the start point. Hit ⌘/Ctrl+D to duplicate the bass. The bass should now extend all the way to the first chorus.

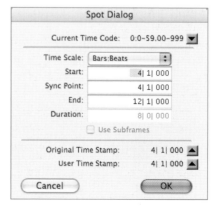

12] **Drag the ChrsBass.** Let's use Grid mode this time, and drag the ChrsBass region to bar 20. I want you to get used to all the different ways of doing things in Pro Tools.

13] **Drag the BreakBass.** Still in Grid mode, drag the BreakBass region to bar 27. You should now have the LiveDrums and LiveBass all the way through the first chorus.

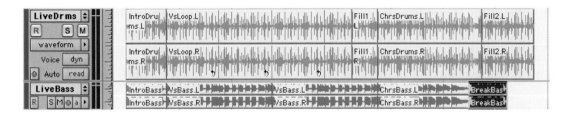

14] **Mute the MIDI bass track.** Mute the MIDI bass, and play back the song with the new bass and drums.

15] **Drag the pad.** Drag or spot the verse pad to bar 4. Drag or spot the chorus pad to bar 20. You may not want to mute the SampleTank MIDI pad track—sometimes layering pad sounds works very well.

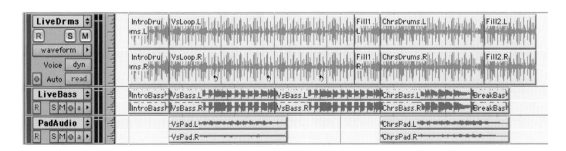

16] **Drag the guitars.** You should be getting the hang of this now. Drag the IntroEgt (electric guitar) to bar 1. Drag the BreakEgt to bar 4. (There will be a gap at bar 3.) Drag the VsEgt to bar 13, and finally, drag the ChrsEgt to bar 19.

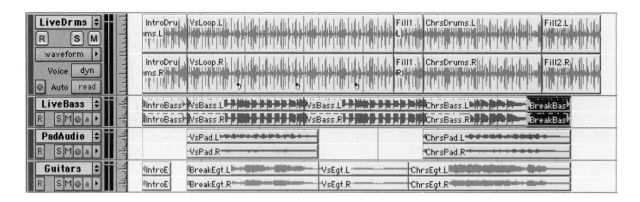

17] **Drag the SynthFX.** Drag or spot the SynthFX region to bar 1.

18] **Save.**

EXERCISE 3:

Hide Tracks and Use Groups

We have now replaced the demo MIDI drums and bass with real instruments, and we don't really need those demo tracks anymore. However, we don't want to delete them, because at some point we might want to go back and use something there, or at least listen to it. So we're going to use a feature called *hiding tracks.* In the Edit window on the left side, you'll see a list of all of your tracks. This is called (big surprise) the Tracks List. Below that are your Edit Groups, which we explored in Chapter 8.

Note

If you don't see the Tracks List, click the arrows at the lower-left corner of the Edit window.

➤ **GROUPS:** *Reference Guide, pp. 114-118*

1] **Hide one track.** In the Tracks List, click the Loop MIDI track. The name will become unhighlighted, and the track will disappear from the Mix and Edit windows. Click the track name again, and the track will come back. This is how you show and hide tracks.

2] **Group the MIDI tracks.** We could hide the Loop, Percussion, and MIDIBass tracks individually, but let's learn some more about Grouping. Make the Loop track visible again by clicking in the Tracks List. Highlight the Loop track (in the main area of the Edit window, not in the List); then hold the Shift key and highlight the Percussion and MIDIBass tracks, too. All three tracks should be highlighted. Now press ⌘/Ctrl+G. The New Group Window opens. Name this Group "Unused MIDI," select Edit And Mix Group, and click OK.

3] **Use Edit Groups.** Now you'll see your Unused MIDI Group in the Edit Groups list. Just to make sure you understand how Groups work, choose the Selector tool and highlight one of the MIDI tracks in the Edit window. They're all highlighted together now. Grouping is great for editing things like drum tracks, where you need one edit to affect all of the tracks. Grouping is also helpful for arranging, as you'll see in the next exercise.

4] **Hide an Edit Group.** To hide an Edit Group, click and hold on its name in the Edit Groups list. You'll see a Group pop-up menu. Choose Hide Tracks In Group. The three Unused MIDI tracks will go away. To bring them back, use this same pop-up menu and choose Show Tracks In Group. Notice that when you hide this group, the names become unhighlighted in the Tracks List.

➤ **HIDING TRACKS:**
Reference Guide, pp. 99-100

Next, we're going to take the first verse and chorus of all the audio tracks and copy them to the second verse and chorus. We could do this one track at a time, or we could create Groups. There are two ways to do this: using Edit-And-Mix Groups or using Region Groups. Let's do it both ways.

5] **Create another Group.** Let's make a Group out of all of the audio tracks except the vocal. Hold the Ctrl key and click the LiveDrums, LiveBass, PadAudio, Guitars, and SynthFX track names. All the names should be highlighted. Press ⌘/Ctrl+G. Name this Group "LiveTracks." You'll now see two groups in your Edit Groups list.

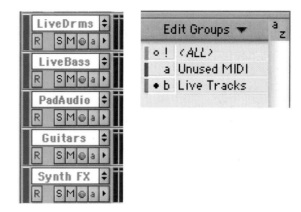

6] **Highlight the new Group.** In Grid mode, choose the Selector and highlight from VoxIntro 1 to VoxIntro 2. Look at your location indicators; they should clearly show that you are highlighted from bar 4 to bar 30.

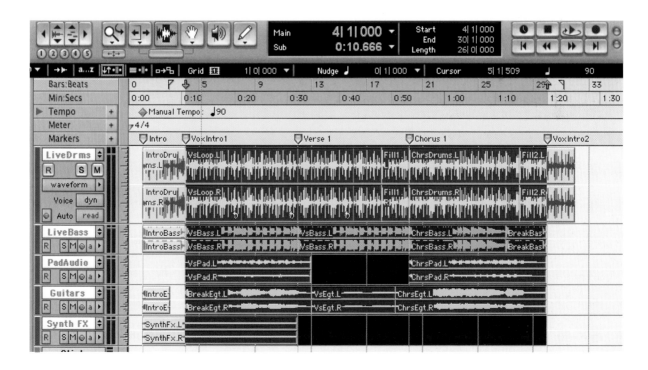

7] **Duplicate the Group.** Press ⌘/Ctrl+D to duplicate the group. You should now have audio all the way up to the bridge.

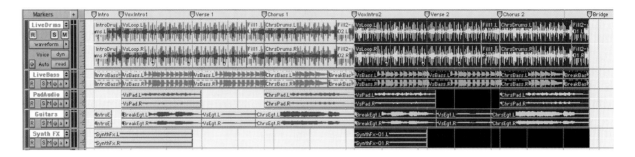

8] **Play the song.** You now have two verses and two choruses.

9] **Undo.** Use ⌘/Ctrl+Z to undo the track duplication.

10] **Create a Region Group.** Let's do exactly what we just did, but this time with a Region Group rather than an Edit-And-Mix Group. Highlight the live tracks again from bar 4 to bar 30. With the tracks highlighted, use the Region Group shortcut, which is ⌘+Option+G/Ctrl+Alt+G —it's the same shortcut as for creating an Edit-And-Mix Group but with the Option/Alt key added. You should now have a Region Group that Pro Tools has named Group-01.

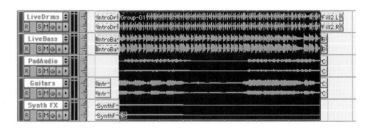

11 **Rename the Group.** Remember that it's a good habit to rename Region Groups. With the Region Group highlighted, press ⌘/Ctrl+Shift+R and rename the Region Group "Verse&Chorus."

12 **Duplicate the Region Group.** Use ⌘/Ctrl+D to duplicate this group. You may notice that you are duplicating over a piece of the Live Drums, but don't worry about it.

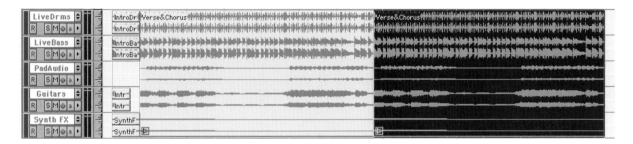

13 **Ungroup the regions.** Choose the Grabber, hold the Shift key, and select both Region Groups. Go to the Region menu and choose Ungroup. Now you should see all your tracks as individual regions again.

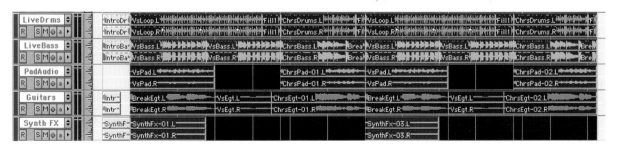

14] **Turn off the Edit-And-Mix Group.** We need to replace a few things on individual tracks before we start adding regions to the bridge. If you try now to click just the LiveDrums track, you'll notice that your cursor highlights all the Live Tracks. So we need to turn off the Live Tracks Group. You can turn off a Mix and/or Edit Group by clicking its name in the Edit Groups list to unhighlight it, just as you did with the Show/Hide feature in step 4 of this exercise.

I constantly use the shortcut ⌘/Ctrl+Shift+G when I want to make an edit to only one region. This shortcut turns off all Groups. Use the same command to turn Mix and Edit Groups back on.

EXERCISE 4:
Finish Arranging the Song

We need to place the last of the audio regions now. This task should go really fast now that you're getting the hang of placing regions at specific bar numbers. Your edit group should be turned off so that you can work just with the LiveDrums track.

1] **Replace Fill1 with Fill3.** You can drag one audio region directly on top of another without having to delete the first one. In Grid mode, drag the Fill3 region directly on top of Fill1 at bar 44.

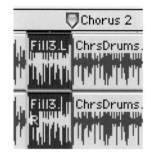

2] **Replace the chorus drums.** Drag in Grid mode or use Spot mode to place the Chrs2Drums region at the Chorus 2 marker at bar 46 on the LiveDrums track.

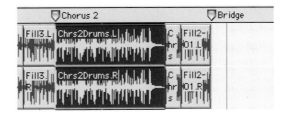

3] **Place the bridge drums.** Drag in Grid mode or use Spot mode to place the BridgeDrums region at bar 53 directly after the Chrs2Drums region.

4] **Place more regions.** In the LiveDrums track, place Fill4 at bar 64. Place the EndLoop at bar 67 and duplicate that region once.

5] **Place the BridgeBass.** Drag in Grid mode or use Spot mode to place the BridgeBass at bar 53 directly over the BreakBass region.

6] **Place the BridgePad.** Drag in Grid mode or use Spot mode to place the BridgePad region at bar 54 directly over the ChrsPad region.

7] **Place the bridge guitar.** Drag in Grid mode or use Spot mode to place the BridgeEgt at bar 53 directly over the end of the ChrsEgt region. Your song should now look more or less like this:

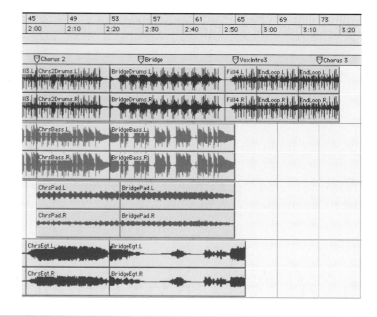

8] **Create a new Group.** Highlight the bass, pad, guitar, and synth tracks (every live instrument track except the drums). Press ⌘/Ctrl+G to create a new Group. Name it "No Drums" and make it an Edit-And-Mix Group.

9] **Turn groups on or off.** Make sure all groups are on. If any are grayed out, use the shortcut ⌘/Ctrl+Shift+G to reenable them. Turn off the Live Tracks Group so that it's not highlighted, but make sure that the new No Drums Group is on and highlighted.

Tip

To delete a Mix or Edit Group, click and hold on its name and choose Delete Group at the bottom of the pop-up menu.

10] **Copy the No Drums Group.** Using the Selector in Grid mode, highlight from bar 30 to bar 38 in the No Drums Group, and use ⌘/Ctrl+C to copy it.

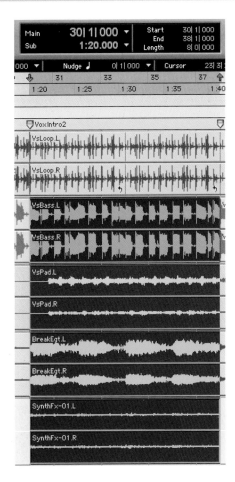

11] **Paste the No Drums Group.** Go to bar 65 and click with the Selector; then press ⌘/Ctrl+V to paste.

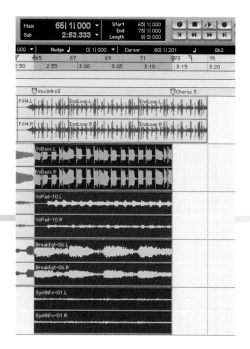

12] **Turn Groups on or off.** Turn off the No Drums Group and turn the Live Tracks Group back on.

13] **Copy 18 bars.** Using the Live Tracks group, highlight from the first chorus at bar 20 through to the beginning of verse 2 at bar 38, and copy.

14] **Paste 18 bars.** Go to bar 73, click with the Selector, and paste.

15] **Turn off all Groups.** Use ⌘/Ctrl+Shift+G again to turn off all Groups. We now need to place individual files again.

16] **Place the EndLoop.** At bar 91, place the EndLoop region in the LiveDrums track and duplicate it three times using ⌘/Ctrl+D. You should now have four EndLoops.

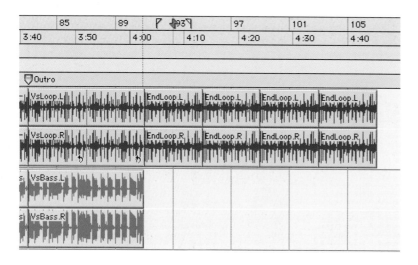

17] **Use Region Looping.** Highlight the VsBass region from bar 83 to bar 91 (you can choose the Grabber and simply click the region once to highlight it). Now let's use the shortcut for Region Looping: Press ⌘+Option+L/Ctrl+Alt+L. In the Region Looping window, type "3" into the Number of Loops field and click OK.

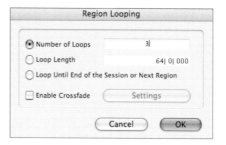

18] **Use Region Looping again.** Highlight the VsPad region from bar 83 to 91, and again use the shortcut and loop this region three times.

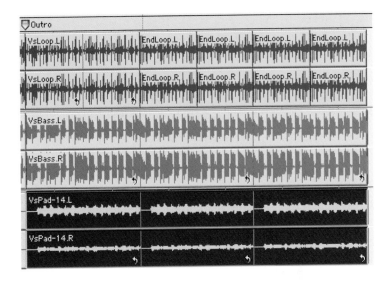

19] **Drag the end guitar.** Drag the EndEgt region to bar 91, and duplicate this region once.

20] Save!

Well, you've done it. You've pieced together your first song.

I created this song in loops for this chapter so you would become comfortable with placing regions into the Edit window, and so that you'd start to understand about editing song arrangements in Grid mode using groups and markers.

This song was obviously not recorded in loops in the way we've pieced them together. The tracks were recorded in the conventional way, using Pro Tools like a tape machine, from beginning to end. I simply cut up the final tracks into loops to teach you about song arrangement and about copying and pasting regions in Pro Tools.

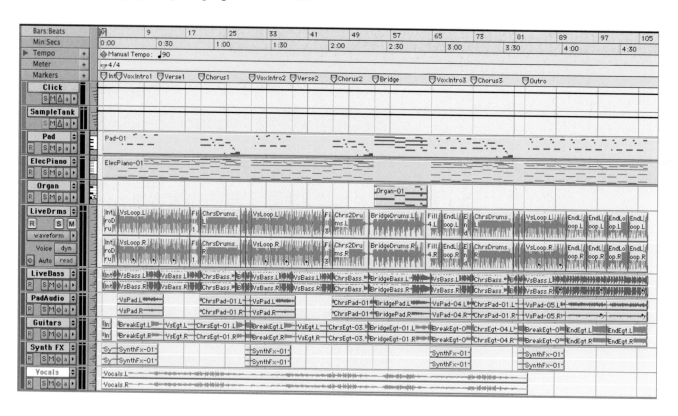

About "Underwater"

German writer/producer Oliver Adolph and I wrote "Underwater" via the Internet between Austin, Texas, and Hamburg, Germany. Olly programmed many of the keyboards and did the original drum programming. I tweaked the chord progressions and keyboards, played the MIDI bass, wrote the lyrics, and sang the vocals in my studio in Austin. From there, I sent the demo version to Pat Mastelotto, who played drums in his studio in Dripping Springs, Texas. I edited these drums and sent them to my friend Tony Levin, who recorded the bass using Apple Logic Audio. The guitars were performed and recorded in Pro Tools by my brilliant friend Teddy Kumpel in New York City. The track is part of a project called "Room to Breathe," slated for release later in 2006. In Appendix B of this book, I'm going to be teaching you how to send your own work to players around the world.

Wrap Up

I hope you have started to grasp what we're doing in these exercises and are beginning to see how to apply these operations to your own music. Coming up in the next chapter are some advanced tips and techniques. Then in Chapter 11 you'll get an introduction to cross-fades, automation, and how to mix a song using "Underwater." So take another break—we only have three chapters to go.

TIPS & TOOLS

Hang on to your Underwater session. We're going to use it in Chapter 11 to learn about automation and mixing. Here in Chapter 10, though, we'll be creating a different session and using it to explore some new techniques.

We're going to start by downloading and importing an entire drum kit so you can get more familiar with using groups of tracks. We'll use these tracks to learn how to find the tempo of a loop and also how to set Pro Tools to work with different meters.

We're going to edit the tempo of each drum group and then create a small arrangement while reviewing the use of Edit Groups, Region Groups, and markers. After we have some tracks to work with, we'll explore a very cool feature called *loop recording*, with which you can record the same part over and over, keeping each take, and then edit them together or layer them to create a more textured sound. We'll also experiment with creating a composite track and doing crossfades.

Multi-Track Loops and Odd-Time Grooves

Though most drum loops come as stereo files, a few companies create loops as multi-track files, giving the user separate control over the kick, snare, hi-hat overheads, room mics, and so on. With this type of material, you can mix the drums however you want. You can even buy these multi-track loop libraries as actual Pro Tools sessions.

In this chapter we're using one of my favorite multi-track loop collections, called Odd-Time Grooves, by a small but innovative company called MultiLoops (MultiLoops.com). They also have some great collections of multi-track loops called Naked Drums, but since I want to introduce other meters to you in this chapter, I chose a couple of beats from Odd-Time Grooves. (Other companies that sell multi-track loop libraries include Discrete Drums, Zero-G, and East West.)

It's easy for me to create drums in my own studio with a real drummer, but most of you aren't set up to record a drum set. I want you to begin to understand the many resources available for your creativity and how to use them in your own music. A collection of loop libraries and plug-ins will be something you'll want to develop as you learn Pro Tools. This book's companion web site lists some of these resources, as well as links for plug-ins and loops, at protoolsformusicians.com.

Ninety-nine percent of all loop collections are in 4/4, but I get bored when I'm writing, and sometimes rather than taking time to program drums in another meter, I want a nice clean acoustic drum loop to write to. Odd-Time Grooves consists of two DVDs full of beats in 5/8, 6/8, 7/8, 9/8, 19/16, and more. The loops are recorded in multiple Pro Tools sessions based on meter and tempo, and each loop gives you 12 tracks of beautifully performed, recorded, and edited loops. So you can open the session, sort through, delete the loops you don't want, and make that session into your song.

I've found only one other loop collection that features additional meters: Brush Artistry by Big Fish Audio. This collection has typical stereo loops, geared more toward a very ambient, brushy snare sound, but there are some nice waltz and 6/8 loops in this collection as well.

EXERCISE 1:

Prepare a New Session

Even though Odd-Time Grooves does provide Pro Tools sessions with the meter and tempo already set up, we're not going to use their sessions, because I want you to learn how to find the tempo and meter on your own. It's important to know how to find the tempo of audio in Pro Tools when you need to.

1] **Download the Chapter 10 files.** Using your browser, go to protoolsformusicians.com and click the Chapter 10 Downloads. Unzip this file on your audio drive.

2] **Create a new session.** Close any open session and create a new session called "Learning PT Ch 10." For the session parameters, choose WAV files, 44.1 kHz, and 24-bit audio.

3] **Open the Pro Tools Workspace.** Use the shortcut Option/Alt+; to open the Pro Tools Workspace, or open it from the Windows menu. Expand your audio drive to show the files within.

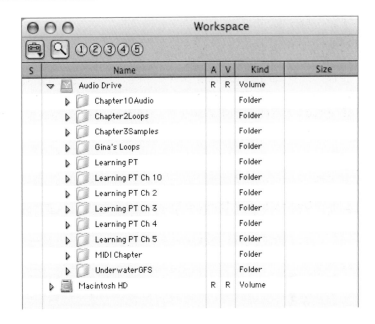

"What is the Workspace?"

The Workspace is Pro Tools' file management system. It shows you any hard drives connected to your computer and lets you listen to and import audio simply and easily into your sessions.

I love the Workspace. I keep a large library of loops on my main G5 Mac in my studio, and a small library of loops on a drive that I travel with. When I begin writing, I can search for loops or sound effects from the Workspace and then audition sounds without leaving Pro Tools. You can even drag files from the Workspace directly to the Tracks List bin or into the Region bin so that they're ready to import.

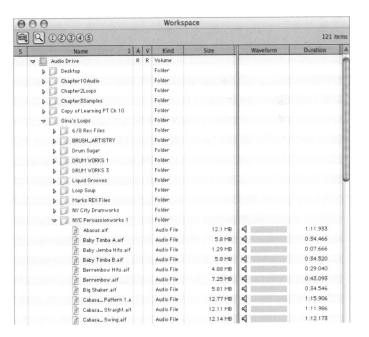

4] **Expand the Chapter10Audio folder.** There are quite a lot of files in here, right? We're going to be working with eight tracks of drums. There are four different loops of eight tracks each that I've put in Groups labeled A through D. Let's select Group A. Hold the Shift key and highlight the eight tracks of drums numbered A-1 through A-8.

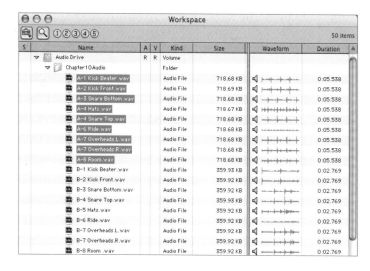

5] **Drag drums to the Tracks List.** Drag all the drums to the Tracks List bin in either the Edit window or the Mix window. This will create eight tracks for you.

6] **Move the overheads.** For some reason, Pro Tools puts the stereo overheads in the wrong order. You can alter the track order in the Tracks List, as well. Click and hold on the Overheads track and drag to place it between Ride and Room. You'll see a line showing that you're placing it in the correct spot.

7] **Unmute any tracks.** Another bug that occurs on my system is that some tracks come in muted. I don't know why. If you have the same problem on your system, unmute them all. Remember, you can hold the Option/Alt key and click one muted track to unmute all of them. Use this same shortcut to change all track sizes to small.

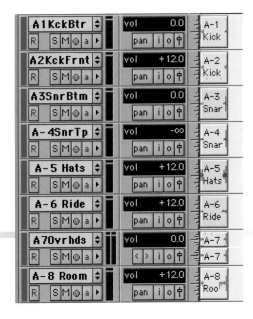

8] Save.

The Danger of Importing Audio from the Workspace

Using the Workspace has one downside, as you'll see in this exercise.

Most of my loops are 16-bit, 44.1 kHz, but most of my sessions are 24-bit, 44.1 kHz. Therefore, when I import loops into my songs from the Workspace, Pro Tools must convert them because they don't have the correct resolution for the song. When Pro Tools converts these Workspace files, it makes a copy of each file in the correct format and places the copies inside the Audio File folder of the session I'm working on. Here's the difficulty: If your Workspace loops happen to be in the same file format and resolution as the session you are creating, importing the loops from the Workspace will cause Pro Tools to use the original copies of these loops in your session, so these files will not be placed in your Audio Files folder. This can turn into a huge problem.

Look inside the Audio Files folder of your new session, and you'll see there's nothing in it. But you just imported eight tracks of drums, right? Why aren't they in there? Because the files you imported are 24-bit WAV files, and the session you created is a 24-bit WAV file session. The new loops are using are the same bit depth and bit rate as the session, so the Workspace has referenced the audio files in the location from which you dragged them, *without* copying the files into your Audio Files folder.

This can be a dangerous situation: If you delete the files from the session, they'll be deleted from your library. Also, if you need to back up your session and you burn a CD of your session folder, the audio files will be missing unless you remember to back up the files that you imported. In order to do that, you'll need to remember exactly where to find them. A quick solution to this Workspace dilemma is to use Save Copy In when you've finished importing audio files.

The most important thing to remember when using Save Copy In is to check the All Audio Files checkbox in the Items To Copy section the bottom of the Save Copy In dialog box. This will save a separate session in a new folder and copy any audio files used in this session to one place. It's a good habit to use the Save Copy In method before you back up your session, to make sure that all related files are in one location. We'll do this in Exercise 14 to reinforce this important lesson.

EXERCISE 2:

Change the Meter and Find the Tempo

1] **Zoom in.** Zoom in to see your loop. Notice that, as always, the Pro Tools default tempo is 120 BPM and the meter is 4/4. Also, notice that our loop is not in sync with the tempo. Play back the loop. What meter is it in?

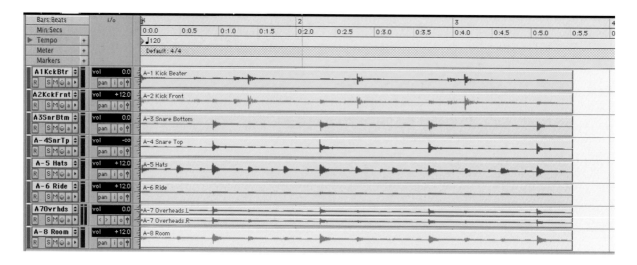

2] **Turn the Conductor on.** Open the Transport window and make sure the Conductor is on. We're finally going to learn how to use it.

The Conductor makes Pro Tools follow the tempo and meter tracks in the Edit window. When the Conductor is off, Pro Tools uses the manual tempo and meter that are set in the Transport window.

This loop is in 6/8, right? You could simply turn off the Conductor and set the meter to 6/8 in the manual meter field—but you still don't know the tempo, so we're going to change the meter and find the tempo.

3] **Change the meter.** If the Meter ruler isn't visible at the top of the Edit window, activate it from the View menu. On the Meter ruler, there's a small + button next to Meter. Click that, and the Meter window opens. Change your meter to 6/8. In this box you can also tell the click track (if you added one) to click on the eighth note if you want it to.

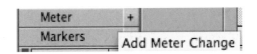

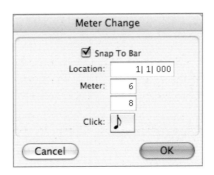

➤ **METER EVENTS:** *Reference Guide, p. 374*

Now the Meter ruler shows 6/8. Changing the meter is that simple. If you want to change the meter at any bar, click that bar number in Grid mode and hit the + key in the Meter ruler. That's it. Remember to make sure that the Conductor is turned on when you use the Tempo and Meter rulers.

We now need to find the tempo of this loop. There are two ways to do this: using Identify Beat or the Beat Detective.

➤ **TEMPO:** *Reference Guide, p. 354*

4] **Use Identify Beat.** Highlight one of the loop regions with the Grabber. Go to the Event menu and choose Identify Beat.

➤ **IDENTIFY BEAT:** *Reference Guide, p. 370*

5] **Set the bars.** This is a two-bar loop, so the start would be bar 1 and the end would be bar 3. Set the End Location to 3| 1| 000 and click OK.

Now the Tempo ruler shows 64.9998—almost 65 BPM. You'll find that some loops don't have tempos in nice round numbers.

6] **Undo.** Undo the tempo change you've just made so we can do this one more time with Beat Detective. Your tempo should be back at the default of 120 BPM.

7] **Use Beat Detective.** With one loop region highlighted as before, go to the Event menu and choose Beat Detective. On the left side of the Beat Detective window are the Beat Detective functions. Keep this set to the first one, Bar/Beat Marker Generation. Set the Start bar to bar 1 and the End bar to bar 3. Click Generate. Your Tempo ruler is back to 64.9998.

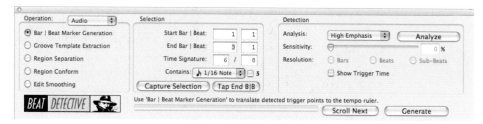

8] **Save.**

Identify Beat vs. Beat Detective

Remember how you learned to use the Pro Tools real-time MIDI properties and then how to do the same functions manually? Well, Beat Detective is the automatic version and Identify Beat is the manual version of finding a tempo.

Beat Detective is a much more powerful tool than what we have just used it for. You can use it to fix entire drum tracks beat by beat. This allows you to quantize real drum performances.

EXERCISE 3:
Change the Tempo

So what if you like a loop, but you want to change its tempo to better suit your song? We did this in Chapter 3 with a stereo loop; let's do it now using multiple tracks.

1]
Create an Edit Group of the drums. We want to make sure we change the tempo of all of the drum tracks together. We don't want to change the tempo eight different times. To prepare for this, hold the Shift key while clicking each drum's track name, and use the shortcut ⌘/Ctrl+G to create an Edit-And-Mix Group. Name it "Drums."

2]
Choose the tempo. Decide what tempo you want to use. I'm going to use 70 BPM. Click the + at the left end of the Tempo ruler and set the tempo to 70 BPM (or whatever tempo you've chosen).

Notice that your loop no longer ends at the downbeat of a bar. It now ends past the downbeat of bar 3. Since our previous tempo was slower than our new tempo, this loop is too long. Let's time-compress the loop to match our new tempo.

Note

You may notice throughout the book that I'm working with slower tempos. When you're learning, it's easier to play along and learn things if the tempo is not too fast.

3] **Use the Trimmer.** Make sure you're in Grid mode with the Grid Resolution set to either bars or quarter notes. Then click and hold on the Trim tool to choose the Time Compression/Expansion tool, which is labeled TCE.

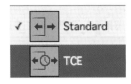

Tip

If you feel you may want to keep the original loops in the original tempo for some other use, get into the habit of duplicating your playlists before you edit anything.

4] **Use the TCE tool.** Click at the end of one of the drum tracks, drag to your left to snap it to the downbeat of bar 3, and let go. A window comes up briefly showing that each track is being compressed. The regions will be renamed with a TCEX in the name. Notice the new regions in the Regions List.

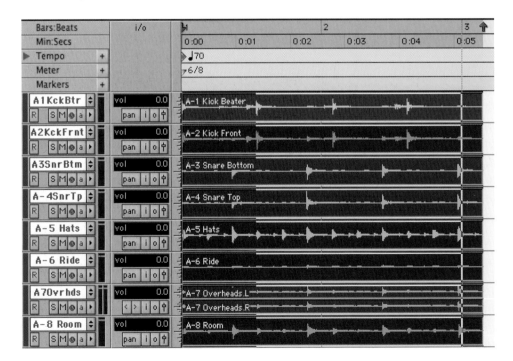

5] **Undo.** What if 70 BPM feels too fast? What if you want a tempo of 68? Use ⌘/Ctrl+Z to undo, thus restoring the original audio files. I want you to get used to doing this, so let's redo this same exercise at 68 BPM.

Tip

It's important to be aware that when you time-compress a file, it degrades the audio quality. So if you later decide to change the tempo again, you don't want to keep time-compressing the already processed file. It's always best to go back to the original files and time-compress them again, so that when you do decide on a tempo, you'll have the highest audio quality of your time-compressed file. Again, the best solution is to duplicate the playlist of every track before you edit it.

6] **Change the tempo.** Click the + again in the Tempo ruler and change the tempo to 68.

7] **Use TCE again.** Use the Trimmer tool in TCE mode again and drag the end of the loop to the downbeat of bar 3.

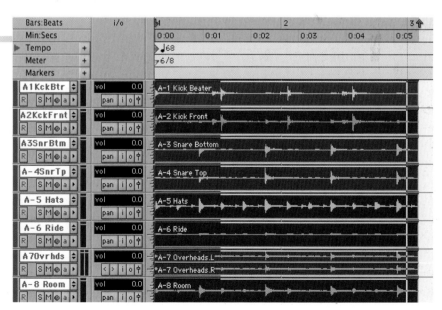

8] **Unselect the Trim tool.** Get in the habit of switching the Trimmer off after you use it. It can be potentially dangerous if you forget you have it selected and then click on one of your regions; the region will become trimmed or time-compressed. If this happens, remember your friend, the Undo command.

9] **Play back and save.** When you find the tempo you want, save your file. (In order to follow some of the exercises later in this chapter, I suggest you leave it at 68 BPM.)

Now let's go ahead and import the rest of the loops.

EXERCISE 4:

Import and Fix More Loops

The first thing we need is to bring in the rest of the audio files. We're going to import them using the Workspace, but this time we won't drag them to the Tracks List. Instead, we'll drag them from the Workspace into the Regions List. Then we'll make a fast, easy arrangement to work with.

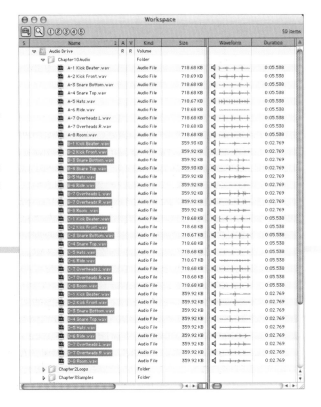

1] **Highlight the audio files.** Open the Workspace and select the drum audio files in groups B–D. Highlight the first audio file, B-1 Kick Beater, hold the Shift key, and highlight the last audio file, D-8 Room. All files in between will be highlighted.

2] **Drag the files to the Region bin.** This time, drag from the Workspace to the Regions bin, not the Tracks bin. As you drag on the Mac, you'll see outlines of all the files. Let go, and your new regions will be in the Regions bin.

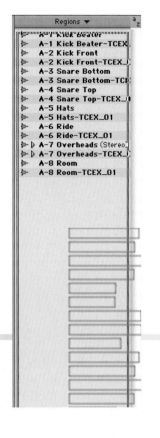

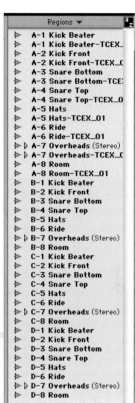

3] **Create a Region Group.** Highlight Region A (the audio segments that are already in the Edit window) and use your shortcut ⌘+Option+G/ Ctrl+Alt+G to create a Region Group.

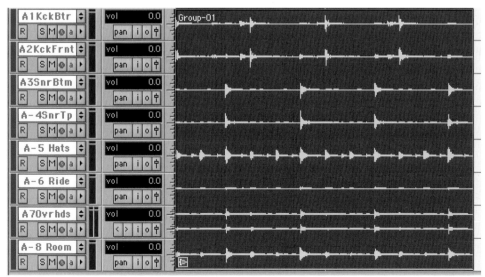

4] **Rename the Region Group.** Rename the Region Group using the shortcut ⌘/Ctrl+Shift+R. Name the Group "Verse Loop."

5] **Duplicate the Verse Loop.** Use ⌘/Ctrl+D to duplicate the Verse Loop once.

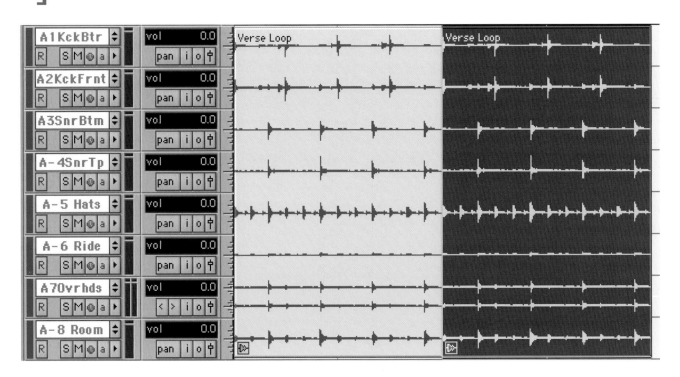

6] **Drag Drum Group B.** In the Regions bin, highlight Drum Group B. Drag Group B to the Edit window in Grid mode. This is a little tricky—be sure to drag to the top of the Edit window so that all eight tracks fit into it. You'll see outlined boxes of your regions. Place these regions directly after the Verse Loop at the downbeat of bar 5.

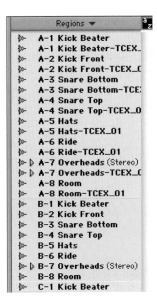

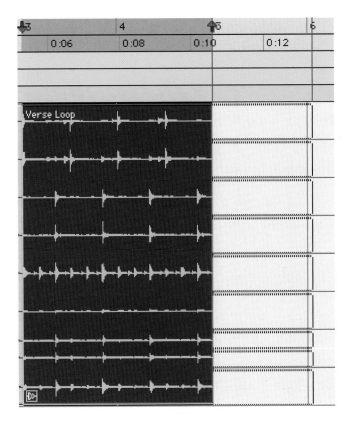

7] **Fix the tempo.** Assuming you left the tempo at 68 BPM at the end of the previous Exercise, you'll notice in your location indicators that this loop is not exactly one bar in length. This means the loop has a different tempo than our session. Let's fix it.

Start	5| 1| 000
End	6| 1| 133
Length	1| 0| 133

Use the TCE tool again in Grid mode and drag the end of the new Group B to the left, to snap at the downbeat of bar 6.

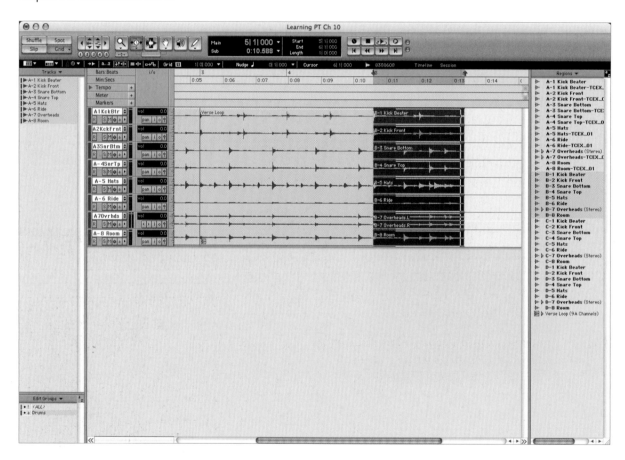

8] **Drag Drum Group C.** In the Regions bin, highlight Drum Group C. Drag Group C to the end of Group B, to the downbeat of bar 6.

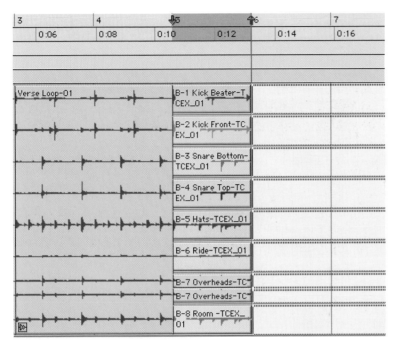

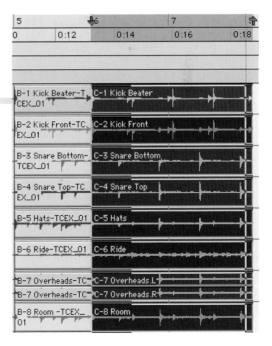

9] **Fix the tempo.** Again, notice that the location indicators show this loop's tempo should be adjusted. Use the TCE tool in Grid mode to fix it.

10] **Drag Drum Group D.** In the Regions Bin, highlight Drum Group D. Drag Group D to the end of Group C, to the downbeat of bar 8.

▷ **D-1 Kick Beater**
▷ **D-2 Kick Front**
▷ **D-3 Snare Bottom**
▷ **D-4 Snare Top**
▷ **D-5 Hats**
▷ **D-6 Ride**
▷ ▷ **D-7 Overheads** (Stereo)
▷ **D-8 Room**

11] **Fix the tempo.** Once again, notice the location indicators. Use the TCE tool in Grid mode to fix the tempo.

Start	8	1	000
End	9	1	133
Length	1	0	133

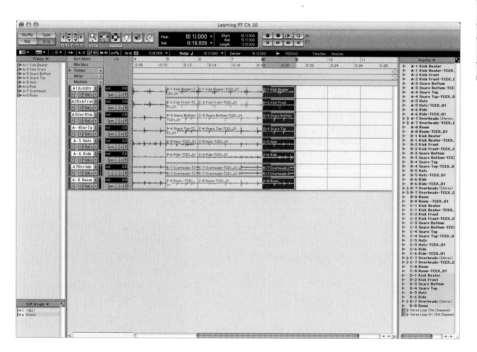

12] **Play back and save.**

EXERCISE 5:

Create Region Groups and Assign Colors

Once the loops are imported and the tempos adjusted, the first thing I do is get all my Regions named and organized so that I know clearly what I'm working with. Let's create Region Groups of the new loops and assign each group a different color.

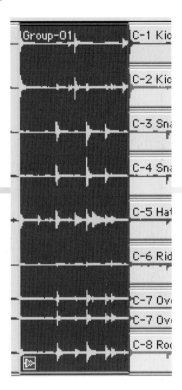

1] **Create Region Group B.** Use the Grabber or double-click with the Selector to highlight Drum Group B. Then use ⌘+Option+G/Ctrl+Alt+G.

2] **Rename Group B.** Use ⌘/Ctrl+Shift+R to rename the group "Verse Fill."

3] **Create Region Group C.** Use the Grabber or double-click with the Selector to highlight Drum Group C. Then use ⌘+Option+G/ Ctrl+Alt+G.

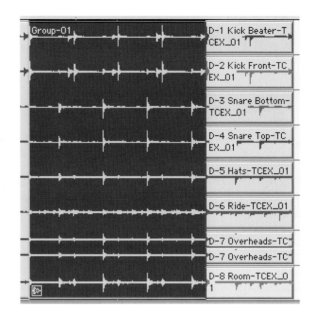

4] **Rename Group C.** Use ⌘/Ctrl+Shift+R to rename the group "Chorus."

5] **Create Region Group D.** Use the Grabber tool or double-click with the Selector tool to highlight Drum Group D. Then use ⌘+Option+G/Ctrl+Alt+G.

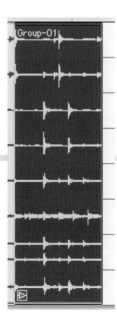

6] **Rename Group D.** Use ⌘/Ctrl+Shift+R to rename the group "Chorus Fill."

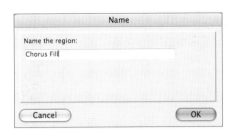

All of the Region Groups are blue. What if we want each region to be a different color? Having different colors won't affect the music, but the colors will make navigating in the Edit window easier.

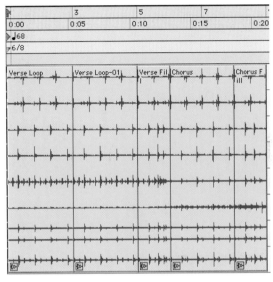

7] **Assign colors.** Go to the Window menu and choose Color Palette. The Color Palette window will open. Use the Grabber with the Shift key to select the two Verse Loops, and then click any color. Click away from the region to see the color change. I'm going to make my Verse Loops purple.

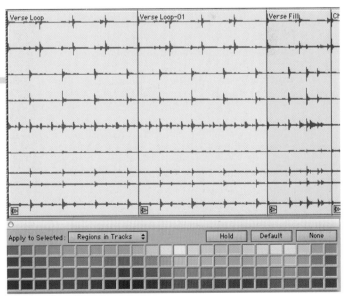

8]

Assign other colors. Make each grouped region a different color by highlighting it and choosing a color.

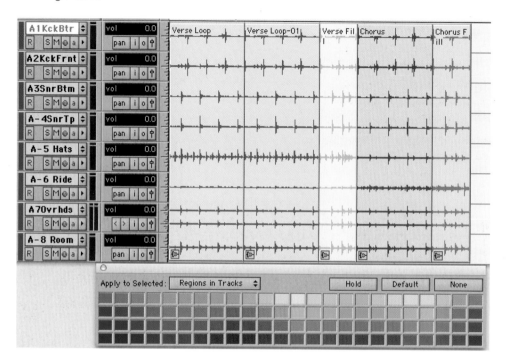

Just as regions have color coding, so do tracks. Assigning colors works exactly the same way. See how the tracks are all blue right now?

9] **Highlight the drum tracks.** A quick way to highlight all track names in a group is to click the tiny circle next to the Drum Edit Group. All of the track names will be highlighted, because we've just been grouping them in the earlier steps of this exercise and there are no other tracks in the session. In other circumstances, if they aren't highlighted, you can click the circle or plus sign to highlight all of the track names in the drum group.

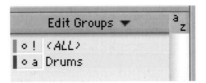

Click the blue color band on one of the tracks, and notice in the Color Palette that the Apply to Selected field changes to show Tracks.

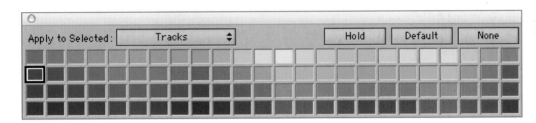

10] **Choose a color.** I'm going to choose teal. Now all of the tracks in my drum group are teal.

11] **Save.**

Color coding comes in very handy when you have large sessions. I always make my drums one color, my guitars another, my vocals another, and so on. Colors make it very easy to recognize specific groups for editing and mixing.

EXERCISE 6:

Use Shuffle Mode

Shuffle mode is used to add time or delete time within an arrangement. Listen to the arrangement of the session we've been working on so far. There are five bars before the chorus. What if we want to delete bar 4 and move the whole song up one bar, so that we have an even four bars before the first chorus?

➤ **SHUFFLE MODE:** *Reference Guide, p. 274*

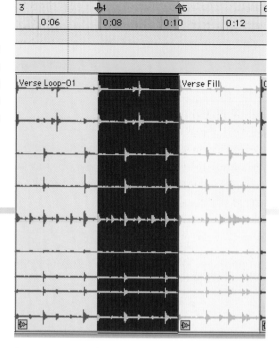

1] **Highlight bar 4.** In Grid mode, highlight bar 4.

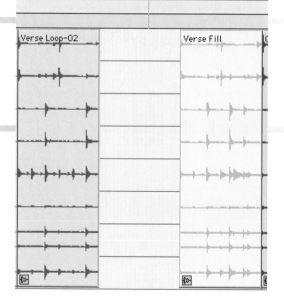

2] **Delete bar 4.** While still in Grid mode, delete bar 4. This leaves a big hole in that space, right?

3] **Undo.** Undo with ⌘/Ctrl+Z.

4] **Choose Shuffle mode.** Choose Shuffle mode and then press the Delete key. Bar 4 goes away, and everything after it is moved up.

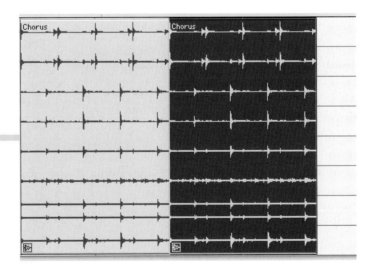

5] **Important: Go back to Grid mode.** After you've used Shuffle mode, it's very, very important to immediately get out of it and choose another mode. I have seen some terrible Pro Tools disasters in which users have left Shuffle selected and started editing with the Selector tool, not realizing that their entire arrangement was being moved and edited. So be alert and get in the habit now of thinking of Shuffle as "the dangerous mode": Use it and get out quickly.

6] **Create a double chorus.** What if you want the chorus to be twice as long? Let's highlight the entire Chorus Region in Grid mode and press ⌘/Ctrl+D to duplicate. But when we do this, we lose our Chorus Fill region.

7] **Undo.**

8] **Use Shuffle mode.** With the Chorus Region still highlighted in Grid mode, switch to Shuffle mode and press ⌘/Ctrl +D to duplicate. Now the Chorus Fill moves back with the new arrangement.

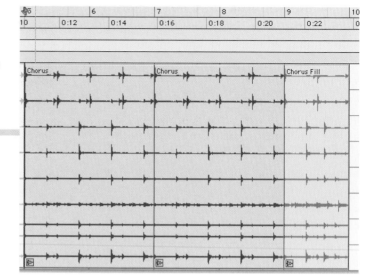

9] **Important: Go back to Grid mode.** Leave Shuffle mode and return to Grid mode. Now listen to the arrangement and hear that the fill makes the chorus five bars long. We want the chorus to be four bars including the fill, so we need to delete bar 8 and have the fill move up. So we're going to delete bar 8 in Shuffle mode.

Tip

It's important to note that Grid mode always must be used before Shuffle mode. Before using Shuffle, you must always highlight, in even bars, the region that you want to affect, to ensure that when you do use Shuffle mode, it will be done in perfect bar numbers. If you use Shuffle mode without Grid mode, your arrangement will no longer be aligned to the tempo and can easily be a mess.

10] **Highlight bar 8.** In Grid mode, highlight bar 8.

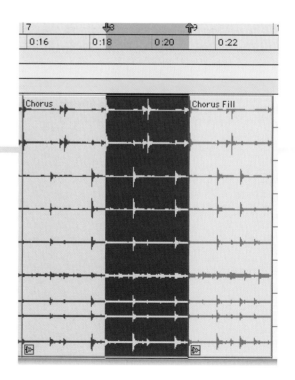

11] **Use Shuffle mode.** Go to Shuffle mode and delete bar 8. Now you have a four-bar chorus including the fill.

12] **Don't forget: Go back to Grid mode.**

13] **Zoom out.** Zoom out to see the whole eight-bar arrangement.

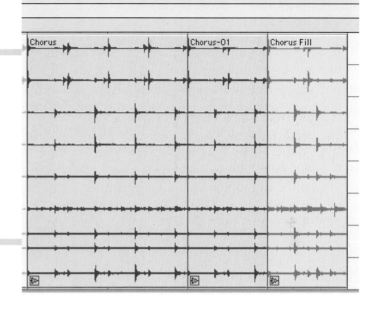

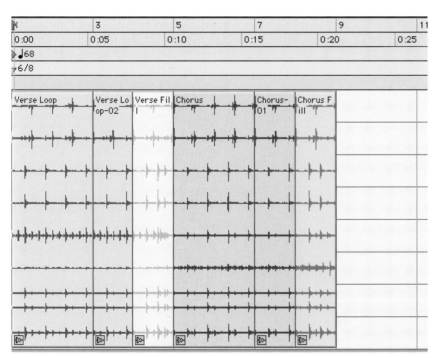

14] Highlight all eight bars.

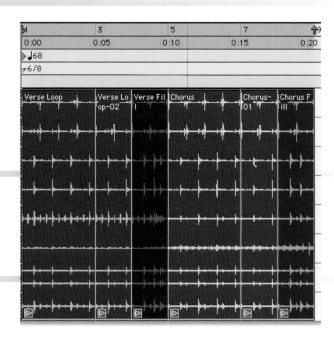

15] Duplicate all eight bars.

16] Save.

Now we have 16 bars to work with. Let's put some markers in.

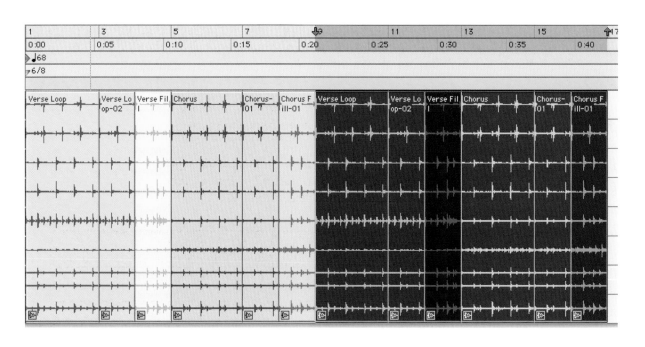

EXERCISE 7:

Create Markers in Playback

You can create markers while Pro Tools plays by pressing the Enter key on the numeric keypad. This can be tricky; let's see how it works.

➤ **MARKERS & MEMORY LOCATIONS:** *Reference Guide, p. 382*

1] **Create marker 1.** Since the first marker will be at bar 1, press Return/Enter to go to bar 1. Click the + button in the Markers ruler, or Ctrl-click (Mac) or right-click (Windows) in the Markers ruler. Name this marker "Verse 1."

2] **Create a marker during playback.** Press the spacebar to play. When the song reaches bar 5, either press the numeric keypad Enter key or click the + in the Markers ruler. Name this marker "Chorus 1."

You can keep playing your song and creating markers in this way, but it gets difficult to type quickly before the next section arrives. So let's tell Pro Tools to name the markers for us during playback, and then we'll rename them later.

Bars:Beats	i/o	1	3	5	7
Min:Secs		0:00	0:05	0:10	0:15
▶ Tempo +		♩68			
Meter +		5/8			
Markers +		Verse 1		Chorus 1	

3] **Set Preferences.** Go to the Setup menu and choose Preferences. Click the Editing tab. At the top of the window are come checkboxes. Check the second option, Auto-Name Memory Locations When Playing, and click Done.

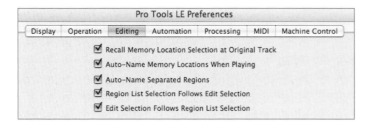

4] **Play from bar 5.** Click at bar 5 and press the spacebar to play. At bar 9, press numeric keypad Enter to create a marker. Do it again at bar 13. Pro Tools will name and number the markers for you.

| Verse 1 | Chorus 1 | Marker 3 | Marker 4 |

5] **Rename the markers.** Click marker 3 to set the playback position at this location. This is very important to do when you want to rename a marker. If you don't click the marker location first, when you rename your marker it will move to the location of the Pro Tools play cursor. Ctrl-click/right-click on the marker and rename it "Verse 2." Then click marker 4 to set the location and rename it "Chorus 2."

| Verse 1 | Chorus 1 | Verse 3 | Chorus 2 |

A marker/memory location can retain more information than just its location. You probably have noticed the Memory Location window has some check boxes below the marker name. I personally don't use these functions very often, but let me show you how they work.

6] **Change the Verse 1 marker.** Double-click on the Zoomer to zoom out and see all 16 bars. Click the Verse 1 marker to set the playback location; then Ctrl-click/right-click to edit it. Check the Zoom Settings and Track Height boxes, and click OK.

7] **Change the Chorus 1 marker.** Click the Chorus 1 marker, make sure the Drum Edit Group is turned on, and change the track height to medium. All drum tracks will change to medium.

Choose the Zoomer tool and zoom so that all you see is the first chorus. Now Ctrl-click/right-click on the Chorus 1 marker, and check the Zoom Settings and Track Height boxes.

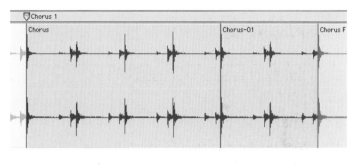

8] Click the Verse 1 marker. Double-click the Zoomer to zoom out and click the Verse 1 marker. Your zoom setting and track heights will change back. Now click the Chorus 1 marker. See how it works?

Tip

You can also move around in the song by opening the Memory Locations window (Window > Memory Locations) and clicking on any marker.

9] Save.

The Memory Location settings can come in very handy, depending on how you work.

EXERCISE 8:
Use Loop Recording

Loop recording is a feature I use all the time. It allows you to highlight a section and record that same section over and over. It may seem that you are actually recording over what you previously recorded (as you would if you were using a tape deck), but you're not. Pro Tools keeps a list of the loop takes and lets you pick and choose. This is a perfect solution for solos where a musician needs to play something over and over to get a part right.

Very frequently I will use loop recording with vocalists. Sometimes a vocalist wants to record a song in sections, as opposed to singing the song from top to bottom. Sometimes the chorus is very high and strains the vocalist's voice, so it makes sense to record the less-strenuous sections of the song first and then come back after the vocalist is warmed up and record the more aggressive sections. In this case, I would use loop recording, highlight the first verse, and let the vocalist sing this verse over and over until they or I feel that they have a great performance somewhere amidst all the different recordings. Then we move on to the next section and do the same thing.

➤ **LOOP RECORDING:** *Reference Guide, p. 177*

Plug in either an instrument or a microphone and get ready to start loop recording.

1] **Create a new track.** Create a mono audio track if you're using a mono source such as a microphone or guitar, or create a stereo track if you're recording a stereo instrument such as a keyboard. I'm using a microphone, so I'm choosing mono. Name this track "MyChorus1."

2] **Set the input.** Select the audio input you're using, put the track in Record, and make sure you have level.

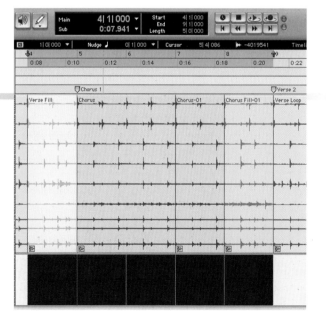

3] **Highlight your loop.** Make the new track medium-sized and highlight from bar 4 to bar 9 in Grid mode.

4] **Turn on loop recording.** The shortcut for loop recording is Option/Alt+L, or you can select Loop Recording from the Options menu. You can also Ctrl-click/right-click the Record button in the Transport window to toggle through a series of options, one of which is Loop Recording.

5] **Play the loop.** Play the loop to become familiar with it, and create something on your instrument or vocally to record. I'm going to sing the first two lines of "The House of the Rising Sun" as my loop, just for something simple to work with.

The secret to loop recording is highlighting a pre-roll and post-roll time as part of the region you're trying to record. This allows you the time to get ready to play or sing the part. It's also important to have something recognizable in your pre-roll so you'll know when to begin recording. Sometimes, when there's no fill or nothing to cue where to record, I'll import a sound effect or audio file that plays one bar before the recording point.

You can choose pre-roll and post-roll in the Transport window, but the pre-roll will only play the first time through the loop. Once the first region is recorded and Pro Tools begins looping, you will not hear the pre-roll again. So highlighting a longer region than you actually need is a better approach.

6] **Record.** Press ⌘/Ctrl+spacebar to record. Your loop will record and then, when it reaches the end, will start over recording at the beginning. Continue recording over and over and over, recording as many takes as you want. When you finish your last take, let the loop begin again and then press stop or hit the spacebar.

Tip

If you stop recording before the second half of a looped region, the most recent take will not be saved. If you stop recording during the second half of your looped region, the most recent take will be saved, but if you stop recording early, the length of this region will be shorter than all the other regions you recorded. It's a good idea for all your regions to be the same length. To manage this, I always complete my last take, let the loop start over, and then stop recording. As a result, all regions from first to last are exactly the same length.

7] **Choose Slip mode.** Switch to Slip mode now, which makes more sense for editing instrument solos and vocals. Grid mode is used more for arranging parts.

8] **Select your loops.** Use the Selector and make sure your entire region is highlighted: Hold the ⌘/Ctrl key down and click the highlighted region. You should see all your loops in one list.

Keep in mind that since you're playing a different instrument or singing something different from what I did for this exercise, our waveforms will be completely different.

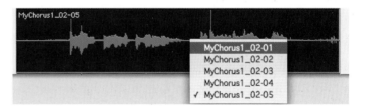

9] **Change loops.** With the region highlighted, hold ⌘/Ctrl and click with the Selector to get your loop list. Choose Take 1 and listen to it.

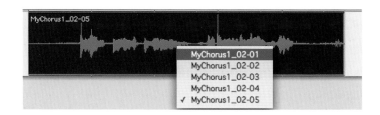

10] **Listen to each take.** Select the takes one at a time from the list and listen to them.

You may decide that you like the beginning of one take and the latter part of another one. No worries—the next exercise will show you how to create a composite.

EXERCISE 9:

Create a Composite with Looped Recording

The next technique we're going to learn can be a bit challenging at first. The most important thing you need to remember after you finish loop recording is to leave one complete unedited loop on one playlist. Once you set this playlist up, don't edit it. This one "safe" playlist becomes the place to which you can return again and again for copying and pasting.

1] **Create a safe playlist.** Duplicate your loop-recorded track and name the playlist "Safe Chorus1."

2] **Create a new playlist.** Create a new playlist and name it "ChorusComp."

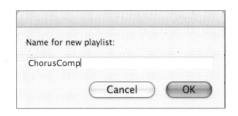

3] **Change to the safe playlist.** Go back to your safe playlist. Highlight the looped region, hold ⌘/Ctrl, and click with the Selector to get your loop list. Choose the take that you want to use in the first part of your composite. I like my take 4 the best.

4] **Highlight your parts.** Since I sang "The House of the Rising Sun," I'm going to highlight the first four words, "There is a house," in Slip mode. Then I'll press ⌘/Ctrl+C to copy those words.

5] **Change to the ChorusComp playlist.** Go to your ChorusComp playlist. Press ⌘/Ctrl+V to paste the audio you just selected into this empty playlist.

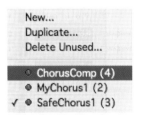

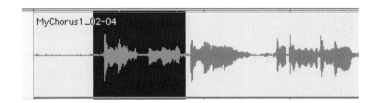

6] **Change back to the safe playlist.** Go back to your safe playlist. Highlight the looped region, hold ⌘/Ctrl, and click with the Selector to get your loop list. Choose the take that you want to use for the next part of your composite track. I'm going to use take 3.

7] **Highlight your parts.** I'm going to use "in New Orleans" from take 3. I'll highlight those words in Slip mode and press ⌘/Ctrl+C to copy.

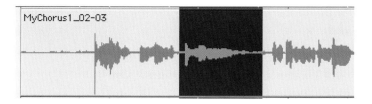

8] **Change to ChorusComp.** Go to your ChorusComp playlist and press ⌘/Ctrl+V to paste into this playlist.

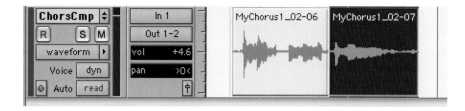

9] **Change back to the safe playlist.** Go back to your safe playlist once again. Highlight the entire looped region, hold ⌘/Ctrl, and click with the Selector to get your loop list. Choose the take that you want to use for the last part of your composite track. I'm going to use take 4 again for the last line, "they call the Rising Sun," so I'll highlight that and copy.

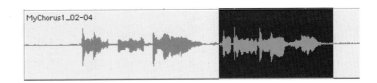

10] **Change to ChorusComp.** Go to your ChorusComp playlist and press ⌘/Ctrl+V to paste into this playlist. Now you have a complete composite.

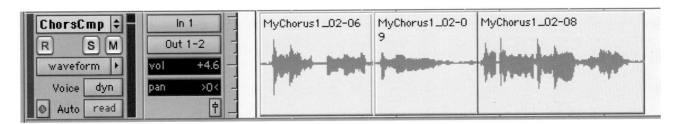

11] **Save.**

EXERCISE 10:
Crossfades, Fades, and Editing Tips

When you solo your composite track, you may notice bad edits between the various audio clips that need smoothing out. If you edited between notes or words, the places where you switched from one take to another may be fine. Regardless, you'll need to know how to create *crossfades* to fix sloppy edits or edits that pop or click. For these edits, we simply need to create crossfades between regions.

Many of you may already be familiar with the term *crossfade*. A crossfade is kind of like a Band-Aid between two regions. The crossfade fades out the end of the first region while simultaneously fading in the start of the next region.

On your composite playlist, zoom in on your first edit. Notice that there's a gap here in my edit. Sometimes in copying and pasting together composites, you will accidentally create gaps. It's important that you try to solo your edited tracks and fix them while listening to them soloed. Sometimes you won't hear tiny gaps like this, but they'll surprise you when you mix. The tiniest flaws can cause colossal problems if you're not vigilant about cleaning up your tracks and checking for bad edits, pops, and gaps. I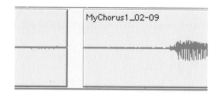
always go through each track and do this digital housekeeping, putting fades and crossfades in my regions, cleaning up noise, and deleting unneeded audio. The Trim tool in Slip mode comes in very handy for these kinds of edits.

When you're doing tricky edits, using the Trim tool becomes an art in itself. You'll learn by listening when to pull the end of a region to the right, or pull the beginning of a region to the left. Sometimes with vocals, you'll have two breaths in different places, and you have to listen while playing with the Trimmer to figure out how to get the most natural-sounding edit. Sometimes the best choice is to delete both breaths. Always use your ears, not your eyes!

Remember that I sang "There is a house in New Orleans, they call the Rising Sun." I created my composite by editing this line in three places. Region 1 is "There is a house," region 2 is "in New Orleans," and region 3 is "they call the Rising Sun." I find that there's a small gap between region 1 and region 2.

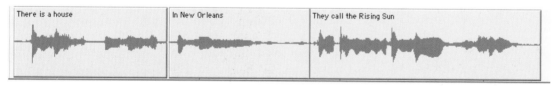

If I pull the end of the left region over to the right with the Trimmer, you can see that this is probably not going to work.

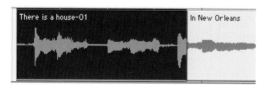

➤ **FADES & CROSSFADES:** *Reference Guide, p. 333*

The best choice is always to find an unobtrusive space in the audio file where there is a breath or a tiny space, and use that to crossfade. Let's get busy with some crossfade editing.

1] **Choose the Trim tool.** When you select the Trimmber, be sure to take it out of TCE mode and set it back to Standard mode.

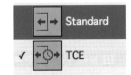

2] **Use the Trimmer.** Use the Trimmer in Slip mode to drag any regions so that they adjoin the neighboring regions, making sure you have a good place to crossfade.

Crossfading when the audio is at a low level is safest. Find spots between audio waveforms, and use the Trimmer to pull the start and end regions to meet in these gaps of silence, and try to crossfade there. When there are no gaps, crossfading sometimes takes patience and finesse. You should always listen to tricky crossfades in Solo mode to make sure the crossfade sounds natural.

3] **Zoom in and highlight.** Zoom in to the seam between two regions and highlight the seam with the Selector.

As you can see, I've also named my regions using the lyrics. This makes it easier to see what you're doing with complex composites involving lots of regions.

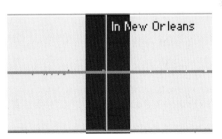

4] **Crossfade.** Press ⌘/Ctrl+F to crossfade. The Fades window pops up and gives you the default crossfade. Click OK to choose the default.

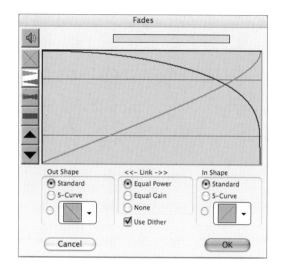

The default crossfade will work for 99 percent of your edits. In the interest of saving time here in our exercise, I'm going to direct you to the Crossfades chapter, which starts on p. 333 of the Reference Guide if you have a deeper interest in the various types of crossfades. If you're not a manual reader, the best way to learn may be simply to change the settings in the crossfade window and listen to the different options.

5] **Change the crossfade size.** You can change the size of a crossfade using the Trim tool. Notice that the Trimmer changes directions based on your choice of the start or end of the crossfade. Drag from both ends to experiment with changing the crossfade size. Try making it drastically large to hear what it does, and then do the opposite. The more you experiment, the better you'll understand how it works.

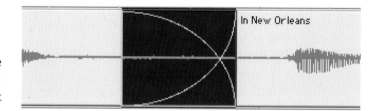

6] **Delete a crossfade.** To delete a crossfade, simply highlight it and press Delete.

7] **Create crossfades.** Highlight each edit seam and create some crossfades. Listen to the track soloed to make sure your crossfades sound transparent and natural.

8] **Create a fade-in.** Zoom out to show the whole chorus. Then with the Selector tool in Slip mode, highlight the first part of the composite track audio and press ⌘/Ctrl+F. The Fades window will open, showing you your fade-in. Click OK.

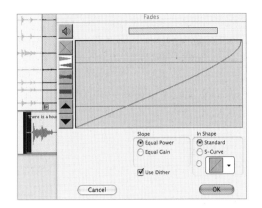

9] **Create a fade-out.** Highlight the end of the composite and press ⌘/Ctrl+F to create a fade-out. Lets choose a different fade shape. Where it says Out Shape, choose the last option and then click the slanted line shape to bring up a menu of shapes. Choose the third option down and click OK.

Look at your entire Chorus composite. You should now have crossfades between your edits, and a fade-in and fade-out at the beginning and end.

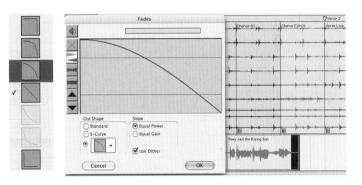

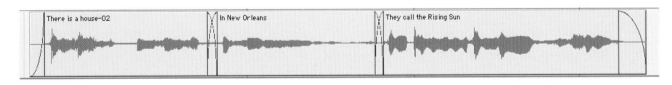

10] Save.

EXERCISE 11:

Punch In with QuickPunch

Sometimes you just want to punch in without loop recording. When you do punch in and out, you should always use the very cool Pro Tools feature called QuickPunch. It's found under the Options menu. To understand what QuickPunch does, let's punch in without it first.

➤ **QUICKPUNCH:** *Reference Guide, p. 205*

1] **Turn loop recording off.** Go to the Options menu and make sure both loop recording and QuickPunch are turned off.

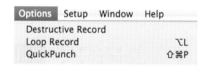

2] **Create a new playlist.** On your Composite track, create a new playlist and name it "QP Lesson."

3] **Highlight bars 5–8.** In Grid mode, highlight bar 5 through the downbeat of bar 9.

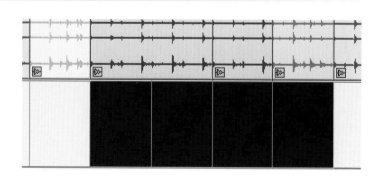

4] **Set pre-roll and post-roll.** Open the Transport window if it's not open. Set one bar of pre-roll and one bar of post-roll. You do this by entering the number "1" in the left-hand side of the field and then pressing the Return/Enter key.

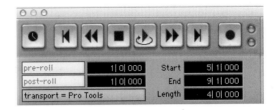

5] **Record.** Sing or play the melody of the first line of "The House of the Rising Sun," or whatever you like.

You may notice that the track goes into Record on the downbeat of bar 5, which cuts off the first word of the song. Most of you probably know this song and realize that there is a pick-up lyric into this downbeat. The lyrics are "There is a house in New Orleans, they call the Rising Sun." The first word, "There," is on the last eighth note of bar 4, and the word "is" is on the downbeat of bar 5. So let's grab the Trimmer and pull the beginning of this region to the left, to bring out the word "There."

6] **Choose the Trimmer.** Choose the Trimmer in Slip mode, and pull the beginning of the new region to the left. It doesn't work, right? Why not? Because we didn't use QuickPunch.

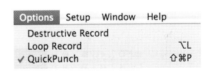

Now turn on QuickPunch in the Options menu, and let's do the same thing again. You can tell QuickPunch is on in the Transport window because the Record button has a *P* on it.

7] **Record.** Sing or play the melody of the first line of "The House of the Rising Sun" while recording, as before.

8] **Extend the region to the left.** Choose the Trimmer in Slip mode, and pull the beginning of the new region to the left. Now, because QuickPunch is on, you can pull the region out one bar to the left.

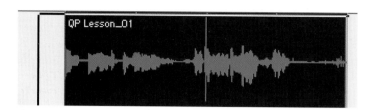

9] Save.

Here's what QuickPunch does: It takes whatever pre-roll and post-roll you have selected and actually records during that time as well. Even though the recording won't be seen on the screen, QuickPunch is actually recording behind the scenes. This feature becomes invaluable when you're punching in and out in the middle of an already recorded track.

Suppose the bass player is recording and you punch in on the chorus. You gave the bass player a three-bar pre-roll, and you have QuickPunch turned on. You tell the bass player to play along with his previous recording before he punches in. So Pro Tools punches in on the new chorus. On listening to the playback that includes the punch, you realize that the few notes before the chorus in the previous take are rushed. Since QuickPunch was on, you can simply use the Trimmer and pull the punch-in point to the left to bring out the parts the bass player played during pre-roll. It works just the same for post-roll.

Remember to always use QuickPunch, and to always tell the person recording to play before and after the spot where they are punching in.

EXERCISE 12:

Using REX Files

Pro Tools 7 includes support for REX files. REX files are a special audio file format that can conform to the tempo of your song without having to be time-compressed or -expanded.

You can buy many loop collections in REX file format, but it's next to impossible to find REX files in anything but 4/4. For this chapter, I called my friends at MultiLoops and asked them to create a few percussion tracks in 6/8. I then converted them into REX files using Propellerhead's application ReCycle. It's normally not this much trouble to find REX files, but since this chapter is using 6/8 time, I had to do a little extra work.

1] **Open the Workspace.** Use the shortcut ⌘/Alt+; to open the Workspace. Find the Chapter10Audio folder again. Inside, you'll find another folder called Rex Files.

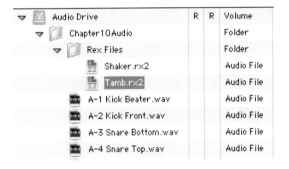

2] **Drag the tambourine.** Drag the tambourine track to the Tracks List. This creates a Tambourine track. Even though the original tempo of this loop is 65 BPM, this REX file will automatically configure itself to the tempo you have chosen, which is 68 BPM.

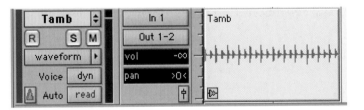

3] **Ungroup the tambourine region.** Notice that the Tambourine REX file came in as a Region Group. Highlight it and choose Ungroup from the Region menu in the main menu bar at the top of the screen. Now look at the Tambourine track. As you can see, a REX file is really just a Region Group.

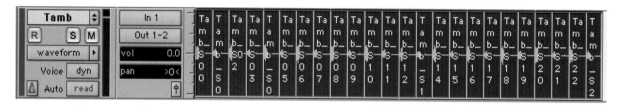

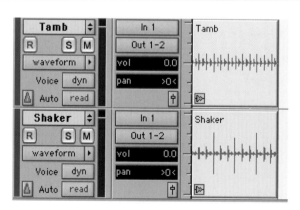

4] **Undo.**

5] **Drag the Shaker REX file.** Drag the Shaker file from the Workspace into the Tracks List to create a Shaker track.

6] **Arrange the percussion tracks.** Arrange the percussion tracks however you want. I'm going to put my shaker in the verses and put both the tambourine and the shaker in the choruses. I'm going to pan the shaker to the left and the tambourine to the right. Use the commands you know, such as Repeat and Duplicate. Use the Grabber to move regions in Grid mode, and remember that you can Option/Alt-drag a region to duplicate it.

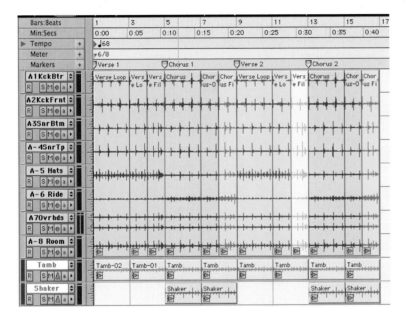

7] **Group the percussion tracks.** Highlight the track names of the two new hand-percussion tracks, and press ⌘/Ctrl+G to create an Edit Group.

8] **Save.**

EXERCISE 13:

Create Groups Within Groups

You can create Edit Groups within other Edit Groups. You can also create Region Groups within other Region Groups. We have a Drum Edit Group and a Percussion Edit Group, but what if we want to create a Drum And Percussion Edit Group too?

1] **Highlight all the track names.** Click the tiny circle (or plus sign) next to All in the Mix Groups list, to highlight all the track names.

2] **Unhighlight the QuickPunch track.** We want to create a group of all these tracks except for the track you recorded. To unhighlight a track, hold the ⌘/Ctrl key and click that track's name.

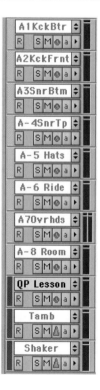

3] **Group the tracks.** Press ⌘/Ctrl+G to create a group. Make it an Edit-And-Mix Group and name it "Drums & Perc."

4] **Solo the shaker.** Solo the shaker track. As you'll see, all of the drum and percussion tracks solo.

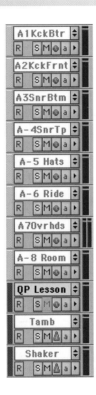

5] **Turn the Group off.** Turn off the Drum & Perc Group.

6] **Solo the shaker again.** Now when you solo the shaker, only the shaker and tambourine tracks solo.

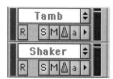

7] **Unsolo.**

8] **Move a track.** We'd like to have the drums and percussion tracks next to each other in the Edit window, so we need to move the vocal track that was recorded. (My track is called QP Lesson.) Drag this track to the bottom of the Tracks List. Now all the drums and percussion are together.

9] **Highlight bars 1–4.** In the Edit window, use the Selector to highlight all the drum and percussion tracks up to the downbeat of bar 5.

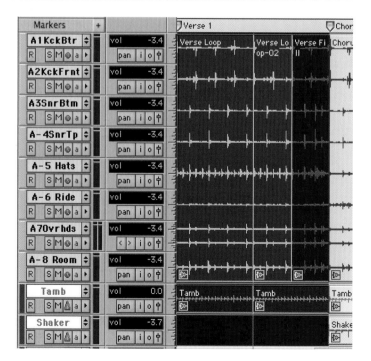

10] **Create a Region Group.** Use the shortcut ⌘+Option+G/Ctrl+Alt+G to create a Region Group.

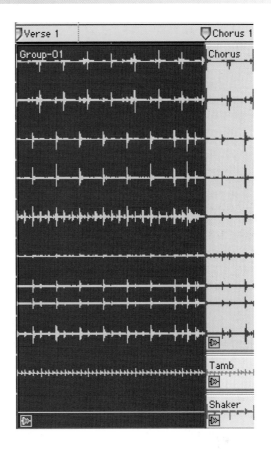

11] **Rename the Region.** Rename the Region Group using the shortcut ⌘/Ctrl+Shift+R. Name it "BigVerse1."

12] **Ungroup.** The Ungroup shortcut is ⌘+Option+U/Ctrl+Alt+U. Notice that if you ungroup this region, it goes back to the previous Region Group name. If you ungroup that, the Region Group disappears back to the original waveforms.

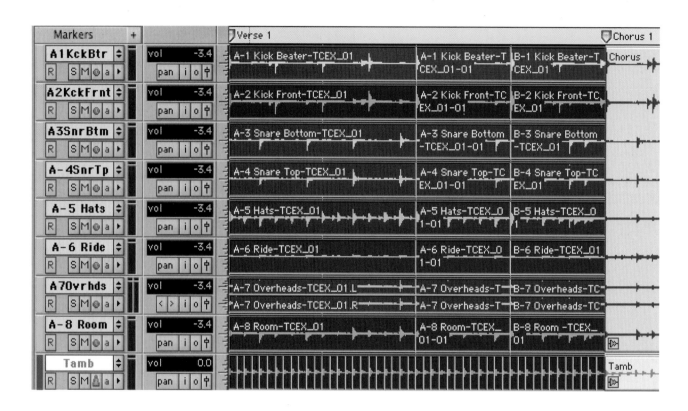

13] **Regroup.** To regroup a region, use the shortcut ⌘+Option+R/Ctrl+Alt+R.

14] **Save.**

EXERCISE 14:

Save Copy In

If you've been paying close attention, you may have noticed that we imported some REX files from the Workspace, but these files never made it into our Audio File folder. To see where your REX files are located, click the Regions Bin menu. Choose Show and then choose Full Path.

You'll have to make the Regions Bin wider so you can read the full path. Click the gray border on the left side of the Regions Bin; the cursor will change to a left-and-right arrow. Pull the Regions Bin border to the left and look at your path names. You'll see that some REX files are in Chapter10Audio and some are in Learning PT Ch 10.

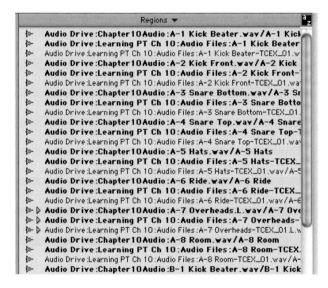

Although all files are on the Audio drive, they're not in the correct folder. Again, this is the danger of using the Workspace to import audio: It leaves the audio you imported in the folder you imported it from, rather than giving you the option to copy the audio into the correct folder, as other importing methods do. Using the Workspace is a simpler method of importing, but it can cause serious file management problems, as you can see. Let's fix this one.

➤ **SAVE COPY IN:** *Reference Guide, p. 50*

1] **Save Copy In.** Choose File > Save Copy In and check All Audio Files in the Items To Copy section at the bottom of the window. As always, be sure to save to your Audio drive. You'll see the files being copied as they're saved.

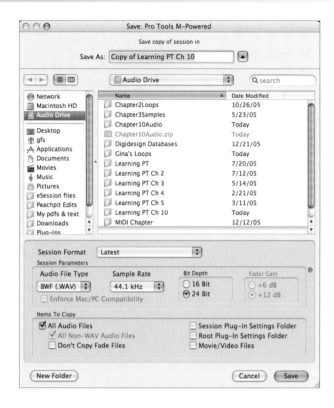

2] **Close this session.** Close this session using the shortcut ⌘/Ctrl+Shift+W, but be sure you've saved before closing.

3] **Open the copy session.** Choose File > Open, and open the file Copy of Learning PT Ch 10.ptf.

If you see this window, no worries— just click No.

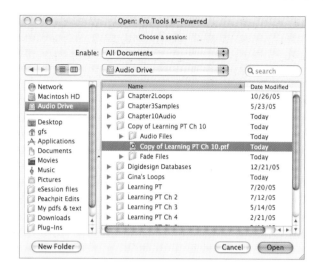

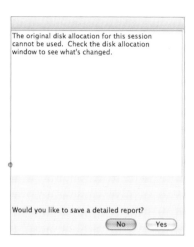

4] **Look at the Regions Bin.** Notice that your Regions Bin now shows all files stored correctly inside this session's Audio Files folder.

5] **Unselect Show Full Path.** Uncheck the Full Path option in the Show menu of the Regions Bin, to unclutter the Regions Bin list. Then make the Regions Bin smaller.

6] Save.

EXERCISE 15:
Delete Unused Audio

The last thing you should do before closing a session is delete your unused audio files. (Some people prefer not to delete anything until the project is completed. This is a matter of personal preference.) Remember, as long as audio is used in a playlist, whether or not the playlist is active, it will not be deleted.

1] **Select Unused Audio.** This is one shortcut you should not fail to memorize: ⌘/Ctrl+Shift+U selects unused audio. This highlights any audio file within your session that is not being used, including any takes you deleted or recorded over.

Look in the Regions Bin now and see all the files that are not being used.

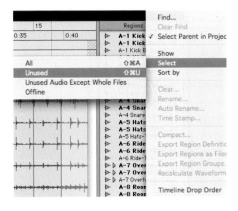

2] **Clear Unused Audio.** The shortcut to clear unused audio from the Regions Bin is ⌘/Ctrl+Shift+B.

3] **Delete files.** In this case, you probably don't want to *remove* files. Removing files takes them out of the Regions Bin but keeps them in the Audio Files folder on your hard drive. You want to *delete* the files, which also deletes them from the hard drive. If you're ready to do this, hold the Option/Alt key and click the Delete button.

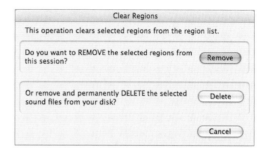

Note

In this particular exercise, the original versions of the drum loops (before we time-stretched them) will be deleted unless you duplicated the playlist of the original files. Should you later need to change the tempo of the session, you'll get better quality by going back to the original audio files and re-stretching than by stretching the already stretched files a second time.

Tip

If you didn't duplicate your playlist and you do want to keep the original loops at their original tempo, do this: Create a new playlist of the drum tracks and drag your original files from the Regions Bin to this empty playlist, to keep them from being deleted. You could also re-import them from the Workspace. As I've often explained, the simple solution and a wise habit to get into is to duplicate your playlist **before** *you time-stretch anything, and then time-stretch the duplicate, so you'll always have the original loop to go back to.*

4] Save.

Wrap Up

Time for another break—this was a dense chapter with a lot of information. In the next chapter, we'll return to the song "Underwater" and learn about automation and mixing.

AUTOMATE & MIX

11

In this chapter you're going to learn about automating and mixing down a song. You'll learn different ways to automate a track's levels, and also how to automate a plug-in. Once the track is mixed and automated, you'll create a Master Fader and add compression to the final mix.

It's a very common practice to put a compressor on the entire mix. This is commonly referred to as "strapping a compressor across the mix bus." *Mix bus compression* serves the purpose of making mixes louder while also smoothing out any abrupt changes in level. Keep in mind that when you apply mix bus compression, you are sacrificing dynamic range for loudness. The consensus of the music industry is that the louder the mix, the better. Also, the sound of compression on a mix has become a signature sound. It's almost used as an effect these days, especially in the rock and pop genres.

You must also understand, however, that it's better to print a mix with little or no compression and let the mastering engineers apply compression later. On the other hand, I realize that many of you will be creating music that may never be professionally mastered. In this case, it's important to learn the principles of mix bus compression so that your mixes sound as professional as you yourself can make them.

While writing this chapter, I tried using Digidesign's dynamics processor for mix bus compression. I tried Compressor, Dynamics III, the BF76, and even Maxim, but I just wasn't happy with the sound. I had my friend, world-class engineer Kevin Killen, try them as well, and he agreed that none of the DigiRack plug-ins work well for mix bus compression. (Digidesign confirms that the plug-ins weren't designed for this usage.) Kevin suggested that the Waves Renaissance Compressor is one of the best, easiest to use, and most affordable mix bus plug-ins. So I did some research and found the Waves Musicians II bundle. This is a five-plug-in bundle for $200. The plug-ins include:

◆ SuperTap, an amazing delay plug-in

◆ Doubler, for doubling and thickening sounds

◆ Renaissance Vox, an excellent vocal compressor

◆ Renaissance EQ, a multiband EQ that's created to sound like analog

◆ Renaissance Compressor, a gorgeous and versatile compressor that works well on many instruments as well as on the mix bus

For the exercises in this chapter we're going to download and install the Waves Musicians II bundle, which will give you a 14-day demo period. (When the demo period has expired, you may need to run the uninstaller program; if you don't do this, Pro Tools may not be able to launch.)

As you'll see, this is a superb collection. If you decide to purchase this bundle, the only other plug-in I'd suggest you have for mixing would be an additional reverb. Although D-Verb, which is included in Pro Tools, is sufficient, it doesn't hold a candle to some of the third-party reverb plug-ins such as Altiverb by Audio Ease. Since we're using Pro Tools LE in this book, our reverb choices are a bit limited; there are more reverb plug-ins available for Pro Tools TDM systems. Altiverb is the best of the bunch for RTAS, but at $795 retail, it's not cheap. Still, it's a relatively inexpensive reverb solution compared with the Sony Oxford Reverb at $1095. Lower-cost reverbs are available, including Trillium Lane Labs Space at $495, which is pretty versatile as well.

For now, let's start with the Waves Musicians II bundle.

EXERCISE 1:
Download and Install the Waves Plug-Ins

1] **Download the software.** Quit Pro Tools if it's running. Go to ProToolsforMusicians.com and download the Waves Musicians II bundle demo.

2] **Expand the file.** Mac users will have a file called WavesMusicians2_V5.0.dmg, and Windows users will have a file called WavesMusicians2_V5.0.exe. Double-click the file to install it. Mac users: The dmg file will mount like a CD on your desktop. Open that and find the installer file.

WavesMusicians2_V5.0

Note

Mac users will also need the admin password in order to install the plug-ins.

3] **Continue.** You'll be led through three windows that require you to click Continue.

4] Agree with the license agreement.

5] **Install.** Choose Easy Install and click the Install button.

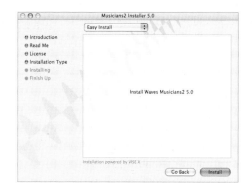

Note

The Easy Install menu includes an Uninstall option. If you don't like this software or want to remove it after the demo period, use this same menu.

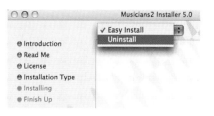

6] **Wait for installation.** You'll see the file installing. It may take up to a minute.

7] **Answer the AudioUnit question.** Mac users may see this window. If so, choose "Let's Go." (AudioUnits are a different format of plug-in that may come in handy for you someday—for instance, if you should need to use Apple Logic Audio as a recorder in place of Pro Tools.) You'll see a window telling you that the AudioUnits plug-in has been installed.

8] **Quit.** You'll see a window telling you that installation was successful. You can quit the installer now.

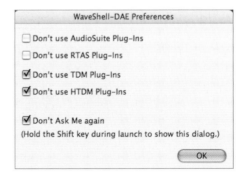

9] **Open Pro Tools.** The first time you open Pro Tools after installation of the Waves Musicians II software, you'll see the Waves preferences. You'll only see this once. Since we're using Pro Tools LE systems, we don't need the TDM or the HTDM plug-ins, so choose not to use those and click OK.

10] **Open UnderwaterGFS.**

EXERCISE 2:

Increase Your Hardware Buffer Size

The first thing you should do before you mix is make sure you have the maximum processing power available for your plug-ins and automation.

The most important Playback Engine setting is the hardware buffer size. Remember to reduce this when you're recording, because if you don't, you'll have a bad latency problem or delay in what you're recording. So keep a high buffer size for mixing, and a low buffer size for recording.

1] **Open the Playback Engine.** Go to the Setup menu and choose Playback Engine.

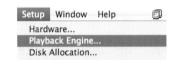

2] **Increase the hardware buffer**. Set the H/W Buffer Size to the maximum setting. Make sure your processor and CPU usage settings are at the maximum setting as well. Leave the DAE Playback Buffer Size set to the default of 2. (If you're recording to an external drive, you may find that a setting of 4 works better.)

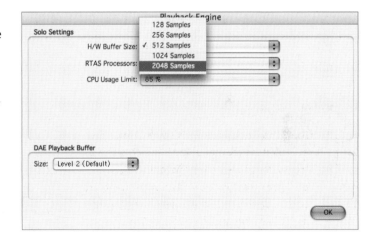

EXERCISE 3:

Set Up Your Effects

Before I start mixing, I usually set up a few aux inputs with effects, to which I can send my tracks. Depending on the song, I usually set up two different reverbs and two different delays, but since this is a relatively small mix, let's create just one of each.

1] **Create two new aux inputs.** Using ⌘/Ctrl+Shift+N, create two stereo aux inputs.

2] **Name each aux.** Name the first aux "Reverb" and the second aux "Delay."

3] **Set the input.** Set the input of the Reverb aux to bus 1–2, and set the input of the Delay aux to bus 3–4.

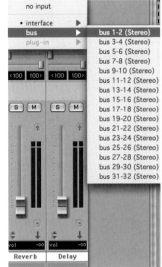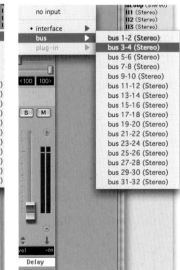

4] **Insert a reverb plug-in.** On insert A of the Reverb aux, insert D-Verb.

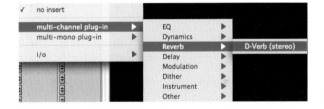

5] **Insert a delay.** On insert A of the Delay aux, insert a Waves SuperTap 6-Taps plug-in.

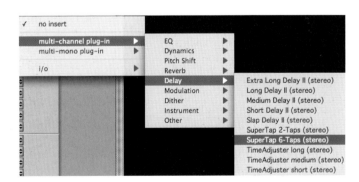

6] **Bring up the aux level.** Hold the Option/Alt key and click each of the aux volume faders to bring them up to zero.

7] **Solo-safe each aux track.** Solo-safe the Reverb and Delay tracks by holding the ⌘/Ctrl key and clicking the Solo button.

8] **Save.**

EXERCISE 4:
Print a MIDI Track to Audio

I want to put a delay effect on the electric piano, but the electric piano track is using SampleTank to make the piano sound. If I put a delay on the SampleTank plug-in, it's going to put a delay on every sound coming from Sample Tank, which would include the pad and the organ sounds as well.

Many new users don't understand why you can't put a plug-in on a MIDI track. If you look at a MIDI track, you'll see there is no insert section, so there is no way to add an effect. The difference is that MIDI is not audio—it's computer information being fed to the instrument plug-in. There is no audio coming out of a MIDI track, and plug-ins affect only audio.

To add delay to the electric piano, we need to record it as an audio track. This is called *printing a track to audio.* "Printing" can also mean recording a track with an effect on it. For example, I printed my vocal tracks for this song with some effects already on them.

1] **Create a stereo audio track.** Highlight the SampleTank track and then use ⌘/Ctrl+Shift+N and create a stereo audio track. This puts the newly created track next to the SampleTank track. Since this new track is quantized, I'm going to choose Ticks as the timebase.

2] **Name the track.** Name this new track "EP Audio."

3] **Set the input for the EP Audio track.** Click the input selector and set the input to any unused bus. Notice how a bus that's being used shows up in bold. Since we're using bus 1–2 for Reverb and bus 3–4 for Delay, we want to use the next bus, which is bus 5–6.

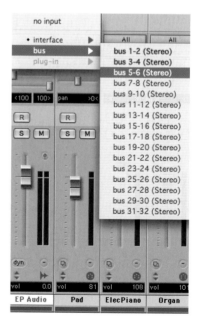

4] **Change the SampleTank output.** We're going to temporarily change the output of the SampleTank track so that its output goes into our new audio track. As you'll see in the Mix window, we're going out of SampleTank into our new EP Audio track.

5] **Solo tracks.** Solo the ElecPiano MIDI track and the EP Audio track.

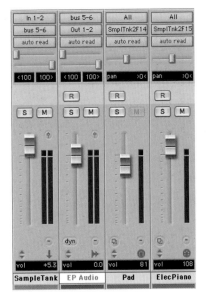

6] **Record the electric piano.** Put the EP Audio track in Record.

7] **Turn on Input Only Monitoring.** Check the Track menu. If you see the item Input Only Monitoring, select it. If you see the Auto Input Monitoring, then you're already using Input Only Monitoring and you don't need to do anything. The reason to use Input Only Monitoring so you can listen to the track and check your level.

Start playback. If your level is low, bring up either the Electric Piano MIDI track or the SampleTank track. Be careful not to peak in the red.

8] **Record the track.** Turn off Input Only Monitoring using the Option/Alt+K shortcut. Hit Return/Enter to go back to the beginning of the song, and press ⌘/Ctrl+spacebar to record. Record the new track for the entire length of the song.

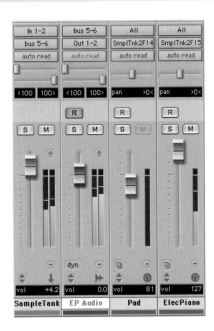

Tip

If you hear the distortion caused by too-hot peaks while recording, you can stop recording by pressing the spacebar, but that method keeps the audio on your hard drive. To cancel recording, which deletes anything recorded, you can use ⌘/Ctrl+. (period). This command works in many Macintosh applications to cancel a function, but it also works in the Windows version of Pro Tools. It's commonly referred to as "Command period."

9] **Play back.** You should now have your electric piano printed as an audio track. Use the Option/Alt key to unsolo one track. This command will unsolo all of them. Rewind to the start of the song, mute the ElecPiano MIDI track, and listen to the new track as part of the mix. You'll notice that it's a little late. We're going to fix that in the next exercise.

10] **Hide the track.** Now we don't need the Electric Piano MIDI track, so let's hide it by clicking it in the Tracks List.

11] **Reset the SampleTank output.** Set the output of SampleTank back to Out 1–2.

12] Save.

Organize Your Tracks

Before I start mixing, I like to move my tracks around into an order that helps my mix go more smoothly. As I mentioned in Chapter 6, I have an order that works for me. I use it all the time, so I always know—no matter what song I'm working on—what my track order is. From left to right in the Mix window and top to bottom in the Edit window, I always have the click (which I hide when I mix), then drums, then percussion, then bass, then guitars, then keyboards, then miscellaneous instruments, then vocals, and then effects. Choose your own method, but here's my final track setup, ready for me to start mixing.

Set Up Your Basic Levels and Panning

Before you start mixing, go through all of your tracks and make sure you have the right basic level for each one. Also, think about the stereo field. Would the guitars be better if they were panned further to the right? Would the electric piano sound better panned slightly to the left? The more stereo spread you can give your mixes, the better. New users tend to put everything right in the middle. Experiment with panning and listen closely to how it affects the sense of space in the mix. Here are the levels I am going to start with.

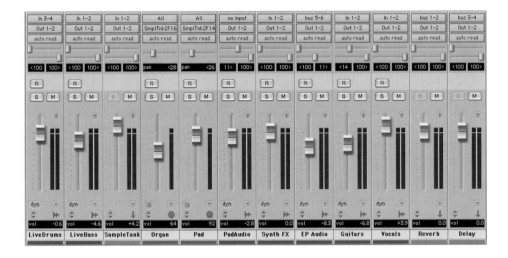

EXERCISE 5:
Shift the EP Audio Track

Although this book is about Pro Tools LE, I know that a lot of you will be using Pro Tools M-Powered. There aren't many differences between them, but I ran into one while writing this book. After I printed the electric piano audio track, as described in the previous exercise, I found that my new audio track was late. This happened because I was using Pro Tools M-Powered, not LE. If you're using Pro Tools LE, you can safely skip the next exercise, because your electric piano audio track will be delayed so slightly that you probably won't be able to hear it. You may want to go through the exercise, though, because we're going to make use of another Pro Tools feature, Tab to Transients.

In Pro Tools M-Powered, increasing the audio buffer size used by the interface will also increase the latency (time delay) when doing a bus mix. Let me show you how to fix a track easily if this happens to you.

1] **Change track size and zoom.** Change the EP Audio track to jumbo, and zoom in so that you can see a close-up of the waveform at bar 4.

2] **Click bar 4.** In Grid mode with the Selector, click the downbeat of bar 4. You'll see that the attack of the electric piano is late.

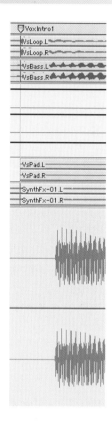

3] **Duplicate the playlist.** I want to show you two ways to shift a track, so let's duplicate the EP Audio playlist. Name the duplicate "EP Shift 1."

4]

Turn on Tab to Transients. We need to high-light the space between the downbeat and the attack of the EP waveform. We could do this manually, but it wouldn't be exact. There is a button called Tab to Transients that does exactly what we need.

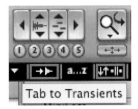

Tab to Transients may sound complicated, but it simply means that if you hit the Tab key, the cursor will advance and stop at the next peak in the waveform. Pro Tools uses the word *transient* to mean a significant peak in the audio, so Tab to Transients means that press-ing the Tab key makes the cursor go from one significant event in the waveform to the next. Option/Ctrl+Tab will go to the preceding one.

The Tab to Transients button is below your zoom settings. Click the button to turn the function on; this will put a blue border around the button.

Note

When Tab to Transients is turned off, pressing the Tab key takes you from edit seam to edit seam rather than from transient to transient.

5]

Try Tab to Transients. With the playback cur-sor at bar 4 and Tab to Transients turned on, hit the Tab key. Your cursor is now at the beginning of the waveform. Look at the location indicator. The beginning of the waveform is a number of ticks late—at least 100, and possibly 125 or moreThe number of ticks will vary depending on which version of Pro Tools you're using, your H/W Buffer Size setting, and possibly your processor speed as well. Take a mental note of how many ticks your track is late.

Main	4| 1| 125 ▼	Start	4| 1| 125
		End	4| 1| 125
Sub	0:10.753 ▼	Length	0| 0| 000

➤ **TAB TO TRANSIENTS:** *Reference Guide, p. 283*

6] **Try Tab to Transients again.** Zoom out a bit and keep pressing the Tab key to get the hang of what this command is doing. Remember that ⌘/Ctrl+Tab goes to the preceding transient.

7] **Highlight the space.** In order to fix this track, we need to highlight the space from the downbeat of bar 4 to the late downbeat of the electric piano waveform, and delete that space from the track using Shuffle mode. When we delete the space in Shuffle mode, it will move the entire track forward.

In Grid mode, click at the downbeat of bar 4, then hold the Shift key and press Tab.

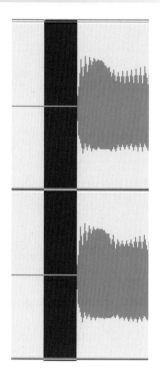

8] **Use Shuffle mode.** Choose Shuffle mode and press the Delete key. This moves the entire EP Shift 1 track to the correct place.

9] **Save.** Go back to Grid mode immediately, listen to the playback if you like, and save.

10] **Switch playlists.** Go back to the unedited EP Audio playlist, and I'll show you another way to shift a track.

New...
Duplicate...
Delete Unused...

▲ EP Audio (6)
✓ ▲ EP Shift 1 (7)

11] **Highlight and choose Shift.** Choose the Grabber and click the entire EP Piano region. Then go the Edit menu and choose Shift. Notice the shortcut, which is Option/Alt+H.

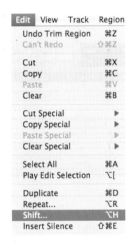

Edit	View	Track	Region
Undo Trim Region			⌘Z
Can't Redo			⇧⌘Z
Cut			⌘X
Copy			⌘C
Paste			⌘V
Clear			⌘B
Cut Special			▶
Copy Special			▶
Paste Special			▶
Clear Special			▶
Select All			⌘A
Play Edit Selection			⌥[
Duplicate			⌘D
Repeat...			⌥R
Shift...			⌥H
Insert Silence			⇧⌘E

12] **Enter the Shift value.** The Shift window opens. Since I know from using Tab to Transients that my EP track was 125 ticks late, I'm going to tell my track to shift earlier by 125 ticks.

When you try to shift earlier, you'll get an error message that says you can't do it. Why? We recorded this track from the very beginning of the song, which in this case is bar 0. How can we shift the track earlier if the track is already at the very beginning of the song? Let's fix this.

Shift

Shift ● Earlier   By
       ○ Later

Bars & Beats: 0| 0| 125
Minutes & Seconds: 0:00.086
Samples: 3828

[Cancel]   [OK]

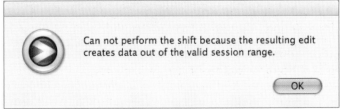

Can not perform the shift because the resulting edit creates data out of the valid session range.

[OK]

13] **Separate the Region.** In Grid mode with the Selector tool, click at bar 4. Choose Edit > Separate Region > At Selection. Notice that the shortcut is ⌘/Ctrl+E.

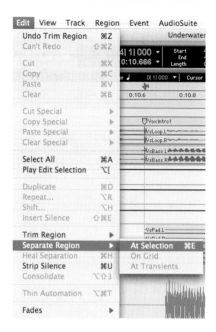

This will create an edit seam at the cursor.

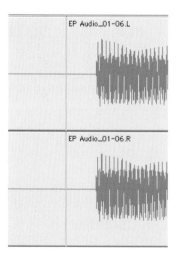

Tip

I use the Edit > Separate Region command a lot. This is how I make drum loops out of a live drum track. I'll find a great two-bar loop within a live track, highlight that loop from start to end, and press ⌘/Ctrl+E to make the highlighted section its own region. Then I usually use ⌘/Ctrl+Shift+R to rename the new region.

14] **Delete the first region.** Double-click with the Selector tool on the empty region to the left of bar 4. This highlights the region. Press the Delete key.

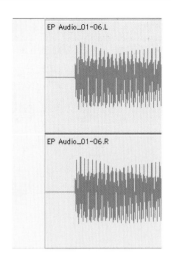

15] **Shift again.** Now double-click the EP region that starts at bar 4 and use the shortcut Option/Alt+H to shift. Shift this region earlier by the number of ticks you observed in step 5. Now the EP waveform will begin exactly at the downbeat of bar 4, where it should be.

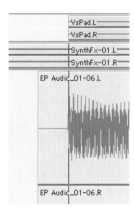

16] **Save.**

You'll find that the more you use Pro Tools, the more you'll use the Shift command. Suppose you want a snare track to be more laid back in a certain section of a song. You can highlight the snare track in that section, use Edit > Separate Region to make the snare its own region, and then shift the region as many ticks as you need to.

EXERCISE 6:

Using the SuperTap Delay and Bussing Effects

Let's put delay and reverb on the new EP Audio track, delay on the vocals, and reverb on the synth effect.

1] **Bus the EP Audio.** On Send selector A, send the EP Audio track to bus 3–4, which is where the delay effect is inserted.

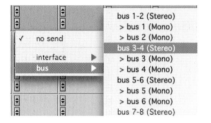

2] **Solo the tracks and bring up the bus.** Solo the EP Audio track and bring up the send level of the EP Audio delay bus. This send fader is sending the EP signal to the delay, so the fader controls how much EP you want to send into the delay effect.

3]
Highlight a loop. I've highlighted from bar 4 to bar 12 in Grid mode and put Pro Tools in Loop Playback mode so that I can tweak my effects while Pro Tools loops.

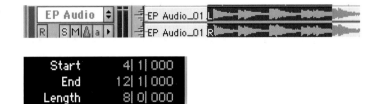

Start	4	1	000
End	12	1	000
Length	8	0	000

4]
Bring up the send. Bring up the send going to bus 3–4 so that you're sending the electric piano to the Delay aux.

5] **Open SuperTap.** Click on SuperTap to open its plug-in window.

We don't have enough pages to examine the Waves plug-ins in depth, but I have included the plug-ins' manuals on the protoolsformusicians.com website. Here in this exercise, I can help you get started so they're less intimidating.

This delay has two versions—a 2-tap and a 6-tap. That means one version has two delay outputs and the other one has six. Unlike the DigiRack delay, which gives you only one delay tap, SuperTap gives you six, plus extra features, as you'll see.

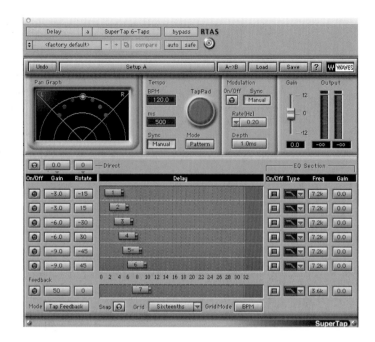

6] **Turn off the direct signal.** Because this delay is on an aux bus rather than inserted directly into the electric piano track, we need it to have a wet-only output. When first inserted, SuperTap has its dry (direct) output turned on, so you're hearing not only the delay but also the direct signal of the non-delayed EP.

Click the button below the Panning Graph, *above* the words On/Off. Click the red circle, and you'll see a dot in the top-center of the graph go dim. Now the output of SuperTap will contain only the delayed sound, without the dry signal.

7] **Turn on the delay.** Below On/Off are six buttons in a column. These activate the delay taps. If you play the loop now, you'll hear no effect because the delays are turned off. Turn a few on by clicking the buttons.

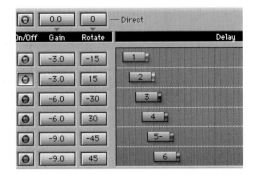

8] **Turn on sync.** You'll notice that these delays are not in sync with the song. At the top of the plug-in, you'll see the Tempo controls. Click the Sync Manual button, which will change to Auto. This makes the plug-in sync to our tempo of 90 BPM.

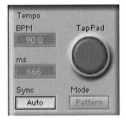

9] **Edit the Delay.** In the top two delay lines are little sliders, currently numbered 1 and 2. At the bottom of the delay line area, your grid is set to sixteenth notes. So delay line 1 is delaying the signal by one sixteenth note. Delay line 2 is delaying the signal by two sixteenth notes or one eighth note. Drag delay line 1 to 4, and you've changed line 1 to delay by quarter notes.

Turn on some other delays. Change the grid setting, move the sliders around, and become familiar with this plug-in.

Note

As you change the delay times, you'll hear little crackling noises. This is normal. You won't be changing the delay times while creating your final mix, so these noises won't be heard.

10] **Experiment with EQ.** To the right of each delay line is each delay's EQ. Just as with the delay line itself, you must turn the EQ on to hear it. I'm boosting my quarter-note delay 12 dB at 1.0 k, to give the delayed sound its own tone color.

11] **Turn on modulation.** To the right of the Tempo and Sync controls is the Modulation section. Click the On button to turn it on. Modulation is used for adding chorusing. It does this by sweeping the delay times up and down slightly. In this case, we don't actually need chorusing because the SampleTank EP track was printed with its own chorusing, but I want to show you how to use the modulation feature.

If you want the modulation rate to sync to the tempo, click the Sync Manual button to change it to Auto. Experiment with the Rate and Depth controls until you find a chorus sound that you like. I double-clicked on my Rate and set it to 1.

12] **Boost the gain.** To the right of the Modulation section is the Gain fader. Use this to boost the level of your delay.

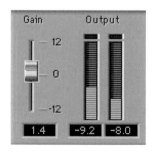

13] **Experiment with panning.** To the left of the Sync button is the Pan Graph. The left edit point is the panning for delay line 1. The center dot that looks like a target is your main source (the dry EP Audio sound), and the right edit point is the panning for delay line 2.

Drag the dots around and listen to the changes. Notice how dragging up and down changes the Gain value in the delay line, and dragging from left to right changes the Rotate value.

14] **Load some presets.** Click the Load button to see a list of presets. Choose a few presets, and you'll start seeing the possibilities of this plug-in. With many of the factory presets, you'll need to switch off the direct signal in order to hear the effect clearly, as explained in step 6.

15] **Create your own preset.** I created a delay for this song that I thought was interesting. Try matching my settings.

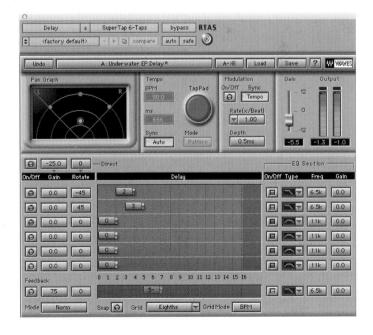

16] **Save your preset.** Click the Save button and choose Put Into Preset Menu As." Name this Preset "Underwater EP Delay."

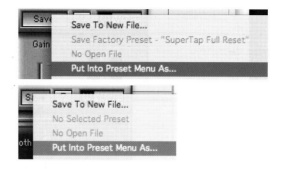

17] **Look at your Preset menu.** Notice that you now have a new preset at the bottom of the list under User Presets—you can recall this delay anytime you need to.

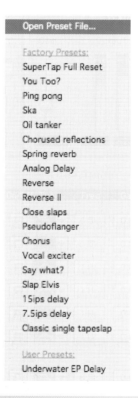

18] **Open send 3–4.** Click the EP Audio send to bus 3–4, and adjust the level as you need to. You may want to unsolo the EP Audio track to hear the balance of this delay with the whole song.

When you have a good send level, solo the EP Audio track again for the next step.

19] **Make the send pre-fader.** Before starting playback, click the Pre button on the bus. This setting sometimes confuses people. The best way to understand it is to use it, so let's do that.

20] **Bring down the EP Audio track.** Bring down the volume of the EP Audio track.

You still hear the delay, right? "Making the send pre-fader" simply means that this send goes to the effect before the signal hits the volume fader. The send level to the delay is not dependent on the volume of the track from which you're sending.

Turn off Pre and listen again. You won't hear the delay anymore, because the track fader is all the way down. Now slowly bring up the EP Audio volume, and you'll hear the delay being gradually added as well.

(continues on next page)

In this song, we want to blend the original dry sound of the electric piano with the delayed sound. There are two ways to do that. We can leave the channel fader up and switch off the delay effect's dry (direct) output, as we did back in step 6 of this exercise. Or we can turn on the direct signal in the delay, make the send pre-fader, and bring down the channel fader. Doing it the second way is pretty much like using the effect as an insert on the EP track, except that we can apply one effect to several tracks at once if we like. Let's see how this works.

Tip

The pre-fader option can come in very handy. What if you're mixing and you want to hear only the reverb of the vocal as a weird effect in a certain section? You'd make the vocal send pre-fader and bring down the level of the main vocal track. Then you'd hear only the reverb of the vocal track.

21] **Bus the EP to the reverb.** On Send selector B in the EP channel, send to bus 1–2, which is the reverb aux effect. Bring up this Send fader so that you're sending some EP into the reverb.

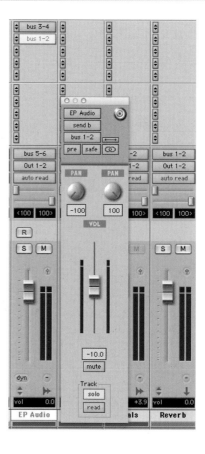

22 **Adjust the reverb plug-in and send level.** Find a reverb that you like. I'm going to use a Large Hall. And I'm going to set my send level to –10 dB.

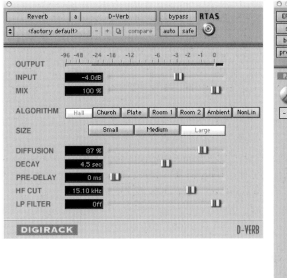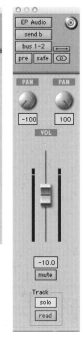

23 **Solo the drums.** Unsolo the EP Audio track and solo the LiveDrums track. Many tracks may solo when you do this, because in an earlier chapter we created an Edit-And-Mix Group called Live Tracks. Turn off that group and then solo the LiveDrums again.

24 **Mute the send**. Start playback. You'll still hear the EP Audio delay. This is because the Delay aux is in solo-safe mode and the EP Audio delay send is pre-fader, so even though the EP Audio track is muted, the audio from that track is still going to the delay plug-in. There are two ways to fix this. (1) Turn off solo-safe by ⌘/Ctrl-clicking on the aux track. (2) Mute the send by holding the ⌘/Ctrl key and clicking on the send to bus 3–4 in the Mix window.

25] **Add reverb to the drums.** Create a send on the LiveDrums track to bus 1–2. Bring up the send level to add as much reverb as you want.

26] Save.

What if you want a different reverb on the bass? You can simply add another stereo aux input, insert another reverb plug-in, set the input to an unused bus (such as bus 7–8 in our exercise), and then create a send on the Bass track to that chosen bus.

Go ahead and add any effects you like using sends and auxes.

Keep in mind that I've done a lot of the work for you in this song, in the interest of saving download time as well as your time doing these exercises. If I had uploaded the entire song in its unmixed form with all the individual drum tracks and vocals and guitars, it would have been over 1 gigabyte in size and would have taken hours to download—and just as many hours to mix the individual tracks.

EXERCISE 7:

Intro to Automation

Notice that on every channel of the Mix window, below the Output selector, is a button that says Auto Read. This is where you set the automation mode. Let's learn what each mode does, using the vocal track as our example.

First we need to make sure that everything we want to automate is turned on.

➤ **AUTOMATION:** *Reference Guide, p. 533*

1] **Open the Automation Enable window.** Go to the Window menu and choose Automation Enable.

2] **Enable All.** Click each parameter to enable it.

3] **Choose Auto Touch for the vocal track.** Change Auto Read to Auto Touch.

4] **Highlight Chorus 1.** Highlight from bar 10 to bar 20 and make sure Loop Playback is turned on.

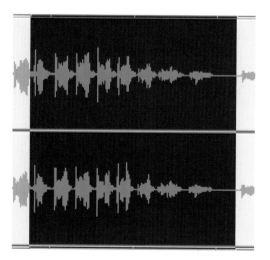

5] **Use Auto Touch.** Notice that in the Mix window, Auto Touch is blinking red on the vocal channel. Play the chorus, and in the Mix window move the fader up, then down, and then let go of it. Notice that as soon as you let go, the fader glides back to the level where it started. This is how Auto Touch mode works. The fader automates as long as you're touching it; when you let go, it goes back to the level it was at before you touched it. Auto Touch is useful for ducking a track briefly to cover up an unwanted sound, or for boosting it briefly to bring out a sound you want to be heard. Play back the music now, and you'll see and hear the fader move you just recorded.

6] **Undo Auto Touch.** Undo your automation moves by using ⌘/Ctrl+Z.

7] **Use Auto Touch again.** Play the end of the first chorus (bars 24–30). Notice how the volume gets lower on the last few lines of the chorus, "I'm faceless, no time or space, underwater." Bring those levels up as the song plays.

8] **Change the track view.** Go to the Edit window. Make the Vocal track large. Click the Track View selector and change Waveform to Volume.

9] **Return to manual editing of automation.** You should now see your automation data. Choose the Selector tool in Slip mode, and highlight your automation data. Now press the Delete key. This is how you delete your automation moves.

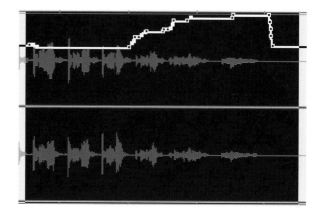

10] **Undo.** Undo the edit so you see your automation data again.

11] **Edit with the Grabber.** What if you want to edit this data rather than deleting it? Zoom in so that you can see it clearly, and choose the Grabber. Notice that when you hold it over one of your automation points, the hand becomes a pointed finger. Click one of the automation points and bring it up or down.

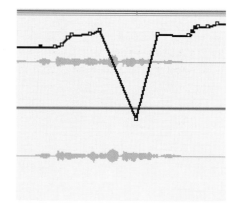

12] **Delete points.** To delete an automation point, hold the Option/Alt key and click the point you want to delete.

13] **Delete the automation.** Zoom out again, highlight your automation data with the Selector, and delete it all.

14] **Use the Grabber again.** Let's say you want to bring up the volume of just one phrase. Find the waveform for the lyric "No time or space, underwater," which is between bar 26 and bar 29. Click with the Grabber on the Volume line, first to the left of the word "No" and then to the right of the word "underwater." You should have two automation edit points on the volume line.

Tip

You can edit mute and pan automation the same way you edit volume automation, using the Edit window and the Track View selector to view the type of data you want to edit.

15] **Use the Trimmer.** Now choose the Trim tool and hold it between the two automation points. The Trimmer turns sideways, right? It's now ready to adjust the automation. Click and drag the Trimmer between these two points and bring the level up.

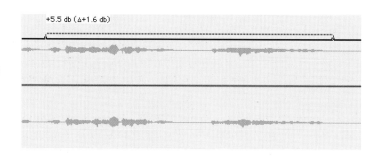

16] **Do fine adjustment.** You may have noticed when executing the preceding step that your volume level jumps way up when you drag it. Now hold the ⌘/Ctrl key while dragging with the Trim tool. This allows you to drag the automation level in smaller increments. Pro Tools refers to this as *fine adjustment.*

Tip

Holding the ⌘/Ctrl key while moving the faders also allows fine adjustment.

17] **Save.**

Tip

The Trim tool is what I use to bring up the level of a whole track. Let's say I have a vocal track with automation from beginning to end, and I decide that the vocal needs to be 3 dB louder throughout the song. I can view the Volume automation data and highlight the entire data line from start to end with the Selector. Then I choose the Trim tool and bring up the vocal track 3 dB, leaving all my automation moves intact.

Auto Write, Auto Latch, Auto Off, and Auto Read

After doing Exercise 8, you know how Auto Touch works. Auto Latch works much the same way: Automation data is recorded starting when you touch the fader. But unlike Auto Touch, which snaps back when you let go of the fader, Auto Latch leaves the fader where it is after you let go. New automation data will be written from the moment you touch the fader to the moment you stop playback. Auto Latch comes in handy for automating things (like panning) that you may not want to snap back to the original position.

Auto Write starts writing automation from the moment you start playing, even before you touch the fader. If you put a track in Auto Write and play the song from the beginning, any previous automation on that track gets erased until you press stop. When you press stop, the automation mode switches back to either Auto Touch or Auto latch, depending on which mode you used most recently. This is a precaution to prevent automation from being recorded when you don't want it to be.

Notice that you also have an Auto Off mode. Sometimes you'll try an automation move or panning effect and then wonder if it really works. It helps to turn off the automation in this one track, listen without the automation, and then turn it back on.

Auto Read is the mode you choose when you've finished automating a track. This mode simply plays back any automation moves.

I often leave most of my tracks in Auto Touch while I'm mixing. Be aware that this can be dangerous: You have to be careful. For example, if you mute a track while a song is playing and that track is in Auto Touch, the mute will be written as automation to the track. If you mute a track before you start playing a song, the mute won't be written.

EXERCISE 8:
Use Timeline Insertion Follows Playback

Let's look at a setting that a lot of people don't know about that comes in very handy while you're mixing. When you press the spacebar to play, your song plays back from the place where the playback cursor is located, right? So say you start playing from bar 10, stop playback, and press play again; if you haven't moved the playback cursor in the meantime, the music will again play back from bar 10.

However, you can change this behavior with a setting in Setup > Preferences > Operation called Timeline Insertion Follows Playback. It sounds more complicated than it is. This setting simply starts playback from the point where you last stopped playing. So if you play from bar 10 and stop at bar 20, the next time you hit the spacebar, the song will play from bar 20.

There's a trick that I use when I'm automating a track. I usually turn on a three- or four-bar pre-roll. So if I'm riding the level of a fader and I stop playback, the next time I start playback, the music will start three or four bars before where I most recently stopped playback. Let's try this so it will make more sense to you.

Note

"Riding the fader" is a term that's been around since the days of large consoles. It simply means to take hold of a fader and move it while the song plays.

1] **Open Preferences.** Go to the Setup menu and select Preferences.

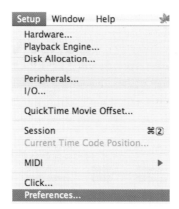

2] **Turn on Insertion Follows Playback.** Click the Operation tab. The top-left setting is called Timeline Insertion Follows Playback. Check the box to enable it.

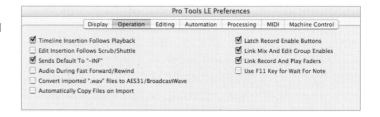

3] **Turn on pre-roll.** Open the Transport window and give yourself three bars of pre-roll.

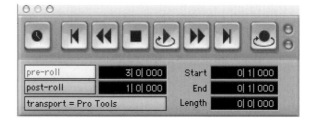

4] **Automate the vocal.** Go to the Mix window. With the vocal track in Auto Touch, play the song from the beginning and start riding the fader as the song plays. Press stop around bar 10. Then press play again.

The music plays from around bar 7, allowing you to get your bearings and begin automating again.

5] **Practice automating.** Finish automating the vocal track using Insertion Follows Playback. Put any other tracks in Auto Touch and automate those, as well. Edit each track's automation data with the Grabber, or delete automation mistakes with the Selector tool.

6] **Save.**

Control Surfaces for Pro Tools

Many people prefer moving an actual physical fader as opposed to moving the mouse on the screen. There are two control surfaces for Pro Tools that retail at $1295: the Digidesign Command 8 (top) and the M-Audio Project Mix. To me, there's no comparison between the two in terms of versatility. The M-Audio Project Mix is the far better deal for the money. The Command 8 is just a control surface with eight moving faders; you still have to buy an interface (such as an Mbox). Command 8 is the better control surface of the two, but of course that's the only thing it was built to do. The new M-Audio Project Mix, on the other hand, is not simply a control surface with ten touch-sensitive moving faders. It also functions as an interface, with eight mic pre's, 18 inputs and 14 outputs, MIDI ports, digital ins and outs, headphone jacks, and even word clock sync. Also, the Project Mix connects via Firewire, which I find to be faster and more reliable than USB, which is what the Command 8 uses.

(continues on next page)

Control Surfaces for Pro Tools (continued)

The big brother to both of these control surfaces is the Digidesign 002 (right), which will cost you over two grand. Given an ample budget, it would be hard to choose between the 002 and the Project Mix. The 002 is also a Pro Tools interface and features eight moving faders, four mic pre's, digital ins and outs, MIDI ports, and headphone jacks. A very cool feature of the 002 is the fact that you can also use it as a stand-alone mixer with effects—very useful if you're performing.

EXERCISE 9:

Automate Plug-Ins

What if, in the bridge, you want the vocal to have a radio voice effect? A simple solution would be to create a new stereo track, highlight the bridge vocals, use ⌘/Ctrl+E to Separate Region (making the Bridge its own region), drag that region to the new track, and then put an EQ plug-in on the new track.

If there are other things happening in the track, however, such as aux sends or effects, you'd have to duplicate them in the new track, which is inconvenient. I want you to learn how to automate a plug-in anyway, so let's put a radio effect on the vocal just during the bridge using the same track. We'll automate an EQ plug-in to do this.

1] **Turn off Timeline Insertion Follows Playback.** Open Setup > Preferences, go to the Operation tab, and uncheck the Timeline Insertion Follows Playback box.

2] **Turn off pre-roll.** Use the shortcut ⌘/Ctrl+K to turn off pre-roll.

3] **Change the track view.** Change the vocal's track view back to Waveform.

4] **Highlight the bridge.** Using the Selector in Grid mode, highlight from bar 55 to 65.

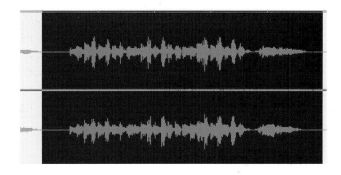

5] **Insert EQ.** Let's use the Waves Renaissance 6-band EQ. Insert it in the vocal track in the Mix window.

6] **Solo the vocal and EQ.** With the vocal track soloed, click the EQ plug-in and EQ the vocal to create a radio effect. The key to a radio effect is to take out all the mid and low frequencies and boost the high frequencies. You can do this by clicking the EQ nodes and dragging them up or down.

First, we need to switch the leftmost band from Bell mode (the default) to Hi-Pass. Do this using the drop-down menu below the band. Now grab the last node to the left and pull that over to the right and down to cut all of the low and mid frequencies.

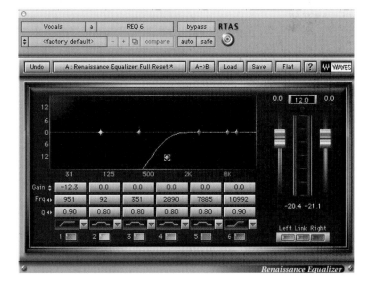

7] **Open the plug-in automation window.**
We want this effect to be bypassed until the
bridge begins, so we have to tell the EQ
plug-in that we want to automate the bypass
switch. In the plug-in window, click the
Auto button. This opens the Plug-in
Automation window.

On the left side of the window you'll see listed
every parameter in the plug-in. You're going
to choose parameters that you want to automate by clicking them and then clicking the
Add button.

Plug-in automation enable

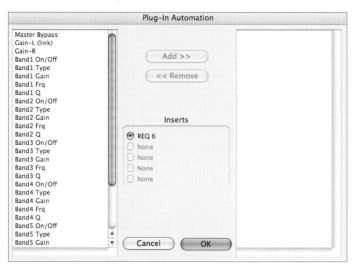

8] **Choose Master Bypass.** We want to automate the Master Bypass, so click Master
Bypass and then the Add button. This moves
the Master Bypass parameter to the right side
of the window. Close the Plug-In Automation
window. Look at the plug-in and notice that
the bypass button is now red.

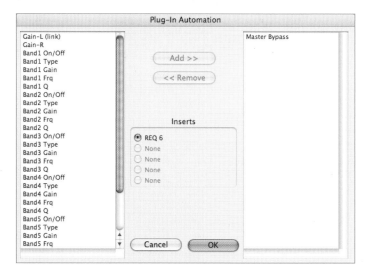

9] **Select Auto Latch automation and turn on bypass.** Put the vocal track into Auto Latch mode. Press the Bypass button so that it's on before you press play.

10] **Automate the Bypass.** Since we started our loop one bar before the bridge vocal actually begins at bar 56, we have enough time to unbypass the EQ before the vocal comes in. Press play with the EQ bypassed and, just after the music starts playing, press the Bypass button to turn bypass off. Let the whole bridge play. After the vocal ends, turn the bypass switch on again.

11] **Change the track view.** In the Edit window, click the Track View selector. You now have a new option because the Master Bypass was enabled for automation. Choose to view the EQ Master Bypass. You'll now see your automation data for the bypass automation.

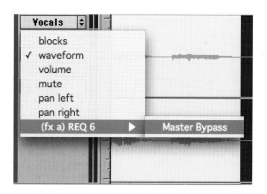

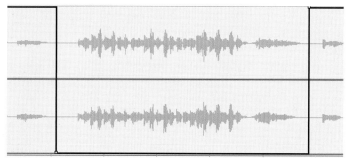

12] **Unsolo the vocal.** Unsolo the vocal and play the bridge. Because we took out a lot of the sound on the vocal using EQ, now its volume may be a bit too low in relation to the rest of the tracks. Let's automate this plug-in's output volume.

13] **Use the three-key trick.** Here's a trick that not too many Pro Tools users know about. I use it all the time. Rather than click a plug-in's Auto button and choose parameters to automate, you can use a shortcut. With the EQ plug-in window open, Mac users hold down ⌘+Option+Control (the three keys to the left of the spacebar) and click the left Gain slider of the Renaissance EQ. Windows users press Ctrl+Alt+Start and left-click. A small submenu will open, in which you can choose to enable this knob for automation.

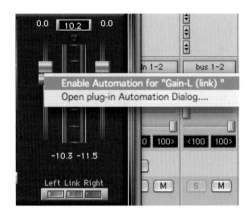

Note

In the EQ plug-in, notice that below the two Gain faders there is a green Link button between the left and right faders With this on, moving just the left fader moves both of them. It's kind of like grouping the faders. Turn the Link button off when you want the left and right gain to be different.

14] **Turn on output gain automation.** Enable the output for automation. You'll notice that the left fader has a small red border.

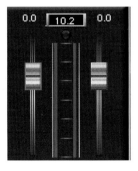

15] **Automate the output.** Play the song with all tracks playing, and ride the output fader to find the right level. If you're in Auto Latch mode, find a level, leave it there, and play until the end of the bridge to write the level. Then press stop.

16] **Change the track view.** Let's view this automation data in case you need to edit it. Go the Track View selector. Now the EQ has two editable parameters—Master Bypass and Gain. Choose Gain.

17] **Edit this level.** Using the Grabber, edit the level if you need to.

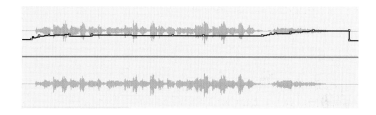

18] Save.

Note

If you hate the radio voice effect, simply turn off the plug-in, as I'm going to do. This was just an exercise to teach you about plug-in automation; it's not anything I would choose to do to this particular song.

EXERCISE 10:
Use AudioSuite Plug-Ins

➤ **AUDIOSUITE PLUG-INS:** *DigiRack Plug-Ins Guide, p. 31*

It's time for you to become more familiar with AudioSuite plug-ins. What if we want a particular effect on the drums for the bridge, as well? Let's put a flanger on the drums.

You'll notice that there is no RTAS flanger plug-in, but there is an AudioSuite Flanger. The downside of AudioSuite plug-ins is that using them adds new audio files to your session. If the old, unprocessed file isn't being used in any playlist, it will be purged when you use the Clear Unused Regions command. So in practice, when you use an AudioSuite plug-in, you're replacing your original file with a processed file. The RTAS plug-ins that we've been using only affect what you hear; they leave the audio folder on your hard drive untouched. If we turn off an RTAS plug-in, we'll hear the original audio file without the effect. AudioSuite plug-ins create a new audio file on your drive, with the effect built into the file.

So what do we do every time before using an AudioSuite plug-in? If your answer was "duplicate the playlist," then you're starting to think like a Pro Tools editor. Duplicating the playlist makes it easy to compare the effected and uneffected versions of the track, and will also ensure that you don't inadvertently get rid of the original take.

1] **Highlight and solo the drums.** Highlight the drums in Grid mode from bar 56 to bar 64, and solo the drum track. (In Chapter 9, we placed a marker at bar 54 for the beginning of the bridge, but there are two bars of lead-in here, so the actual bridge music starts at bar 56.)

2] **Duplicate the playlist.** Duplicate the LiveDrums playlist and name it "DrumFx."

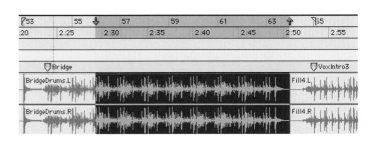

Name for duplicated playlist:

DrumFX

Cancel   OK

3] **Open the AudioSuite plug-in.** Go to the AudioSuite menu and choose Modulation and then Flanger.

4] **Preview the effect.** You always want to preview AudioSuite plug-ins before processing the audio through them. Click the Preview button in the bottom-left corner of the Flanger window.

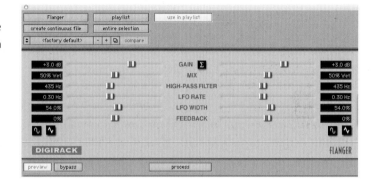

5] **Change the preset.** Click the Preset menu. You'll see a list containing a few presets. Choose Slow n Deep. To hear it, click Preview.

Go through the presets and move the sliders around to change the sound.

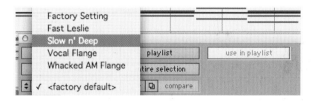

6] **Choose a preset.** I like the Vocal Flange effect on the drums, so I'm going to choose that one. Now I'm going to process my file by clicking the Process button at the bottom of the window.

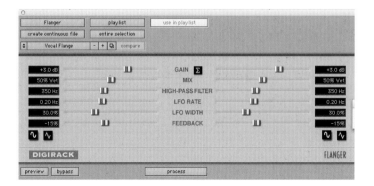

7] **Unsolo the drums, and play back.** Close the Flanger window. Notice that your drum track now has a new region. Unsolo the drums, and play back your newly effected drum track.

8] **Save.**

Experiment with the AudioSuite plug-ins, but remember *always* to duplicate your playlist before you process anything.

EXERCISE 11:
Automate a Send

What if you want reverb on the bass but only in the bridge? Let's learn how to automate a send.

1] **Bus the bass.** On the bass track, create a send to bus 1–2.

2] **Put the bass track in Auto Touch.** Put the bass track in Auto Touch mode. You'll notice that the Send fader also goes into Auto Touch mode.

3] **Highlight the bridge.** Highlight from bar 53 to bar 65.

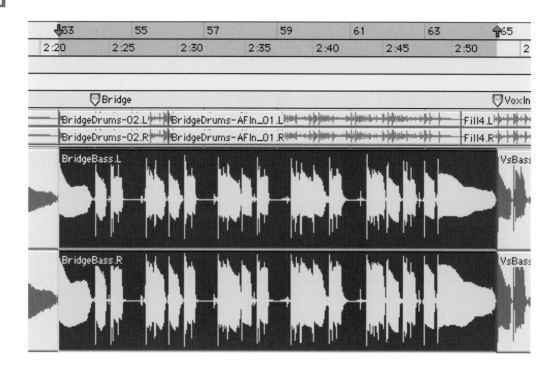

4] **Change the Track View.** Click the Track View selector. You now have a Send A in the list. Also notice that you can automate not only this send's level, but its mute and panning as well. Choose Level.

There are many ways in which we can use this send to put reverb on the bass but only in the bridge. We could keep the Send fader down, as it is now, and then ride it during the bridge until we have the right level of reverb. We could also set the perfect level of reverb on the Send fader and then mute that send everywhere but in the bridge, which is very similar to what we did in Exercise 10 using the Master Bypass (which is basically the Mute button for a plug-in). We could also simply set a level with the Grabber tool in the automation data after displaying it with the Track View selector. Let's choose this last method, since you already know how to ride a fader.

5] **Make an automation point.** Choose the Grabber and click the line at the bottom of the bass track to create an automation point at bar 53.

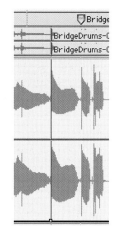

6] **Make another automation point.** Click at bar 65 to create an automation point.

7] **Bring up the level.** Choose the Trim tool and click between the two points to get the sideways Level Trimmer. Bring up the send level a little more than halfway.

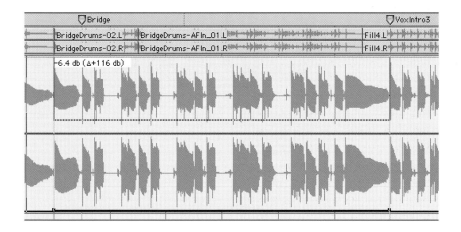

8] **Look at your Send fader.** Play the bridge, and notice that the Send fader is no longer at zero level.

9] **Move an automation point.** You may notice the reverb came in a bar early. Let's move the send start time one bar over. In Grid mode, using the Grabber tool, grab the top automation point and move it to bar 54.

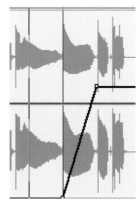

10] **Move an automation point again.** Click the bottom automation point and move that to bar 54, too.

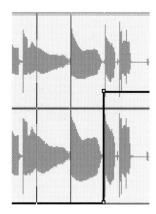

11] **Save.**

EXERCISE 12:
Tidy Up Your Tracks

It's important that you go through your regions and do any fade-ins or fade-outs that may be needed. It's a good idea to solo each track before you mix, cleaning up pops or noise and creating fades. Let me show you how to clean up a few things, using the guitar track in this song as an example.

1] **Set all track views to Waveform.** Holding the Option/Alt key, click the Track View selector of one track and set it to Waveform. This changes all tracks to Waveform view.

2] **Change track size and zoom.** Make the guitar track large, and zoom in to the first few bars.

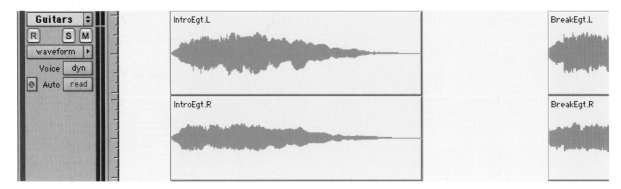

3] **Turn on Slip mode.**

4] **Turn off Tab to Transients.** In the Edit window, make sure the Tab to Transients button doesn't have a blue border. Now the Tab key will not go to the next significant waveform, but rather to the next Edit Point.

5] **Get familiar with the Tab key.** Using the Selector tool, click the guitar track before the first region begins, and then hit Tab. Your cursor goes to the beginning of this region. Press Tab again, and the cursor moves to the end of the region. Press Tab yet again; this time the cursor moves to the next region, which is at bar 4. Now press Option/Ctrl+Tab. The cursor goes backward, to the end of the first region. Play with the Tab key until its function make sense to you.

6] **Use Shift+Tab.** Click the guitar track between bar 2 and bar 3; then hold Shift and press Tab. This highlights from where you clicked to the end of this region.

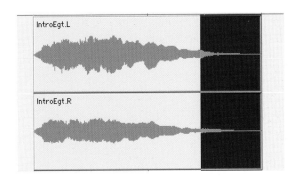

7] **Create a fade-out.** Use the shortcut ⌘/Ctrl+F to create a fade in the highlighted area. Choose the straight diagonal shape, and click OK.

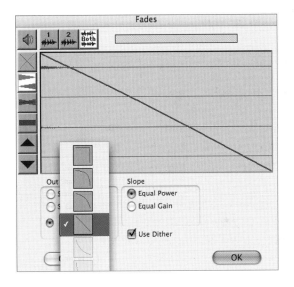

8] **Highlight for a fade-in.** Hit Tab twice to go to the beginning of the next region. Hold the Shift key and click just after the attack.

9] **Create a fade-in.** Use the shortcut ⌘/Ctrl+F to create a fade. Choose the third curved shape and press OK.

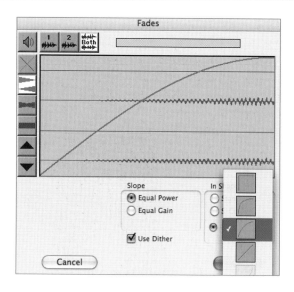

10] **Create another fade-out.** Hit Tab twice. This takes you to the VsEgt region at bar 13. Lets create a fade-out on the region before bar 13.

Click between bar 12 and 13, hold Shift, and press Tab. Again, this highlights from where you clicked to the next edit point. Press ⌘/Ctrl+F and choose the fade shape of your choice.

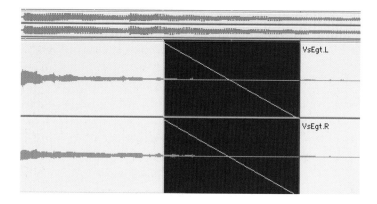

11] **Create another fade-in.** Hit Tab once. This takes you to the beginning of the VsEgt Region. Hold Shift and click around the second beat of bar 13. This highlights from your In Point to where you clicked. Press ⌘/Ctrl+F and choose the fade shape of your choice.

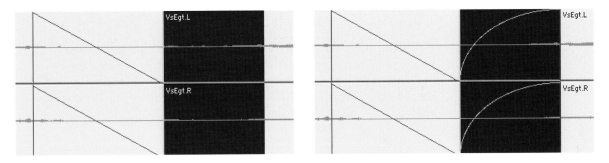

12] **Handle crossfade errors.** Press Tab twice, which takes you to the downbeat of bar 19 and the beginning of the ChrsEgt region. Highlight the seam between these regions, and press ⌘/Ctrl+F to create a crossfade. Choose any shape and press OK. You'll get an error window.

I wanted you to see this error so that you'll know what it is when it happens in your next song. What this window is saying is, "Hey, there's no audio on one side or both sides of this region boundary, so I can't create a cross-fade." Even if you click Adjust Bounds, it won't create a crossfade, because there's no extra audio at the end of the left region and no extra audio at the beginning of the right region. So there's nothing to create a crossfade with. To verify this, you can choose the Trim tool and try to pull out audio from either side of both regions. You won't be able to.

Let me show you a place in the song where we can make this work and fix it.

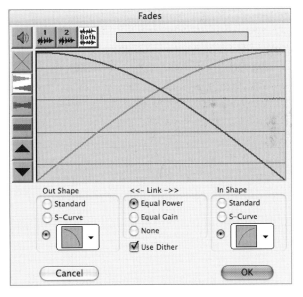

If you get in the habit of recording with QuickPunch on, you'll rarely get the invalid fade error, because QuickPunch will be recording during your pre-roll and post-roll times, giving you the extra audio you need to create crossfades.

13] **Go to bar 65.** Click the Main counter, type "65," and press Return/Enter. This takes you to bar 65.

14] **Listen to this edit.** Solo the guitar track and play this edit. You might hear a small pop. This one isn't bad, but in case you do have edits with pops or clicks, you need to know how to fix them.

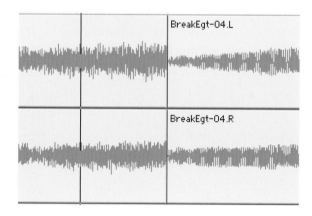

15] **Highlight the seam.** Highlight the seam, press ⌘/Ctrl+F to crossfade, choose the default shape, and press OK. You'll get the same error as in step 12. This time, press Skip Invalid Fade(s).

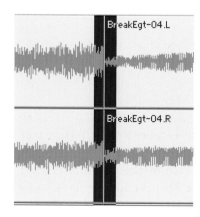

16] **Use the Trimmer.** Choose the Trim tool in Slip mode and drag the end of the left region a little bit to the right, into the attack of the next BreakEgt region.

The reason we're doing this is to extend the left region into the right region, which now gives the right region the extra audio we need to create a crossfade.

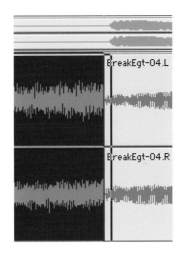

17] **Fix the seam.** Now highlight the seam and crossfade. If you see the error message, click Adjust Bounds.

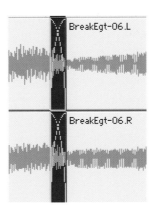

Tip

Make sure you don't make your highlight wider than the extension you made with the Trim tool; otherwise, you'll get the same invalid fade error.

18] **Save.** Unsolo the guitars and save.

Okay, I'm going to leave you on your own for a bit to get this song into shape and ready to print our final mix. There is some nasty noise on the guitar track from bar 28 to 30. Using ⌘/Ctrl+Shift+Tab, create a fade-out to fix that. Add EQ or compression plug-ins to any channels that you feel would benefit. Experiment with the Waves plug-ins. Try the Doubler plug-in on a track, bus additional effects, do some automation, or process regions using AudioSuite plug-ins. When you feel that your mix plays back just as you want it to from top to bottom, move on to the next exercise.

EXERCISE 13:

Create a Master Fader

The Master Fader is like a global fader for the whole song. You use it to adjust the level of the entire song, to create a fade-out for the entire song, and to put compression on the final mix. Before you create a mix for a CD, you usually create a Master Fader and make any adjustments that are needed.

1] **Create a Master Fader.** Create a new track and make it a Stereo Master Fader. I usually keep my Master Faders on the far-right of my Mix window.

2] **Use the Master Fader.** Play the song and get used to how a Master Fader works. It adjusts the levels for the whole song, mutes the whole song, and so on.

3] Save.

EXERCISE 14:

Use Mix Bus Compression

Mix bus compression should be applied sparingly, with a less-is-more approach. Technically speaking, mix bus compression is typically used with a high threshold, so that only the loudest peaks will pass the threshold and be compressed. Mix bus compression is also appropriate with a very low 1.5:1 or 2:1 compression ratio, and with long attack and release times.

1] **Insert a compressor.** Insert the Waves Renaissance Compressor on the Master Fader.

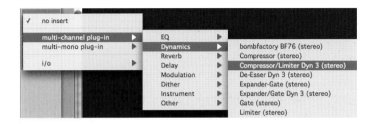

2] **Tweak the compressor.** I brought the Master Fader down to –4. Remember, you can hold the ⌘/Ctrl key while moving the fader to move the levels in smaller increments, making it easier to be more exact. In the plug-in, I set my threshold to –3 dB. I set the ratio to 2 and brought the gain back up, adding 3 dB of what is called "make-up gain" to compensate for the loss in level caused by the compression.

At the top of the plug-in are three buttons.

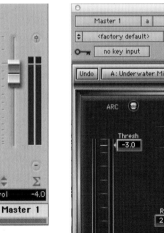

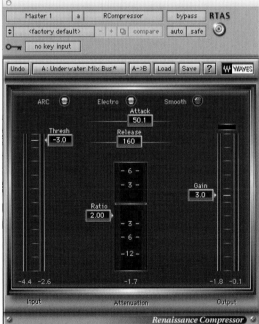

◆ The first, labeled ARC, is the Waves Auto Release switch. With this switched on, the plug-in sets its release time automatically.

◆ The next button is the Compression Behavior button. Use Electro for mix bus compression. Opto tends to give tracks a vintage compression sound, which is great for drums.

◆ The third button is the Character button; the two options are Smooth and Warm. Choose Smooth, which does not add much character to the compression, which is what we want for mix bus compression.

Be sure to read the Waves Musicians II manual to learn more about each of the plug-ins. These manuals are very well written and are easy to understand. (Remember, they're available at protoolsformusicians.com.)

3] **Save your settings.** Save this preset, as you did earlier with the other plug-ins. Name it "Underwater Mix Bus."

4] Save.

Creating a Song's Fade-Out

A simple solution to making a whole song fade is to create a Master Fader, put that Master Fader in Auto Latch, and record the fade automation manually.

You can also edit the Master Fader's automation data as we did in Exercise 7, using the Grabber tool to click and create edit points. I want this song to begin to fade around bar 90 and fade out completely by bar 102. I also want the end of the fade to be a little more gradual.

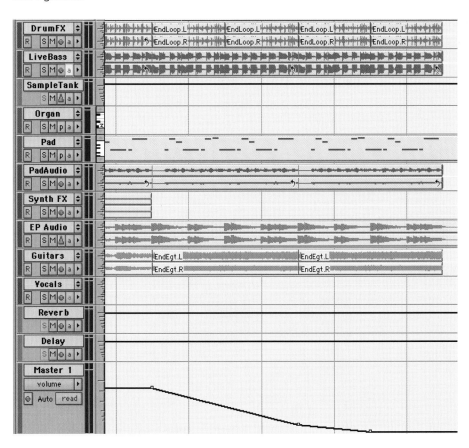

As an exercise, create your own fade-out for this song.

EXERCISE 15:

Bounce to Disk

Many times as I'm working, I'll want to take my song with me in the car, so I'll burn a quick CD of my mix to listen to while I drive. I simply highlight the song from start to end and choose a function called Bounce to Disk.

I'm sure you're familiar with the term "bouncing." In the old days of multi-track tape recorders, bouncing meant sending a combination of tracks to another track, so as to free up more tracks on tape to record to. Today, bouncing usually means taking everything out of the main outputs and making that into a CD-quality audio file to burn to CD. You can choose to bounce things other than your whole mix, which can be useful in certain situations. Let's give it a try.

1] **Check for overs.** Because we've used compression and make-up gain to get the song as loud as possible, we need to check and make sure the output doesn't go over the maximum and clip, even for a moment. So play back the whole song and watch the Mix Bus meters. If there's an over, you'll see one or both red clipping lights at the top of the meters.

If the mix has clipped, reduce the output gain of the compressor and try again. Remember to hold the ⌘/Ctrl button when you bring down the output gain so that it moves in small increments.

2] **Highlight the song.** Highlight in the Edit window from bar 1 to the end of the fade on the Master Fader.

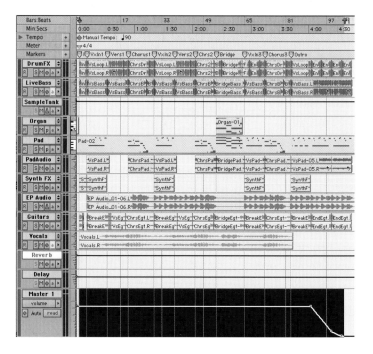

3] **Choose Bounce to Disk.** In the File menu, choose Bounce to Disk. The shortcut is ⌘+Option+B/Ctrl+Alt+B. You'll be using this a lot, so memorize it now.

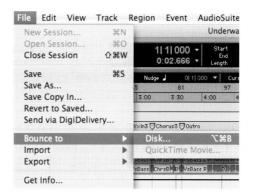

4] **The Bounce options.** Our ultimate goal is to use the bounced file to burn a CD.

First, we need to make sure that the bounce source is correctly set to Out 1–2.

Next, we need to set the Bounce options for a stereo CD-quality file. You can use either AIFF or WAV, but use WAV as your default. Set the format to Stereo Interleaved. Make the resolution 16-bit and the sample rate 44,100 (44.1 kHz). I usually use Convert After Bounce.

Click the Bounce button. If you should change your mind while the song is bouncing, use ⌘/Ctrl+. (period) to cancel.

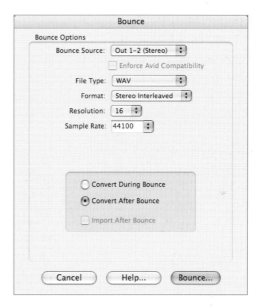

5] **Save the file.** Here is the window you want to be cautious of. Don't get into a hurry and click the Save button. You want to stop and think here: "Where do I want to put my mixes?"

I like to create a folder on my Audio drive and name it My Mixes. Then anytime I need to burn a CD of any song, I know where to look. Let's create a new folder. Click the Audio drive; then click New Folder and name the folder "My Mixes."

6] **Name your mix.** Name your mix "Underwater Mix 1." That number will help you know which mix this is. Believe me, you'll have more than one mix, so numbering is a good way to name them. Click Save.

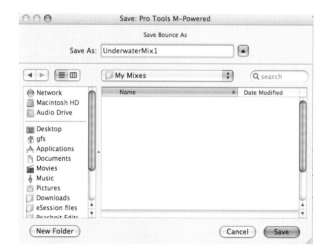

7] **Bouncing.** Your song will begin playing. You'll be locked out of Pro Tools and the song will play in real time, displaying a window to let you know that you're bouncing.

> Bouncing to Disk...
>
> Time Remaining: 4:25
>
> (type Command-period or Escape to cancel)

8] **Save.**

Congratulations—you've just mixed your first song. Let's burn a CD.

EXERCISE 16:
Burn a CD

For burning CDs, Macintosh users can use Roxio Toast; Windows users can use Roxio Easy Media Creator. These are the most common CD burning applications and are far superior to anything that comes with your computer. iTunes does allow you to burn audio CDs, but it doesn't allow you to back up computer files.

Do yourself a favor: Go to Roxio.com and purchase and download Toast or Easy Media Creator. Both retail at $79.95, but it will be money that you'll never regret spending because you'll use these applications constantly. (Most stores such as CompUSA and Fry's sell both applications, but I buy most everything on the Internet these days.) If you have a separate audio editor program, it may be able to burn audio CDs, but it probably won't burn data CDs, so having a program that will do either type of CD is useful.

After you download them, you have to install them. Roxio will email you a serial number that you'll need before installing these applications.

The Importance of Being Organized...

I have been accused of being anal-retentive, but I can't afford not to be. When you've spent thousands of dollars and you have thousands of files and loops, and countless software applications and plug-ins, you really must be well organized.

When you need technical support for something you've paid for but you can't find your serial number, and you have a client standing over your shoulder waiting, you can lose business. You should have a fail-safe system to find anything you need, whether it be your serial numbers, your manuals, your installation CDs, or whatever. Make a commitment to yourself and spend a day or two getting organized.

I have one file drawer for all of my installation CDs. I also have an emergency CD carrier that I carry with me, which has my most important CDs (such as operating systems) and my Pro Tools installer CDs. I have a bookshelf dedicated to my manuals, and I keep a book of print-outs detailing what's on each hard drive and each back-up tape. I label every CD and every tape with a title and date. I don't like frantically searching for my client's work or my own.

For serial numbers, I've created an Excel spreadsheet. I keep the same thing for my passwords. Every time I buy a new plug-in or application, I paste the serial numbers into the spreadsheet, as well as the tech support phone numbers. I save these files on two different computers. This documentation comes in handy frequently.

Manufacturer	Product	Version	Serial No	Additional Codes	Tech Support
Digidesign	ProTools LE	6.7			650-731-6300
	ProTools LE	6.4			
Digidesign	Pro Tools TDM				
Digidesign	Mbox				650-731-6300
Apple	Logic 7				
Native Instruments	Absynth	2			323-372-3676
Native Instruments	Absynth (Update)	3			
Sony	Oxford EQ		Authorization Code:	OS9 ...... OSX	
				...... OSX	
				Resp ...... ADAM	
Spectrasonics	Atmosphere				888-870-4223
Spectrasonics	Trilogy			Code:	888-870-4223
Spectrasonics	Stylus RMX				
Yellow Tools	MVI Culture	1		Challenge Code:	
WebSTAR	Server Suite	5.2		Cust ID	1.408.557.4600
WebSTAR	4D Mail	5.2		Cust ID	www.webstar.com
Antares	Autotune	3			831-461-7800
Micromat	Drive 10				707-566-3806
Waves	TDM Bundle				865-909-9200
Waves	Renaissance Collection			......	865-546-6115
Wave Mechanics	UltraTools Upgrade 1.0 to	2.2			802-951-9700
Mezzo Technologies	Mezzo	4.5		Password:	
Mezzo Technologies	Mezzo			Password:	408-557-4682
SynchroArts	VocAlign	2.8		Product Key:	www.synchroarts.com
				Authorization Code:	
			product key	......	
Emagic	XSKey				530-477-1050
Microsoft Word	Microsoft Word				
				Reg #:	
Intuit	Quickbooks	6		......	
Macromedia	Dreamweaver	2004			
				Cust number:	
Final Draft	Final Draft	7			
SnapZ Pro	SnapZ Pro		...... - Name Gina C. Fant-Saez		
Arkaos	Arkaos	3.02			
Apple	DVD Studio Pro	3			
Apple	Final Cut Pro	4.5 HD			
Apple	Quicktime				
Apple	Quicktime				
Apple	Motion				
Boris FX	Boris FX	3		831-461-7800	

So often I've gone to a commercial studio and asked for an installation disk or a manual, only to have some intern looking frantically in drawers and closets while I wait and am expected to pay their hourly fees for *their* disorganization. Get into good habits now—organize all your materials in one place, and your clients will appreciate it down the line.

1] **Mac users: Open Toast.** Open the Toast program and click the Audio tab. Find your My Mixes folder and drag the Underwater Mix 1 file to the Toast window. Click the red Record button and insert a CD. The Record window will open. The basic setting are fine. Click Record. When the CD is done, the Mac will chime like a toaster and you can eject the CD.

2] **Windows users: Open Easy Media Creator.**
Open Easy Media Creator. On the left side of
the window, click Audio to expand the Audio
section. Then click Audio CD. Find your My
Mixes folder and drag the Underwater Mix 1
file to the window on the right. Click the red
Record button and insert your CD. The CD will
show you the progress as it burns.

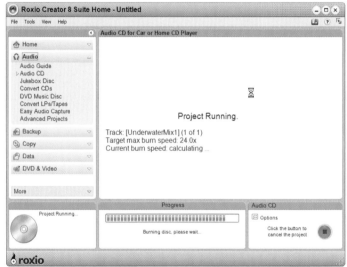

3] **Label your CD.** Whether it's with a real label, a CD printer, or a Sharpie marker pen, get in the habit now of labeling your CDs immediately after they're burned.

Wrap Up

I hope you've learned a lot in this chapter and are starting to grasp the ins and outs of mixing in Pro Tools. The more you practice, the sooner mixing will become second nature to you, and the sooner Pro Tools will become like an instrument you can just pick up and play fluently.

We have just one chapter to go. I appreciate your hanging in there with me. Take a rest, and as soon as you're ready, we'll dive into Chapter 12.

EXPORT YOUR SONG

12

This chapter contains a series of exercises designed to round out your knowledge as a Pro Tools engineer. They'll also give you a few more computer skills that you'll find helpful in managing files.

You'll learn how to record a mix back into Pro Tools the way the professionals do. You'll also learn how to punch into a mix and then create one consolidated file out of an edited mix. We'll cover how to export this mix into a CD-quality file without using the File > Bounce to Disk function.

You'll also learn how to back up your session using Toast or Easy Media Creator. Throughout the chapter, I will stress the importance of clearing unused audio files; if you fail to do this, your backups will take far more space than they need to.

In today's music, being able to create mp3 files is essential. We'll cover the process of creating mp3 files using both Pro Tools and Apple iTunes.

In Chapter 9, I discussed briefly the purpose of stem tracks. Now you'll find out how to create them for yourself. During this exercise, you'll also learn how to import tracks from one Pro Tools session to another.

We'll be using our stem session to prepare a hypothetical session to send to another musician. Many people are using the Internet to collaborate with other songwriters and musicians around the world. In Appendix B, we'll look at the many ways in which large audio files are sent across the Internet using Digidesign's DigiDelivery, FTP applications, Apple File Sharing, iDisk, iChat and other chat applications, and finally, my new company eSession.com.

Off we go....

Recording Back into Pro Tools vs. Bouncing to Disk

There are several reasons why you may want to record your mix back into Pro Tools rather than using Bounce to Disk as we did in Chapter 11.

First, sound quality. There is a huge debate about whether using Bounce to Disk negatively affects the sound quality of a final mix. Personally, I don't hear a difference, but many people whose ears I trust more than my own say there *is* an audible difference. There are also people whose ears I trust more than my own who say there is *no* difference. I use Bounce to Disk quite frequently and have never had a problem sonically. Most professional engineers, however, don't use it, because the consensus is that mixes recorded back into Pro Tools are superior in stereo image, depth of field, and sound quality when compared with mixes created using Bounce to Disk. In this chapter I'll give you the tools to do it both ways and let you decide for yourself.

Most people recording back into Pro Tools are using consoles or Pro Tools systems with multiple outputs, so—due to the fact that Bouncing to Disk only bounces two outputs—they have no choice in the matter. Bouncing outputs 1 and 2 might give them only the drum tracks, not the entire mix. There is another huge debate here: Many professionals say Pro Tools sounds better coming out of multiple outputs. They argue that the audio of Pro Tools should be sent out of multiple outputs and then mixed to stereo outside the computer using analog technology. This is called *summing*.

Throughout this book, we have let the computer do all of our summing. The professional argument is that internal summing within the Pro Tools software, using the computer's processor, distorts the stereo image. Some people feel there is an audible difference when the multichannel output is sent through analog mixing gear and back into Pro Tools.

My philosophy is that you should work with what you have and be grateful for it. As I was always reminded as a child, there are starving children in Africa who will never have a Pro Tools studio. But seriously, I've heard music done on an Mbox with no hardware that was better than music done in a $3000-a-day commercial studio. It's not about your gear or your finesse as an engineer. In my humble opinion, it's about talent and it's about the song. A bad song played by incompetent musicians with an out-of-tune vocalist won't sound any better on a $25,000 Pro Tools system. A great musician and a great singer recording a great song on an Mbox or FireWire Solo will beat out the "professional" recording system every time.

Given the choice of where to invest your time and money, focus on refining your talent and material first, and then invest in gear when you have quality material to record and the talent and skills required to record it.

But I'm digressing. Let's talk about the practicalities of recording your mix back into Pro Tools. When you choose Bounce to Disk, you have to make sure your song is ready to go from top to bottom. If your song is bouncing to disk and you're at 3 minutes out of a 4-minute song when you hear a mistake in the mix, you have to cancel the bounce, fix your mistake, and rebounce. This can be time-consuming and frustrating. In contrast, if you're recording your mix back into a track in Pro Tools, you can stop recording at 3 minutes, fix the mistake, and then manually punch in on the mix track from where the mistake was.

Another advantage of recording back into Pro Tools is for mastering purposes. When you're getting your music mastered, you always want to send the mastering engineer a final mix that is the exact same file format and bit resolution as your Pro Tools session. This allows the mastering engineer to use all of his or her high-end gear to do any digital audio file conversions that may be needed. For songs going to a mastering engineer, you also probably don't want to record your final mixes with a fade-out. You should leave that step for the mastering engineer as well. But when the mix is for your own use, then you probably do want to record your fades into the mix. Again, there are no wrong choices, just lots of options.

I'll shut up now and teach you how to do this.

EXERCISE 1:
Record Back into Pro Tools

1] **Create a new track.** Create a stereo audio track and name it "Underwater." Set the input of this track to any unused stereo bus. For this exercise, let's use bus 7–8.

2] **Set all tracks to the bus output.** If we need to set all tracks to be sending their output to the bus, how do we do that? I hope your answer was "hold down the Option/Alt key and change one track." Doing this will change them all.

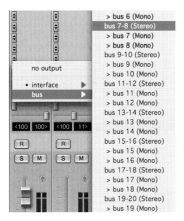

3] **Set the master fader output to the bus.** The preceding step doesn't change the master fader, so we need to set its output to the bus.

4] **Change the Underwater track's output.** Change the output of the Underwater track back to outputs 1–2 so that you can hear what you're recording. This should be the only track coming out of outputs 1–2.

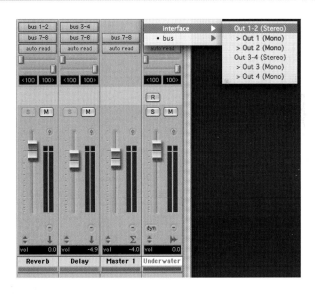

5] **Put the Underwater track in Record.**

6] **Check your levels.** Put Pro Tools in Input Only Monitoring so you can hear what's coming into the Underwater track. Play the music and check the input level to make sure you're not peaking. If you are, bring down the output level of your Renaissance Compressor, or bring down the entire volume of the master fader's automation data using the Trim tool. Hold down ⌘/Ctrl to drag the volume in small increments.

7] **Record the mix.** Record the mix from bar 1, and press stop at the end of the fade.

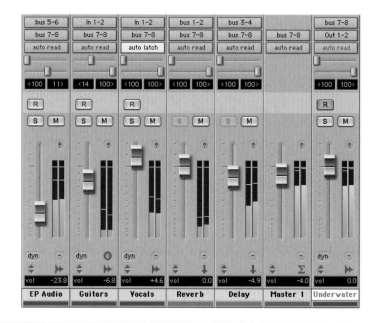

8] **Solo your mix and play it back.** Turn on Auto Input Monitoring to hear your newly recorded track. Solo it and play it back.

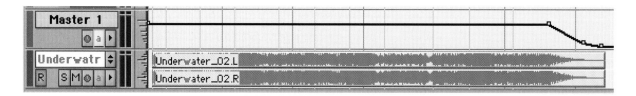

9] **Rename the mix.** I like to use ⌘/Ctrl+Shift+R to rename my mixes. This way, on the hard drive I can find the file easily without wondering if it's the right one. Highlight the region, and use the shortcut to rename your mix "UnderwaterMix1."

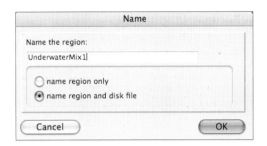

10] Save.

EXERCISE 2:

Punch In on a Mix

Punching in to mixes is one of the coolest things about recording back into Pro Tools. Let's say that as you're printing your mix, you hear a drum fill that's too loud or a vocal phrase that's too low. You would stop recording your mix, put the offending track in Auto Touch, and fix the level manually or edit the track's volume automation data. Then you would simply need to punch in at this one spot and re-record the mix. You don't have to record the mix again from bar 1, as you would with Bounce to Disk.

Let's punch in on bar 89 and re-record the outro of the mix without a fade.

1] **Delete the fade.** Use the Selector, highlight the volume automation data on the master fader, and press Delete.

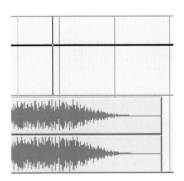

2] **Turn on pre-roll.** In the Transport window, set one or two bars of pre-roll.

Note that you don't really need post-roll in this case because we're at the end of the song, so feel free to turn it off.

3] **Highlight the punch.** In Grid mode using QuickPunch, click at bar 89. Use the shortcut ⌘/Ctrl+Tab to highlight to the end of UnderwaterMix region.

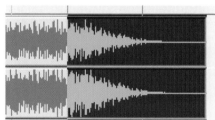

Tip

You don't have to highlight punch points. Using QuickPunch, you can simply play the song up to the area you want to fix and manually punch in and out rather than highlighting punch-in and punch-out points.

4] **Record.** Record the new ending without the fade.

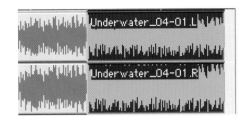

5] **Solo the mix and listen.** Make sure Auto Input Monitoring is on. Also make sure your Delay track is either muted or not in solo-safe mode, so that you don't hear the delayed EP track.

Turn off pre-roll using ⌘/Ctrl+K, click before the punch-in point, and check for a pop or click. You shouldn't have one—but if you do, QuickPunch makes things easier. Because we used it, we can zoom way in to the mix track and put a tiny crossfade at the punch-in point.

6] **Save.**

EXERCISE 3:
Consolidate Files

You'll notice that your UnderwaterMix track consists of two separate audio regions, because you punched in.

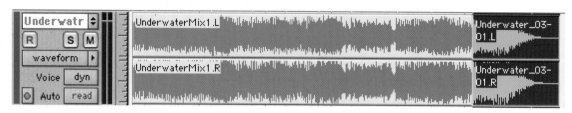

Hide or minimize Pro Tools. Open your audio drive and open the UnderwaterGFS session folder. Now open the Audio Files folder. Tell your computer to sort the list by Date Modified.

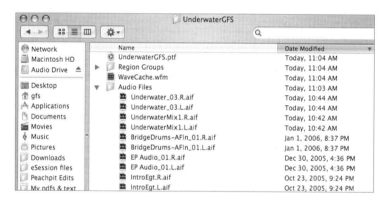

You should see your mixes at the top of this window because they're the most recent files recorded. Notice that there are two pairs of mixes—the main mix, UnderwaterMix1.L and UnderwaterMix1.R; and then the punched-in audio files from the end. On my hard drive these are called Underwater03-01.L and Underwater03-01.R. Remember that Pro Tools doesn't record stereo files. It creates what are called *dual mono files*—that is, separate files for the left and right sides of a stereo track. (Your files may not have the same names as mine, and you may have more files than I do, depending on how many times you punched in.)

I wanted you to see these files because I want you to understand that you always want your final mixes to be one cohesive audio file from end to end, without edit points and without being made up of edited regions. If you ever need to give the 24-bit mix to a mastering engineer, you'd want to give him the dual mono mix from bar 1 to the end, not a mix consisting of audio files in pieces.

So how do we make this punched-in mix into one region? We're going to do what's called *consolidating a region*. When you highlight multiple regions in a track and consolidate them, all of your edits will be gone. The operation creates one cohesive region out of whatever you highlight. And here's a familiar reminder: I always duplicate my playlist before I consolidate anything, so that I can go back to my original regions if I need to and change crossfades or re-edit the file.

1] **Duplicate your playlist.** As always, before you do anything that could mess up your mix, duplicate the playlist and edit the duplicate. Name this new playlist "MixEdit1."

2] **Create a fade.** Highlight the end region of MixEdit1 at the point where you want the fade to begin. Using ⌘/Ctrl+F, open the Fade window. Click Standard in the Fade window.

And here's a new trick: Click the blue fade line and drag down. See? You can make your own fade shapes. Click OK.

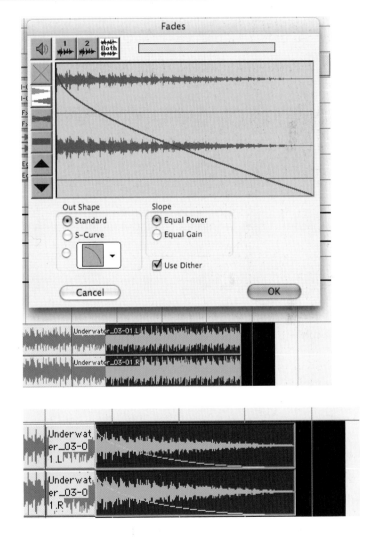

3] **Highlight the whole song.** Double-click the Zoomer to see the whole song. Then use the Selector and triple-click the MixEdit1 track to highlight it from end to end.

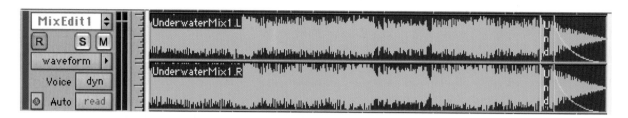

Tip

If you double-click with the Selector, you only highlight one region, but triple-clicking highlights the entire track.

4] **Consolidate.** Under the Edit menu, choose Consolidate.

Note

Consolidating creates a new audio file, so any fades or crossfades will be incorporated in the new file.

Edit	View	Track	Region
Undo Create Fades			⌘Z
Can't Redo			⇧⌘Z
Cut			⌘X
Copy			⌘C
Paste			⌘V
Clear			⌘B
Cut Special			▶
Copy Special			▶
Paste Special			▶
Clear Special			▶
Select All			⌘A
Play Edit Selection			⌥[
Duplicate			⌘D
Repeat...			⌥R
Shift...			⌥H
Insert Silence			⇧⌘E
Trim Region			▶
Separate Region			▶
Heal Separation			⌘H
Strip Silence			⌘U
Consolidate			⌥⇧3
Thin Automation			⌥⌘T
Fades			▶

5] **Rename the mix.** The regions become one consolidated region that takes its name from the playlist.

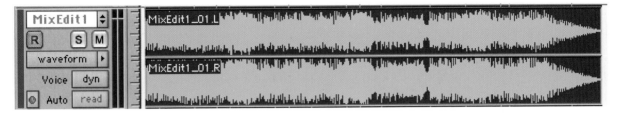

Let's rename this mix using ⌘/Ctrl+Shift+R and call it "UnderwaterMix2."

6] **Save.**

It's crucial that you grasp the importance of renaming these files. Look in your Audio Files folder now. If you hadn't renamed this file, it would be called EditMix1. If you gave this file to someone, how would they know what song it was?

EXERCISE 4:
Export Regions as Files

The new mix in our Audio Files folder is a pair of mono 24-bit files, which is not what we need for CD. To burn a CD, we need to make this mix into a 16-bit, 44.1 kHz stereo file. We could solo this track and use Bounce to Disk—but if you buy into the idea that Bounce to Disk hinders the quality, doing it this way would defeat the purpose of recording back to Pro Tools in the first place. Most pros use a simple method called Export Regions as Files.

The advantage of using Export Regions as Files is that (unlike Bounce to Disk, which is a real-time function requiring that you listen to the song in real time) this method exports the file without playing it. As a result, it can do so much faster.

The disadvantage is a result of the advantage. Because Bounce to Disk requires that you actually listen to your final mix being created into its final format, this last playback gives you a time to listen intently. With Export Regions as Files, you don't get to listen.

A few months ago, I did a 30-minute radio program for a very boring promotion for vitamins. I chose Export Regions as Files because I couldn't bear listening to the spot one more time. There was a mistake in volume around 20 minutes in, and this was due to two things: first, my impatience; and secton, the fact that if I had been using Bounce to Disk, I would have heard the problem and fixed it. As a result, my client was not happy and I had to credit them for the time to fix the mistake. Using Export Regions as Files cost me time and money. Let this lesson of mine be something for you to think about. But since you may find it useful to know how to do it, let's give it a try.

1] **Find the mix.** In the Regions bin, your newly renamed mix, UnderwaterMix2, should be highlighted. If it's not, click it to highlight it.

Regions ▼
BreakBass (Stereo)
BreakEgt (Stereo)
BreakEgt-02 (Stereo)
BridgeBass (Stereo)
BridgeDrums (Stereo)
BridgeDrums-01 (Stereo)
BridgeDrums-02 (Stereo)
BridgeDrums-AFIn_01 (Ste
BridgeEgt (Stereo)
BridgePad (Stereo)
Chrs2Drums (Stereo)
ChrsBass (Stereo)
ChrsDrums (Stereo)
ChrsEgt (Stereo)
ChrsPad (Stereo)
EndEgt (Stereo)
EndLoop (Stereo)
EP Audio_01 (Stereo)
Fill1 (Stereo)
Fill2 (Stereo)
Fill3 (Stereo)
Fill4 (Stereo)
IntroBass (Stereo)
IntroDrums (Stereo)
IntroEgt (Stereo)
SynthFx (Stereo)
Underwater_03 (Stereo)
Underwater_03-01 (Stereo)
UnderwaterMix1 (Stereo)
UnderwaterMix2 (Stereo)
Vocals (Stereo)
VsBass (Stereo)

2] **Choose Export.** In the Regions menu of the Regions bin, choose Export Regions as Files.

Note

Export Regions as Files does not export any fades. All fades must be done prior to consolidating.

3] **Choose a destination.** In the Export Selected window, click the Choose button to choose the destination for this file. Remember the folder we created for mixes, in Chapter 11? Find the My Mixes folder on your Audio drive and click Choose.

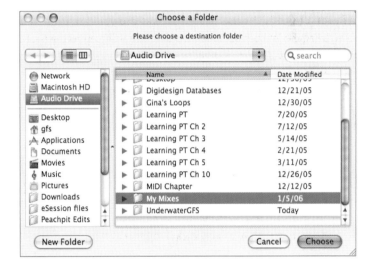

4] **Choose the correct settings.** In the Export Selected box, choose WAV as the file type and Stereo as the format. Bit Depth should be set to 16 and Sample Rate should be 44100. Leave the default filename setting at the bottom; don't worry about that right now. Click Export.

Your mix will be converted and exported into your My Mixes folder.

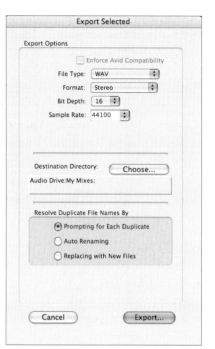

5] Save.

6] Hide or minimize Pro Tools.

7] **Open My Mixes.** Open your My Mixes folder. You should have two mixes, one created at the end of Chapter 11 using Bounce to Disk, and now a new one.

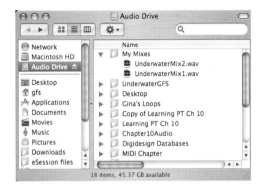

8] **Burn a CD.** Using your CD-burning application, burn both of these mixes to CD. Mix 1 was done using Bounce to Disk, and mix 2 is using the "more professional" method. Now you can judge for yourself whether you can hear any difference.

EXERCISE 5:

Create an Instrumental Mix

It's always a good idea to create an instrumental mix of your songs. That way, if you ever need to re-sing the vocals or perform to your track, you have a copy. The instrumental mix is also useful in case you need something to rehearse to.

1] **Create a new playlist.** On the MixEdit1 track, create a new playlist and name it "Inst. Mix."

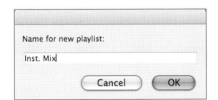

2] **Mute the region.** Let me teach you a trick. Rather than muting the Vocals track, we're going to mute the region. Why? If you had a send on this vocal track and the send was pre-fader, then your vocal would still be going to your effect and your instrumental mix would have the effects of the vocals in it, which is not what you want. You could bypass the send, but if you had 10 tracks including background vocals, you'd be doing a lot of bypassing and muting. Here's the best way to turn off tracks when you're creating custom mixes like this one:

Highlight the entire Vocals track in the Edit window. Press ⌘/Ctrl+M. The region will become grayed out. Now this region is muted regardless of any sends. You won't hear it because it's disabled.

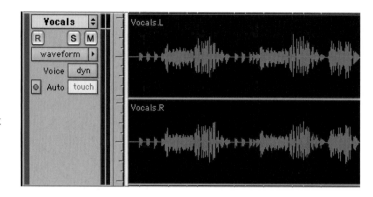

3] **Record the track.** Put the Inst. Mix track in Record at bar 1, and record this track to the end.

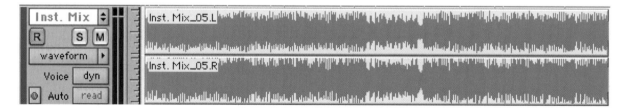

4] **Trim the end and fade.** Using the Trim tool in Slip mode, pull back the Inst. Mix region to where you feel the song should end. Then highlight a fade area starting around bar 99 and press ⌘/Ctrl+F.

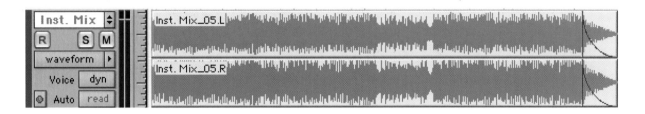

5] **Bounce to disk.** Solo the Inst. Mix and Bounce to Disk. Make sure to bounce into your My Mixes folder, and clearly name the file "UnderwaterInst."

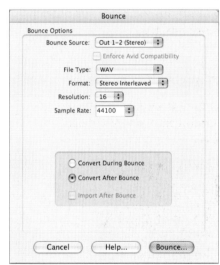

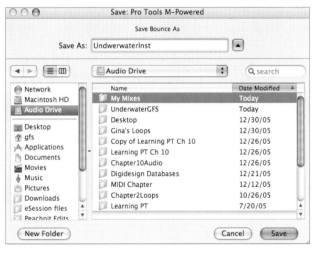

6] **Save.** For those who use Bounce to Disk, you're done with this exercise.

If you don't want to Bounce to Disk, do it this way:

7] **Duplicate the playlist and rename.** Duplicate the Inst. Mix playlist and name the duplicate "Inst. Mix Cons," meaning the consolidated version of the instrumental playlist. (I always try to make my track names suggest what is different about each track.)

8] **Consolidate.** Highlight Inst. Mix Cons, and press Option/Alt+Shift+3 to consolidate this file.

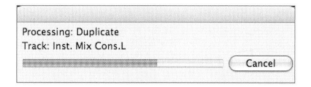

9] **Rename the region.** Use ⌘/Ctrl+Shift+R and name this region "UnderwaterInstMix."

10] **Export the region as a file.** In the Regions bin, make sure your Inst. Mix is highlighted. Use Export Regions as Files from the Regions menu of the Regions bin—or try the shortcut ⌘/Ctrl+Shift+K. The Export window keeps your previous settings, so you should be able to click Export and go.

11] Save.

Although Bounce to Disk does requires real-time playback, the process doesn't take as many steps as exporting. However, exporting gives you a cohesive 24-bit file that you can give to a mastering engineer.

Tip

If you forget to rename your bounced or exported mixes properly, you can always rename the files in your My Mixes folder. Be sure to do this while your memory is still fresh, otherwise you'll forget which mix is what.

EXERCISE 6:

Clear Unused Audio

We went through the process of clearing unused audio in previous chapters, but I want to remind you again. These are two shortcuts that should be etched into your brain: ⌘/Ctrl+Shift+U to select unused audio, and ⌘/Ctrl+Shift+B to delete it. You should always choose to delete rather than remove unless you're creating a stem session (as we will do later in this chapter).

This should be your rule: Clearing unused audio is the next-to-last thing you do at the end of a session, whether it's a recording session or a mix session. The last step, after deleting unused audio, is backing up your files.

1] **Select unused audio.** Using the shortcut ⌘/Ctrl+Shift+U, select unused audio. Any unused regions will be highlighted in the Regions bin.

Anything that's used in a playlist will not be deleted. Everything you see highlighted as unused will be outtakes and recordings that you recorded over or chose not to keep.

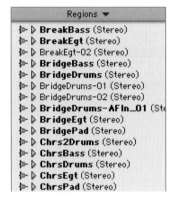

2] **Clear unused audio.** Use ⌘/Ctrl+Shift+B to open the Clear Regions window. Always choose to delete, unless you're creating a stem session.

Clicking on Remove leaves the files on your hard drive, which will cause your hard drive to become fragmented and ultimately give you errors because you've left a bunch of unused files all over it. Don't be paranoid that you're going to delete something you need. Simply get into the habit of duplicating playlists before you edit or change anything, and you'll never have to worry.

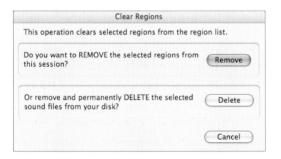

3] **Delete the files.** Click Delete. A window asks if you're sure you want to delete this file. If you hold down the Option/Alt key and click Yes, it will delete everything else without asking you to confirm each deletion.

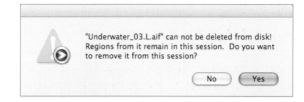

"Underwater_03.L.aif" can not be deleted from disk! Regions from it remain in this session. Do you want to remove it from this session?

No   Yes

4] Save.

5] Hide or minimize Pro Tools.

EXERCISE 7:
Back Up Your Session

There are two ways to back up files. The first and easiest is to spend $100, buy another external hard drive, and name it Back-Up Drive. Then, after working on any session, you do three things: (1) save; (2) delete unused audio; and (3) drag your entire session folder to your back-up drive.

The second way to back things up is by using your CD burning application. You should have a CD and DVD burner built into your computer. If your burner is just a CD burner, you should think about replacing it with a CD/DVD burner. I've seen these selling for as low as $30.

Why do you need a DVD burner? DVDs aren't strictly for movies, just as CDs aren't strictly for music. Think of CDs and DVDs as just little round hard drives that can hold your data. A standard CD holds 650 megabytes of data, but most sessions are much larger than this—which is why you need a DVD burner. DVDs hold 4.7 gigabytes.

"I have no idea what a megabyte or gigabyte is!"

You're not alone. I answer this question all the time. Although the words *megabyte* (MB or meg) and *gigabyte* (GB or gig) get casually tossed around quite a lot, not everyone really grasps what they mean.

Here's the secret: Think about megs and gigs as being like money. Megs are dollars, and gigs are thousand-dollar bills. That's all it is: 1 gigabyte = 1000 megabytes.

You've seen files that say 200K, or maybe you get email with pictures attached that take up 120 KB (which may be shortened to 120K). What is K? The K means kilobytes, and these are kinda like pennies. Or actually, tenths of a penny. 1000 kilobytes = 1 megabyte.

Pretty simple, huh? So here's a quiz. If you have a 200 gigabyte hard drive, how many megs is that? The answer is 200,000.

For technical reasons, there are two ways of counting the number of bytes in a file. For example, you might see an audio file that Windows describes this way: "Size: 3.71 MB (3,895,172 bytes)." Don't worry about this discrepancy—whether it's 3.71 or 3.89 megabytes doesn't really matter. This happens because 1 megabyte is actually equal to 1024 kilobytes, not 1000. Likewise, 1 gigabyte is actually 1024 megabytes. But as a rule of thumb, thinking of it as 1000 rather than 1024 is easy and close enough.

◆ For Mac users, to find out how large your session is, go to your Audio drive, find your UnderwaterGFS folder, click it once to highlight it (not twice to open it), and press ⌘+I. You can also choose Get Info from the File menu in the Finder. My UnderwaterGFS folder is 569.7 MB, so in this case I can back up this session to a standard CD.

◆ For Windows users, find your UnderwaterGFS folder on your Audio drive, right-click and choose Properties.

We used the CD-burning application in Chapter 11 to burn an audio CD. This time we're going to burn a data CD. This is just as easy.

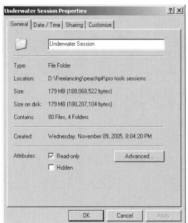

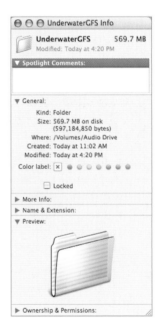

1] **Open Toast or Easy Media Creator.** Click the Data tab.

2] **Drag the session.** Open your Audio drive and drag the UnderwaterGFS Pro Tools session to the Data window of Toast or Easy Media Creator.

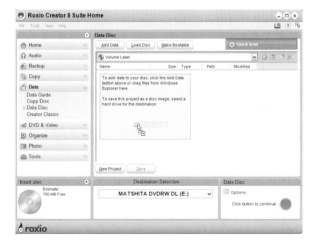

3] **Check the Data window.** Make sure you see your files in the Data window.

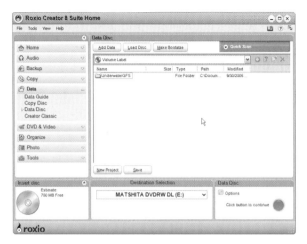

4] **Click the red button.** In both Toast and Easy Media Creator, you simply click the red button in the lower-right corner. On the Mac, you'll see this window: Now insert a CD or DVD to burn. Since this file is under 650 MB, we can use a CD.

In Windows, you'll see this window: Insert a CD or DVD, depending on the size of the folder you are backing up.

5] **Quit.** Quit your CD-burning application. You don't really need to save Toast or Easy Media Creator files, because you can easily drag your folder again to the window. I rarely ever save a Toast file. When I do, it's when I create a CD with many songs in a specific order and I don't want to have to drag these songs again. But for one folder or one song, I usually choose not to save.

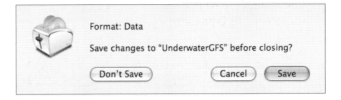

6] **Eject and label.** Eject the CD. Mac users can click the CD on the desktop and press ⌘+E. In Windows Explorer, right-click the CD and choose Eject.

Now label your CD "Underwater Back-Up" and add the date.

7] **Test the CD.** Insert the CD in the computer and make sure your data shows up.

Note

You can't run a Pro Tools session from a CD or DVD. When restoring from a back-up CD, you have to copy the files to your hard drive first.

EXERCISE 8:
Create a Folder for the Mixes

It's important to remember that you never, never want to move files out of the Audio Files folder of your session. But what if this song is going to be mastered, and I want to send a folder of my mixes to a mastering engineer? In that case, I need to create a folder for my 24-bit files. But if I create this folder on my Audio drive and drag the files out of my Audio Files folder into this new folder, it will remove the files from the Audio Files folder, which is not what I want.

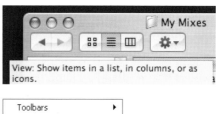

If I create this folder on my internal hard drive and drag the files to it, the computer will copy them and leave copies in the Audio Files folder because I'm copying to a different drive. But I don't want audio files on my internal drive. I want to use the Audio drive, because that's what it's for. Let me show you how to accomplish this without accidentally moving files out of your Audio Files folder.

I always view my files as lists, not as icons. When you view files as lists, you can choose what order you see them in. Alphabetical order is the default, but you can also view by date, which comes in very handy, as you will soon see. (In Windows Explorer, clicking on the column header causes the files to be sorted according to the information in that column.) So if you're in the habit of viewing files in icon view, get over it. You'll just spend much more time looking around the screen for the file you're trying to find.

Would you rather find a file in a window like this?

Or like this?

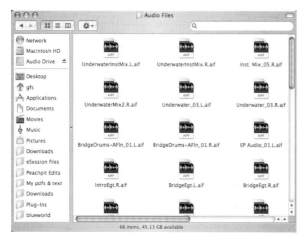

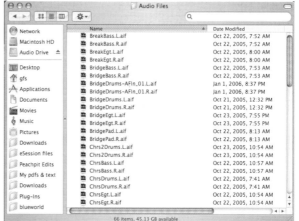

1] **Create three folders.** Let's organize everything into the My Mixes folder. Open My Mixes and create three new folders, using the File menu or the shortcut ⌘+Shift+N. Windows users can right-click inside the folder and choose New > Folder, or use the keystrokes Alt+F (to open the File menu), then W, then F.

Name the first folder "Underwater Mixes," the second folder "Underwater 16 Bit," and the third folder "Underwater 24 Bit."

2] **Highlight the 16-bit files.** Hold the Shift key and select all three of the 16-bit stereo mixes.

3] **Drag these files.** Drag these files to the Underwater 16-Bit folder and let go. Expand the 16-Bit folder.

4] **Drag the 16-Bit folder.** Now Drag the 16-Bit folder into the Underwater Mixes folder.

5] **Open another window.** On the Mac, hold the Command key and double-click your Audio drive. This leaves your My Mixes window open and opens up a separate, new one. (Windows users don't need to open another Explorer window, as you'll see shortly.)

Move the two windows side by side. Choose List View in the new window. Click the Date Modified column to organize the folders by date, putting the most recent files at the top of the window. In this new window, expand your UnderwaterGFS folder. Expand the Audio files folder. You'll see your 24-bit mixes inside this folder.

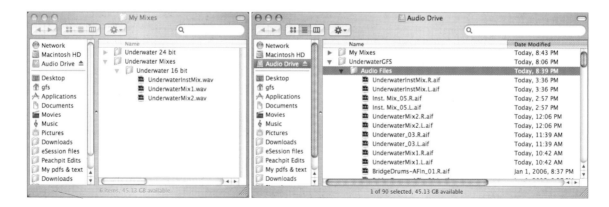

6] **Highlight the 24-bit mixes.** Because you renamed your 24-bit mixes after recording them into Pro Tools, you know which three files are the 24-bit mixes. See how important renaming is? Hold the ⌘/Ctrl key and click on the left and right sides of all three mixes.

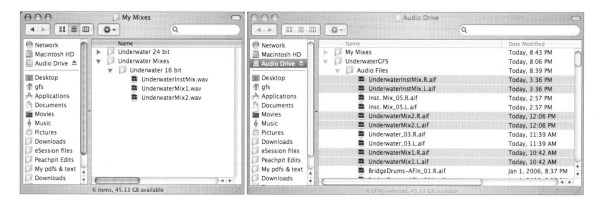

Note

You may notice that we're not using the Shift key to select multiple files in this exercise. This is because the Shift key only selects multiple files in a row. We need to skip some files between the mixes, so we need the ⌘/Ctrl key to do this.

7] **Mac users: Hold Option and drag.** Hold the Option key and drag the six 24-bit files from the right window into the Underwater 24-Bit folder of the left window. Your cursor turns green and shows a + symbol, and you see a ghost image of the files as you drag them. A window comes up showing that the files are being copied.

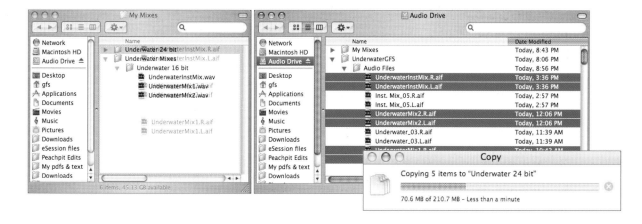

8] **Windows users: Right-click and copy.** In Windows, Alt-dragging won't work, because it will create a shortcut to the files, which is not what you want. After selecting the files, right-click any of them and choose Copy. Then navigate to the folder where you want to put them, right-click, and choose Paste.

9] **Move the 24 Bit folder.** Your 24-bit files should still be in your Audio Files folder, and you should now see them inside the 24 Bit folder in the My Mixes folder as well.

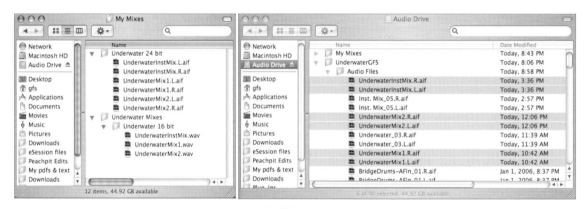

Move the 24 Bit folder into the Underwater Mixes folder. You should now have two folders inside the Underwater Mixes folder.

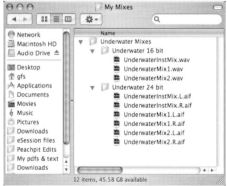

EXERCISE 9:
Create MP3 Files in Pro Tools

CD-quality stereo audio uses 10 megabytes of disk space per minute of music. So a 4-minute song occupies 40 megabytes. If you have a 30-gigabyte iPod, you'd have room for 750 songs of this length. The popular mp3 file format is a compressed audio format; it decreases the file size by an average of 90 percent. A 4-minute song will be around 4 megabytes when converted to an mp3 file. So using mp3 files rather than CD-quality audio means your 30 GB iPod can hold 7500 songs.

In the next exercises, we're going to learn two ways to create mp3 files: using Pro Tools and using iTunes.

To create mp3 files using Pro Tools, you have to install the mp3 conversion files required to make this work. These files are on your Pro Tools installation disc. Let's do this installation first and then see how simple it is to create mp3 files.

Unfortunately, the Pro Tools mp3 functionality does not come free with the software. Due to some licensing issues, in order to export mp3 files from Pro Tools you have to either use the 30-day demo or spend $19.95. I wish they would build this into the basic installation and the price of Pro Tools, because every other audio software application I've ever used incorporates mp3 functionality without added installation hassles or fees. But let's just grin and bear it.

1] **Insert the Pro Tools CD.** Quit Pro Tools. Insert your Pro Tools CD and double-click the icon that says Install Pro Tools.

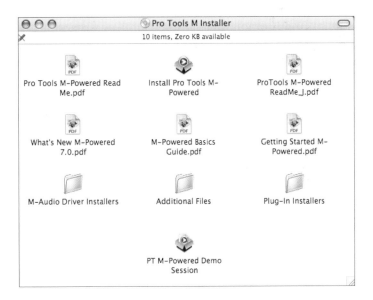

2] **Choose what to install.** When you get to this window: unselect Pro Tools and select either the Mp3 Codec Demo, which gives you 30 days of free use, or the Mp3 Codec Upgrade.

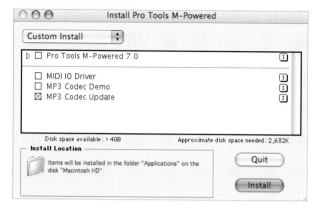

If you choose the upgrade, after installation you'll need to go to the DigiStore at www.digidesign.com, choose the mp3 option, and pay your $19.95. You'll be emailed a serial number.

3] **Open UnderwaterGFS.** Your computer will restart after installing the Mp3 Codec file. If it doesn't restart automatically, restart it manually. Then open UnderwaterGFS.

4] **Highlight a mix.** In the Regions bin, highlight the mix you want to convert to mp3.

5] **Use Export Regions as Files.** Start using the shortcut ⌘/Ctrl+Shift+K. You'll see the by-now-familiar Export Selected window. For File Type, choose MP3.

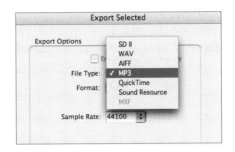

6] **Choose a destination.** In the Choose a Folder window, click Choose, and in the destination folder field, find your My Mixes folder. Once you're inside the My Mixes Folder, don't click Choose yet. Click New Folder in the bottom-left corner and create a new folder called "Underwater Mp3s." Click Create. This will put you inside the new folder. Now press Choose.

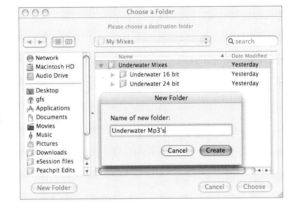

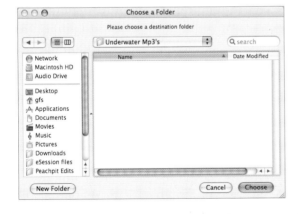

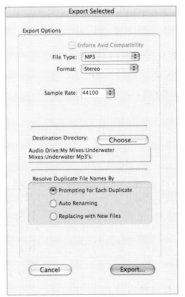

7] **Authorize.** Those of you who chose the Mp3 Codec Update will be asked to authorize. Click Authorize and enter your serial number.

8] **Choose the mp3 format.** After selecting the mp3 format in the Export Selected window, you'll see a new window with lots of fields, the MP3 window.

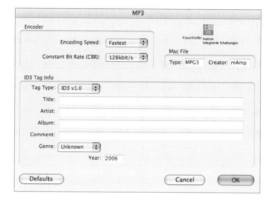

9] **Learn about encoders and bit rates.** The MP3 window may appear intimidating. It's not. Let's work our way through it.

At the top, in the Encoder section, you'll see Encoding Speed. Encoding simply means converting. Pro Tools wants to know, "Do you want to convert this file quickly or slowly?" I don't hear much of a difference, and it doesn't affect the size of the file. So if you're in a hurry, use Fastest. If you're patient, use the slower Higher Quality setting.

The second Encoder choice is Bit Rate. Don't worry about the technicalities here; just understand that the higher this number, the higher the audio quality. But as always, the higher the quality, the larger the file. Most people's email servers won't accept large files, so if you're planning to send the file via email, smaller is better. I try never to send anyone a file over 5 MB, because most the time it bounces back to me. I usually create two versions of my mp3 files—one larger for my iPod, and one smaller for emailing. As a rule, you don't want to go below 128 kbit/second). I use 160 kb/s as a good average. Let's use that for now.

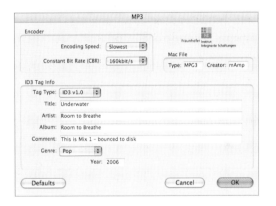

10] **Add the ID3 Tag Info.** I'm sure you've seen in iTunes or some other mp3 player that most mp3 files show the artist's name, the album title, the song title, tempo, genre, and so on. In technical terms, this is called mp3 metadata. In the MP3 window, I always fill out my ID3 Tag Info fields. For Tag Type, use Version 1; it's the most widely used. Complete this form and click OK.

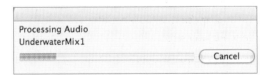

11] **Processing.** Wait while the file is processed and placed in your My Mixes folder in your new Underwater Mp3 file folder.

12] **Change the bit rate.** Let's convert the same mix at a different bit rate so that we can compare file size and sound quality. Press ⌘/Ctrl+Shift+K again and click Export. In the MP3 window, make your Bit Rate 128 kb/s. Don't change anything else, not even the title.

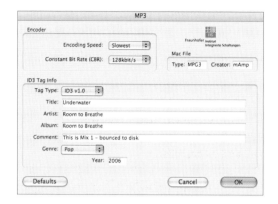

13] **Rename.** Pro Tools will ask you to rename the file. Mp3s take their name from the file you highlighted in the Regions bin, so when you convert the file again, Pro Tools will see that you have a duplicate filename and prompt you for a new one. When I make a smaller mp3 file, I always put the bit rate in the name. Click Save, and the file will be processed.

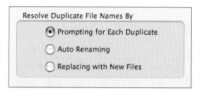

14] **Save.**

15] Hide or minimize Pro Tools.

16] **Open the My Mixes folder.** Inside this folder should be three folders, one each for mp3s, 16-bit mixes, and 24-bit mixes.

EXERCISE 10:
Create CDs and MP3 Files with iTunes

Apple iTunes is a very popular application for burning CDs and creating mp3 files. Let's learn how to use it to burn CDs and convert Pro Tools audio to mp3 files. iTunes comes installed on all Macs, and it's available for free to Windows users. If you don't have it, use Google and type in exactly what you're looking for. The first link is what you need.

1]

Open iTunes. After installing iTunes, open it, go to the iTunes menu (Mac) or the Edit menu (Windows), and choose Preferences.

2]

Display the Advanced Preferences. Click the Advanced tab.

Under the General tab of this window, notice the checked box that says, "Copy files to iTunes Music folder when adding to library." This means everything you drag into iTunes will be copied. This setup can be good or bad—good because it creates a back-up of your mixes, but bad because it can fill up your hard drive pretty fast if you use it a lot to convert files.

3] **Click the Importing tab.** This is where you choose what kind of file you want to create in iTunes. For Import Using, choose MP3 Encoder. For Setting, choose High Quality. Click OK.

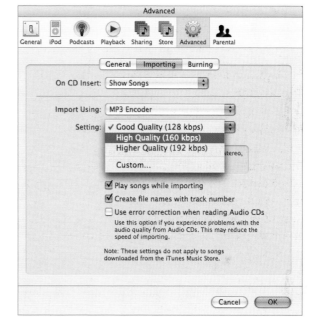

Tip

If you want to create smaller mp3 files, you'll need to come back to the iTunes Preferences Advanced/Importing tab and choose Good Quality. If you want to use the highest mp3 file settings in iTunes, choose Higher Quality. The Pro Tools mp3 converter has many more options than these three.

4] **Create a playlist.** In the bottom-left corner of the iTunes main window, you'll see a + button. Click this to create a new playlist. Name this playlist "Underwater Mixes."

5] **Drag files to the playlist.** Open your My Mixes folder and set it side-by-side with iTunes.

Expand the Underwater 16-Bit folder and drag Mix 1 into the iTunes window.

6] **Use Get Info.** You'll see the mix inside your iTunes playlist. Click it; then go to the iTunes File menu and choose Get Info.

Click the Info tab, choose the settings that I have in my window, and then click OK. I've renamed the song UnderwaterMixIT, so that we'll know this version came from iTunes.

7] **Change the View options.** You may notice that you some of your columns are not showing up. Go to the Edit menu and choose View Options. Here are the views that I use:

8] **Burn a CD.** In the top-right corner of iTunes is the Burn Disk button. Click that button, insert your CD, and off you go. That was easy.

9] **Convert to mp3.** Highlight the mix in the iTunes window, go to the Advanced menu, and choose Convert Selection to MP3. The file will begin playing and will convert at the same time.

10] **Where is the file now?** You'll eventually hear a sound that says you're finished. But where is the file? iTunes has put this converted file into your main iTunes library, so click Library to see all the songs in iTunes. (I have quite a lot of them.) The columns at the top organize the order in which you see songs. If you clickon the Name column, it will organize the list in alphabetical order by song title. Click Artist, and the list will show the artists in alphabetical order. Assuming you've added the information I showed in step 6, you'll be able to scroll down to the R's and find Room to Breathe.

Name		Time	Artist	▲	Album		Genre	Year	Bit Rate	BPM
☑ All I Really Want	○	4:44	Alanis Morissette	○	Jagged Little Pill	○	Rock	1995	192 kbps	
☑ You Oughta Know	○	4:09	Alanis Morissette	○	Jagged Little Pill	○	Rock	1995	192 kbps	
☑ Perfect	○	3:07	Alanis Morissette	○	Jagged Little Pill	○	Rock	1995	192 kbps	
☑ Hand In My Pocket	○	3:41	Alanis Morissette	○	Jagged Little Pill	○	Rock	1995	192 kbps	
☑ Right Through You	○	2:55	Alanis Morissette	○	Jagged Little Pill	○	Rock	1995	192 kbps	
☑ Forgiven	○	5:00	Alanis Morissette	○	Jagged Little Pill	○	Rock	1995	192 kbps	
☑ You Learn	○	3:59	Alanis Morissette	○	Jagged Little Pill	○	Rock	1995	192 kbps	

11] **Highlight the mp3 file.** If you set your view in step 7 to show Bit Rate and Comments, you can easily tell the difference between the 16-bit mix and the mp3 file. The 16-bit mix is at 1411 kbps, and the mp3 is at 160 kbps. Highlight the mp3 file of "Underwater."

☑ NoRulesNew	○	4:56	Room to Breathe	○	Room to Breathe	○	Pop	2005	125 kbps (...		
☑ PlugMeIn	○	3:50	Room To Breathe	○	Room to Breathe	○	Pop	2005	192 kbps	95	
☑ SayAPrayer	○	4:09	Room To Breathe	○	Room to Breathe	○	Pop	2005	160 kbps	86	
☑ TakeARide	○	3:32	Room to Breathe	○	Room to Breathe	○	Pop	2005	192 kbps		
☑ UnderwaterMix1	○	4:34	Room To Breathe	○	Room to Breathe	○	Pop	2006	1411 kbps	90	This the first mix using Bounce to Disk
☑ UnderwaterMix1	○	4:34	Room To Breathe	○	Room to Breathe	○	Pop	2006	160 kbps	90	This the first mix using Bounce to Disk

12] **Drag to the Underwater playlist.** Drag the mp3 file to the Underwater playlist and let go. You'll see the familiar green +.

13] **Open the Underwater playlist.** Click the Underwater playlist. You should see both versions now.

	Name		Time	Artist		Album		Genre	Year	Bit Rate	BPM	Comment
1	☑ UnderwaterMix1	⊙	4:34	Room To Breathe	⊙	Room to Breathe	⊙	Pop	2006	1411 kbps	90	This the first mix using Bounce to Disk
2	☑ UnderwaterMix1	⊙	4:34	Room To Breathe	⊙	Room to Breathe	⊙	Pop	2006	160 kbps	90	This the first mix using Bounce to Disk

14] **Drag the mp3 to My Mixes.** Open your My Mixes folder and expand the Underwater Mp3s folder. Move this folder next to the iTunes window. Click the mp3 version to highlight it, and drag it to the mp3 folder of My Mixes.

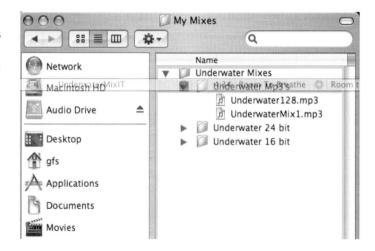

15] **Quit iTunes.** You don't have to save your setup in iTunes. It automatically does that for you. For quitting, you can use the shortcut ⌘+Q (Mac) or Alt+F and then X (Windows).

16] **Open My Mixes.** You should now have three mp3 files in your Underwater Mp3s folder. Two we created in Pro Tools, and one we created in iTunes.

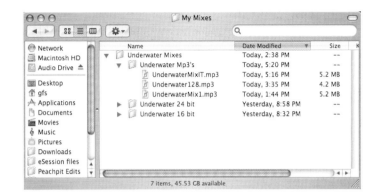

17] **Where are the iTunes files?** On a Mac, you can find your iTunes files here: HardDrive > Users > User Name > Music > iTunes > iTunes Music. In Windows, they'll be in My Documents > My Music > iTunes > iTunes Music.

Within this folder will be folders named for the artist or band. If you don't name something, it goes into a folder in the same location called Unknown Artist.

So now you can listen to these mp3s, compare them, and see if you can hear the difference. Then choose whichever mp3 method works best for you.

EXERCISE 11:
Create a Stem Session

In Chapter 9, I explained stems and why we use them. Now let's learn how to create them. Imagine that you need to prepare this mix to send to two other musicians so they can add tracks. Musician A is in Paris and uses Apple Logic; Musician B is in New York and uses Pro Tools LE. So what do you do?

You could take the easy way out and send them one of your 24-bit mixes, or even, as a last resort, an mp3 file. Only slightly more difficult would be to send an instrumental mix with an a cappella vocal. But think about it. Suppose Musician A, who uses Logic, is a cellist. Your track will be so much better if this musician can solo the keyboards to hear the chord changes, or mute the guitars to better hear their pitch. Ideally, you'd like to create a session that allows this. To do this, you need to create stems. While you're at it, you should probably separate the bass and drums because the cellist may need to solo the bass. You may also want to keep the guitars separate.

You're probably wondering, "Can I send this session to Musician B, who uses Pro Tools?" The answer is yes technically, but no musically. Musician B can open your session and hear the plain audio files, but unless they have whatever virtual instruments and plug-ins you have in your system, they won't hear any of the MIDI sounds or effects you've been using. So you'll have to make sure to print any of those sounds as audio files, as well as all of your automation moves. Here's how to do it:

1] **Open UnderwaterGFS.**

2] **Save As.** Save in the same folder as your UnderwaterGFS session, and name this session "UnderwaterStem."

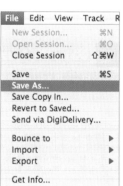

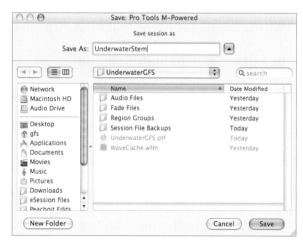

3] **Create a new track.** Create a new stereo audio track and name it "UWBassStem" or something similar.

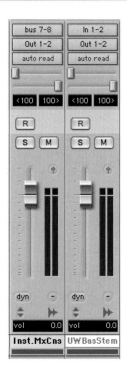

4] **Create a new playlist.** On the Instrumental Mix track, make a new playlist and name it "UWDrumStem."

5] **Set the inputs.** On the drum stem track, make the input bus 9–10. Make the input of the bass stem bus 11–12.

6] **Change the outputs.** Change the output of the main drum track to bus 9–10. Change the output of the main bass track to bus 11–12. Solo these two tracks. We're sending each track to a new track, and we're going to record them.

But wait: The bass has some reverb in the bridge. Set the reverb channel's output to bus 11–12 as well, so it will be recorded with the bass.

7] **Put the stem tracks in Record.** Put the stems in Record, and solo them as well.

8] **Record from bar 1.** Click bar 1 in Grid mode and record the drum and bass tracks. Press stop when the song ends. Your session should now look like this:

Tip

I never give musicians tracks with fade-outs. I like the musician to have the entire song to play to. Sometimes the coolest parts they play are in the fade of the song. If that happens, I can copy what they played during the fade and paste it somewhere else in the song where it can actually be heard. It's always better to give someone too much to work with than too little.

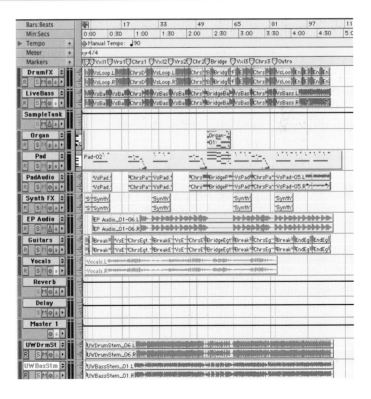

9] **Delete the original tracks.** Highlight the bass and drum tracks, not the new stems. Make sure these two tracks are the only tracks highlighted.

Go to the Track menu and choose Delete. A small window will come up telling you that you have active regions on this track. Click Delete.

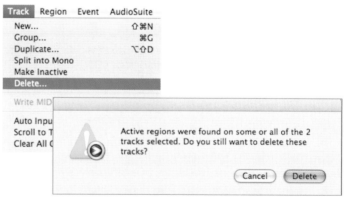

Since we have an uneffected Drum playlist, another window pops up and says, "Hey, there are playlists in here, too—are you sure you know what you're doing?" Click Yes. These two tracks will disappear. No worries: We're not going to lose anything.

10] **Create two new tracks.** Create two new stereo tracks. Name the first one "Pad Stem" and the second one "Guitar Stem." Set the input of the Pad Stem to bus 9–10, and make the input of the Guitar Stem bus 11–12. Unsolo any other tracks and take any other tracks out of Record. Now solo the new tracks and put these new stem tracks in Record.

11] **Set the pad track output.** Now we need to record the pad into the Pad Stem track, so we need the output of all pad tracks to go to bus 9–10, which is the input of the Pad Stem track. (I hope this is starting to make sense.) Solo SampleTank, solo the Pad MIDI track, and solo the PadAudio track. Set the output of the SampleTank track and the PadAudio track to bus 9–10. Remember, MIDI is not audio but computer information, so leave the MIDI track alone.

Technically, you don't have to solo the SampleTank track because it's in solo-safe mode, but I do it anyway as a visual guide. Then I can easily see what tracks I've created stems of.

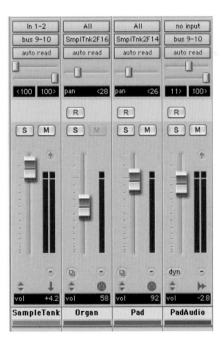

12] **Set the guitar track output.** Solo the guitar and send this track out of bus 11–12.

13] **Record the stems.** Click at bar 1 in Grid mode, record these files to the end, and stop.

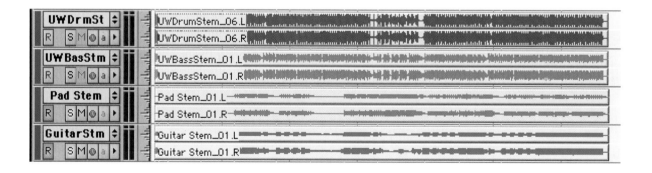

14] **Highlight and delete three tracks.** Highlight the pad MIDI, pad audio, and guitar tracks. Delete the tracks by going to the Track menu and choosing Delete.

We're not deleting the SampleTank track because we still need it for our organ sound.

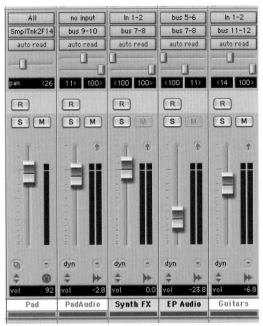

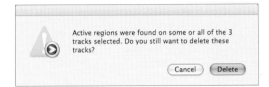

Active regions were found on some or all of the 3 tracks selected. Do you still want to delete these tracks?

Cancel   Delete

"But isn't there an easier way to create a stem session?"

Question: Why can't I consolidate my audio tracks from bar 1 and use those same tracks in my stem session?

Answer: You can, but any plug-in effects or automation won't be recorded in the consolidated audio files. Also, these tracks won't be recorded at the level at which you mixed them, so when another musician imports the files into their DAW, all the levels will be wrong.

Question: Can I record all my stems at once, using many busses?

Answer: Yes. I find that it's best to record stems in pairs and listen as things are recorded to make sure that the person who will be receiving the files will get them without errors. It's very easy to make careless mistakes and record the wrong things on tracks if you're not paying close attention.

15 **Create two more tracks.** Name the first track "Key&FXStem" and the second track "EPStem." Set the input of the Key&FXStem track to bus 9–10, and the EPStem track to input bus 11–12. Solo both tracks and put them in Record. Unsolo any other tracks.

16 **Set the Key&FXStem outputs.** Solo the SampleTank track, the Organ MIDI track, and the Synth FX track. Set the output of the Synth FX track to bus 9–10.

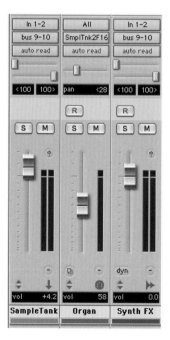

17 **Set the EPStem output.** Solo the EP Audio track and set the output to bus 11–12. We also want to record the EP with reverb and delay, right? So set the output of the Reverb and Delay channels to bus 11–12, as well, so that these effects are recorded with the EP sound.

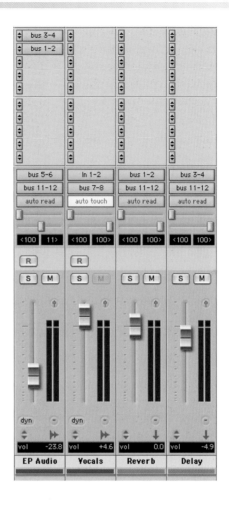

18 **Record these last stems.** Click at bar 1 in Grid mode, and record these last stem tracks. You should now have six stem tracks.

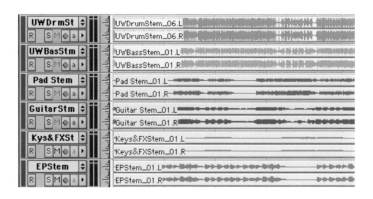

19] **Delete more tracks.** Highlight all tracks but the stem tracks and choose Delete in the Track menu. Click Yes when it asks if you want to delete playlists as well.

I know, I know, we forgot the vocal. I'm forgetting and deleting the vocal on purpose so I can teach you how to import a track from another session. Act like you don't know this and are making a mistake, which will inevitably happen sometimes.

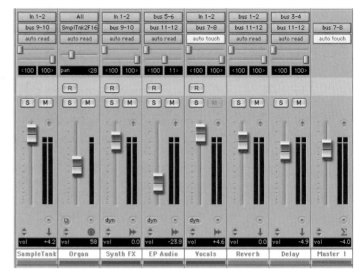

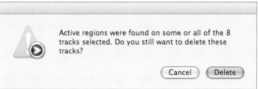

Active regions were found on some or all of the 8 tracks selected. Do you still want to delete these tracks?

Cancel   Delete

20] **Delete the hidden tracks.** You'll see in the Tracks List that we have some hidden tracks. Hold the Control key and click (Mac) or Ctrl+right-click (Windows) the All option under Edit Groups. This will make all of the hidden tracks reappear.

21] **Delete the MIDI tracks.** Highlight the four MIDI tracks, but not the click track. Again, choose Tracks > Delete.

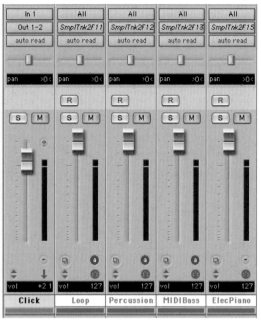

22] **Delete unused playlists.** You're nearly done. The next step in creating a stem session is to delete any unused playlists, so that the session contains only tracks and audio files that you're using. On the drum stem track, in the Edit window, go to the playlist menu and choose Delete Unused. The window showing all the unused playlists appears. Highlight all of them and click Delete.

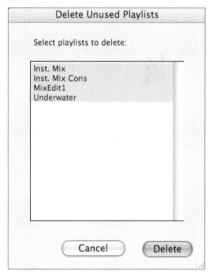

23] **Remove, don't delete!** Now here's the tricky part—pay very close attention. Use your newly memorized shortcut ⌘/Ctrl+Shift+U to select unused audio files and ⌘/Ctrl+Shift+B to clear them. But you *won't* be pressing Delete this time in the Clear Regions window. Instead, you'll use Remove. Why? Because the audio files in the Regions bin in this stem session are also used in the main UnderwaterGFS session. If you delete them, you'll be deleting audio that you still need. When creating stem sessions, *always* choose Remove to clear unused audio, *not* Delete.

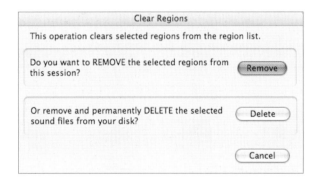

Now look at your Regions bin. If you correctly followed the steps of this exercise, you should have only six stereo files.

24] **Save Copy In.** The very last step in creating a stem is to use File > Save Copy In, *not* File > Save As. This command allows you to save the file in other formats and convert to another sample rate or bit depth.

The most important check box in the whole window is All Audio Files in the Items To Copy section at the bottom-left. *Make sure* this box is checked. Click your Audio drive, and name this session "UnderwaterStemNew."

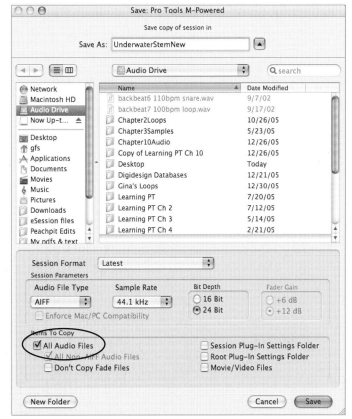

A separate stem session with its own set of audio files is now created on your hard drive.

25] Save and close this session.

Gina's Nine Steps to Stem Sessions

1. Use File > Save As in your original session.

2. Record all tracks into stem tracks, making sure to include any send effects.

3. Delete the original tracks after recording into stems.

4. Delete any extra effects tracks.

5. Delete any hidden tracks.

6. Delete any unused playlists.

7. Select unused audio.

8. Remove, *do not delete,* the unused audio.

9. Select File > Save Copy In and be sure to check All Audio Files.

Printing a Click Track to Audio

Most software programs have their own click generators. But occasionally, a musician will ask for a printed click track as well. Here's a quick and easy way to print a click track to an audio track:

1. Create a mono audio track and name it "Click A" (*A* for *audio*).

2. Insert a click plug-in and choose your click sound.

3. Put the track in Record, and record from bar 1.

EXERCISE 12:

Import Tracks from a Pro Tools Session

Oops, we forgot the Vocals track. Do we have to go back to the original session? No. We can import a track into Pro Tools from one session to another session.

1]

Open the new stem session.
Open UnderwaterStemNew. If it asks you about saving a report regarding disk allocation, choose No.

The original disk allocation for this session cannot be used. Check the disk allocation window to see what's changed.

Would you like to save a detailed report?

No   Yes

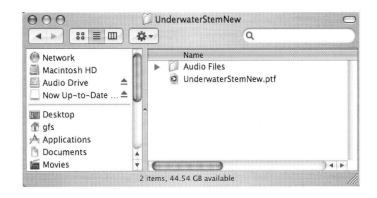

2]

Choose Import > Session Data. Go the File menu and choose Import > Session Data.

3] **Choose the session to import from.** Pro Tools wants to know which session to import tracks from. Find the UnderwaterGFS session and select it.

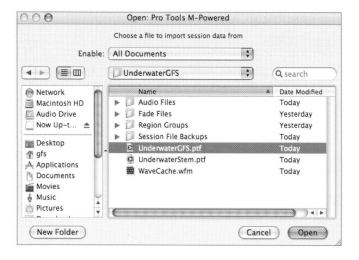

4] **Choose to copy the vocals.** You will now see the Import Session Data window. Don't let this sizable window scare you. At the bottom of the window, you'll see all the tracks in UnderwaterGFS. Scroll down and find the Vocals track. In the Destination column, where it now says "(none)," set it to New Track.

If you want to import more tracks, you can do the exact same thing. In the Audio Media Options field, choose to copy from source media. This meansthat we're not borrowing the audio file from the UnderwaterGFS session but rather making copies for this session.

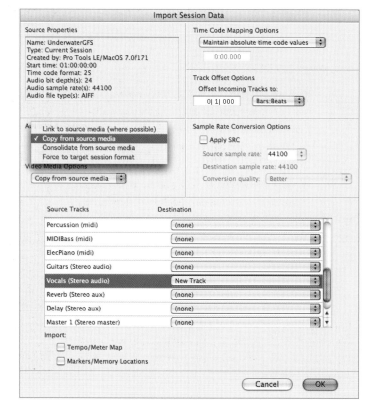

5] **Unmute the vocal.** The Vocals track now imports, but why is the track grayed out? Remember that this region was muted so that we could create an instrumental mix. We now need to unmute the region, so click this region with the Grabber and press ⌘/Ctrl+M.

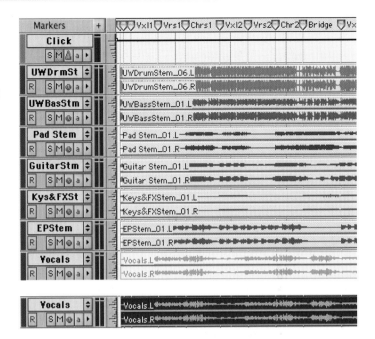

6] **Create a vocal stem.** This track has volume and plug-in automation, including an automated EQ radio voice effect. Let's record our last stem and then we'll never have to hear this song again.

Create a new stereo track and name it "Vocal Stem." Since the Vocals track is already going to bus 7–8, let's make the new Vocal Stem track's input bus 7–8. You don't have to, but I like to solo what I'm recording.

Tip

You can save significant disk space and upload time by creating stems in mono. I personally would rather give the musicians better mixes, even at the cost of longer download times.

7] Record the stem vox.

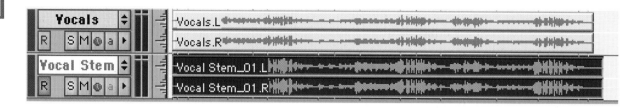

8] **Delete the Vocals track.** Highlight the original Vocals track and delete it.

9] **Clear unused audio.** Use ⌘/Ctrl+Shift+U to Select Unused Audio and then ⌘/Ctrl+Shift+B to clear it.

So do we delete or do we remove? The answer is Delete. I'm intentionally throwing you a curve ball here so that you'll start making the right decisions when you work on your own. When we imported this vocal track from the UnderwaterGFS session, we chose a setting that made a copy of the audio and imported it into our new session. We no longer need the file that we copied. Since it's a copy, we know the original is still there, so choose Delete in this case.

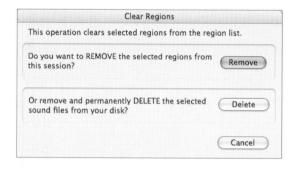

10] **Rename the Drum file.** Remember that we're going to use these same files to send to two hypothetical musicians. Musician A uses Logic, as you'll recall from the beginning of Exercise 11, which means you want to name the audio files clearly so Musician A will know what's what. And we don't really need the numbers after the names. I'm going to start each audio file name with "UW" so that we'll know these files come from Underwater in case we ever lose track of them.

Starting at the Drum track in the Edit window, use the Grabber and the shortcut ⌘/Ctrl+Shift+R to rename. Name this track "UWDrumStem."

11] **Rename all files.** Using the same ⌘/Ctrl+Shift+R shortcut, rename each file with "UW" in the name. When you're done, your tracks should look like this in the Edit window: Your Regions bin should look like this:

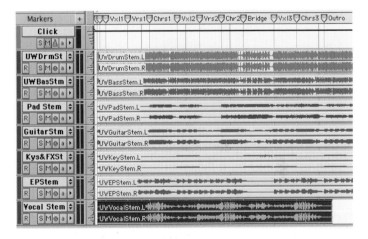

12] **Save and quit.**

We're officially done with this song in Pro Tools. If you play back the stem session, you'll hear that all tracks have been recorded with the right effects and the right levels. When anyone hears this session, regardless of what plug-ins they have, it will sound exactly like our session.

And now you have what you need to send to both musicians. Musician A, the Logic user, will need just the Audio Files folder, not the whole session. You'll need to let this musician know what tempo, key, and sample rate and bit resolution you used. Musician B will receive the whole stem session, and regardless of what Pro Tools system he or she has, the song will sound perfect.

The Logic user simply needs to create a new Logic song, set the tempo to 90 BPM, and import your audio files, placing them all at bar 1 of his/her song. That's it.

If you flip back to Appendix B, at the end of this book, you'll find some specific suggestions of ways to collaborate with other musicians in distant locations using the Internet.

Compressing Your Session Folder

You've learned a lot in this book about compression, but the term can still be confusing because it can mean several different things. In our mix, we used the Waves Musicians II plug-ins to compress the levels of the audio signal. This is using audio compression. When we created mp3s, we used the Mp3 Codec to perform audio-based data compression. Now we want to create a zip file of our session folder. Zip files use data compression, which is completely unrelated to audio compression. Compressing and later uncompressing the data in an audio file by zipping it or using another method such as Stuffit will have no effect on the sound, unlike mp3 compression.

The benefit of compressing files is that it makes them smaller for sending. It also creates one cohesive file, which is easier to deal with than sending many different files. Another benefit is for file protection. A lot can happen to a file traveling across the Internet. Files occasionally get corrupted in transit. Compressing files can help protect them from corruption as well.

Mac users will probably have seen .sit and .sitx files. These files are made using the standard Mac compression utility, Stuffit. For many years I compressed my files into .sit files, but I kept running into PC users who couldn't open them. I find that if I use Stuffit to create .zip files rather than .sit files, then everyone, whether they're using a Mac or Windows, can open them.

While working your way through the exercises in this book, you've encountered many .zip files, so you should know how to uncompress them. Now let's see how easy it is to create them. Mac users can use Stuffit Standard Edition, which costs $49.95. You can find this at Stuffit.com. Windows users can use either WinZip, which is $29.95 at WinZip.com, or Stuffit Standard at $24.95. Demo versions of both are available at the respective Web sites for you to try.

There are other compression utilities, but trust me—use Stuffit and WinZip; they're the standards for a reason. If you'll be sending files to other people, compressing your files with a commonly used utility is a must.

Download and install the application of your choice, and let's get started. If you buy the software, you'll be emailed a password or registration code. Simply copy that number from your email and paste it when you're prompted for it.

Mac Users

While installing, click Yes when Stuffit asks to be added to the Dock. Click DropStuff in your Dock after installation, and click the Zip tab. Now you've told DropStuff that any file or folder that you drag and drop to this application will become a zip file.

The rest is easy: Just drag your UnderwaterStemNew session to the DropStuff icon in the Dock. After the compression process is finished, look on your hard drive and you'll see your zip file. You'll see that it is a 500 MB file. So how big was our session? Click the UnderwaterGFS folder and get info with ⌘+I. You'll see that the session is around 620 MB. So zipping the file saved 120 MB of download time. Not bad.

Create a folder on your Audio drive and name it "Zipped Files." Drag UnderwaterStemNew.Zip into this folder.

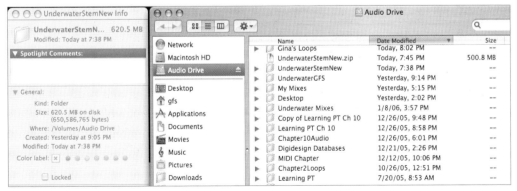

Windows Users

After installing, right-click the UnderwaterGFS session folder and choose WinZip > Add to Zip.

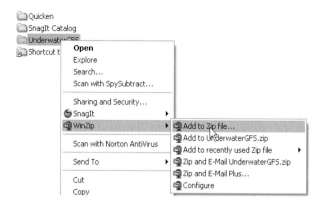

A window opens, and you can choose another location for the zipped file if you wish. Leave the settings as they are for now, and click the Add button.

The default settings place the zipped file in the same directory as the session folder.

You can compare sizes by right-clicking the zip file and then the UnderwaterGFS session and choosing Properties.

On your Audio drive, create a new folder and name it "Zipped Files." Drag your UnderwaterGFS.Zip file into this new folder.

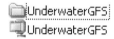
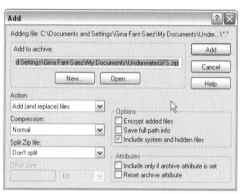

All Together Now...

We're going to compress one more file: the Audio File folder of the UnderwaterStemNew session. Open the UnderwaterStemNew folder. Mac users, if you installed what's called the Magic Menu with Stuffit, press ⌘+S in the Finder. Or you can drag the Audio Files folder to your DropStuff application. Windows users, right-click and choose WinZip or Stuffit.

When the folder compression is done, move it into your new Zipped Files folder. You should now see both zip files.

Your Zipped Files folder now contains exactly what you need to send to Musicians A and B. You have a zipped Audio Files folder that contains all the stem files for Musician A to import into Logic, and you have a zipped Pro Tools stem session for Musician B.

Let's rename AudioFiles.zip and call it "Underwater90BPM." Now Musician A knows the title and the tempo. And if you see this file six months from now, you'll know what it is.

A Little Spring Cleaning

If you've been following along, you now know where all your files are—your mp3 files, your 24-bit mixes, your 16-bit CD quality files, and your zips.

Let's create one more folder, since our hard drive is getting a little messy from all the files we've created while working through this book. Create a new folder on the Audio drive and call it "PT Book Files." Now highlight every folder on your drive that you've created with this book's exercises. Remember to use the ⌘/Ctrl key to select multiple files that aren't in a row. Now drag one of the files into the new PT Book File folder. They'll all follow along.

Ahh, now your hard drive is neat and organized. You have a clean slate ready for you to take everything you've learned and create your own music.

Congratulations...

You have now completed *Pro Tools for Musicians and Songwriters*. I hope this book enables all of you to sit down and be the creative musical geniuses you are without being overwhelmed by the process of using your computer and Pro Tools to record. I hope you have your shortcuts memorized and know where you're saving your songs. I hope I have instilled good habits for naming your tracks, duplicating your playlists, deleting your unused audio files, and so forth.

I encourage all of you to stay in touch with me at protoolsformusicians.com in my blog area. Feel free to post any questions you may have, or let me know if you're confused about some aspect of using Pro Tools. I'll be checking this website frequently, and I'm available to help any of you whenever I can.

I sincerely appreciate the time you put into reading this book and doing the exercises. I wish all of you the greatest success with your music.

Thank you all for your time and attention.

—Gina Fant-Saez

HELP YOURSELF

As you learn Pro Tools, it's important to have a variety of resources that you can tap into when you have problems or questions. In this appendix, I'll give you a list of Web sites and online resources that I use when I have problems. We'll also take a look at ways to make backup copies of important files.

Google It First!

I find Google.com to be the best resource for anything I'm looking to do. I've mentioned using Google throughout this book. If I get an error code or forget how to do something, I type into Google exactly what I'm looking for. The key to using Google successfully is to type in as much information as you have. For example, let's say I want to learn how to export an mp3 file from Pro Tools. If I type just "mp3 file" into the Google search field, I'll have to wade through thousands of pages. But if I type "exporting mp3 files from Pro Tools" I'll get exactly what I'm looking for.

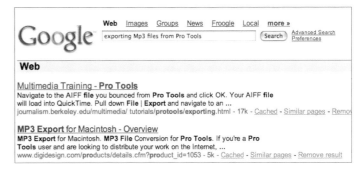

The Pro Tools Help Menu

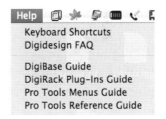

The secret to efficient use of the Pro Tools Help menu is to open the Reference Guide and then use the search feature of Acrobat or Preview. If I'm looking for help on quantizing, I type "quantize" into the Search field to find pages that have the word "quantize" in them.

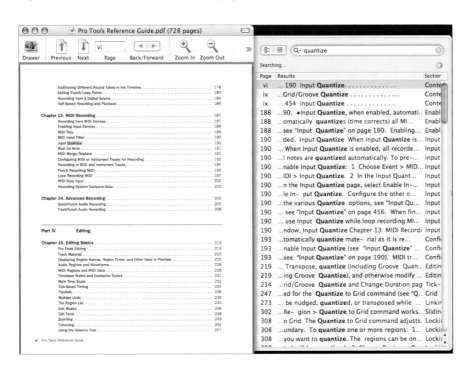

The Digidesign Website Support Options

Digidesign's Web site has an excellent support section. There are three routes to take when you need technical help from Digidesign:

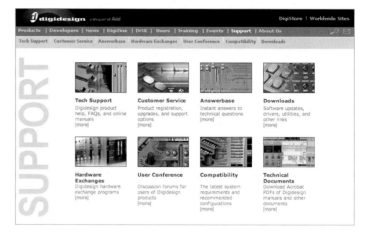

1] If your gear and software are still under warranty, you can call Tech Support (650-731-6100). I find Digidesign's Tech Support to be among the best; they can usually resolve any issue I'm having.

2] You can search the Answerbase. The Answerbase is a technical database of all known technical problems. You can type in your error code or a description of the technical issue you're having, and read possible solutions. For example, if I have an error 9128, I type "9128" into the Answerbase search field and choose my operating system. This gives me a list of results where I can look for the answer to my problem.

3] You can create an account and use the Digidesign User Conference (DUC). I'm a huge fan of the DUC. Not only does Digidesign's tech support staff monitor it frequently and answer questions, but many times the best and fastest technical support answers are posted there from users who have had the same problems and know how to fix them. Each version of Pro Tools has its own forum section at the DUC. I can post a question and, sometimes as little as five minutes later, have the answer. Again, the key is using Search. I type in "9128" or whatever error I'm having, choose the date range of postings that I want answers from, choose which forum(s) I want to search, and then click Submit. I then get a list of posts that apply to whatever I searched for, and I can start reading about how other people solved the same problem.

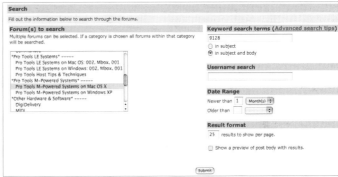

Tip

Unlike Google, where you get better results if you enter more information, both the Digidesign User Conference and the Answerbase tend to give you better search results when you type in less information.

Online Digital Audio Forums

I spend a fair amount of time reading, searching, responding to, and posting questions on digital audio forums. They can become quite addicting as you learn Pro Tools, and you can learn a lot from them. Here are a few of my favorites.

The DAW-Mac List

One of the first and best digital audio forums is a group called the DAW-Mac Group, found at Yahoo.com. This group covers not just Pro Tools but most other Mac audio software as well. There are daily discussions about everything from hard drives, back-up software, and networking to tips and tricks. I learn something from this group every day. I've been a member for almost seven years now, and I've come to refer to the other members as my gurus. In all honesty, many of them can run circles around me technologically. So much of what I know is from this small, generous group of people. Thank you Arthur, Lou, Hiro, Rich, Rail, Ray, Ian, Paul, Mike, Nick, Bob, Monte, and all the rest.

You'll find them at http://groups.yahoo.com/group/daw-mac.

Gearslutz.com

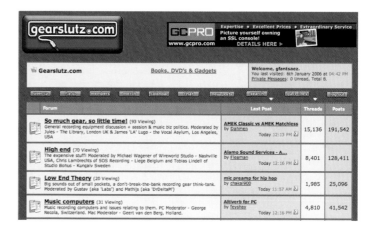

Another great resource is the forums of Gearslutz.com. One of my heroes, Eva Manley, moderates a forum there. Very frequently they have high-end guest moderators such as George Massenburg, Ed Cherney, or Elliot Scheiner.

Some fairly hot-headed discussions occur here, which is not my thing. I'm passionate about my Mac and Pro Tools, but I'm not going to get into a heated discussion defending any of my views, or insult someone who doesn't use the same gear I do. You'll find a lot of knowledge at Gearslutz, but be prepared for a certain amount of attitude.

ProToolsUsers.org

ProToolsUsers.org has a nice Pro Tools forum and is generally a good resource for new users.

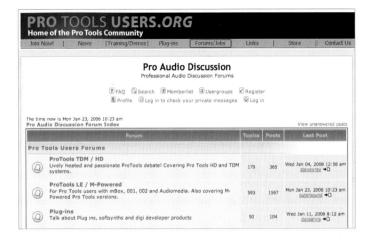

Harmony-Central.com

Harmony-Central is one of the oldest music technology sites, and has digital audio guru Craig Anderton moderating a great forum called Sound, Stage and Studio. This forum provides more discussion and debate rather than problem-solving, but it's a great place to learn new things.

Obedia.com

Obedia is for those who want hands-on training and/or one-on-one telephone support. This is a very cool new company; their staff includes some of the most technically astute people in the country. You can buy a block of time at a discount, as you do with a phone card, or you can pay $1.99 a minute and talk with someone in person who will help you through any audio or computer problems, regardless of whether the problems are Pro-Tools-specific or not. Obedia supports all computer platforms, all operating systems, and all digital audio software. Based on your issue, you'll be transferred to a specialist. The really outstanding thing is that they work 24/7.

Clone Your Hard Drive

I can back up my songs and my documents by dragging them to another hard drive or burning a CD, but every week I also create a clone of my hard drive. Why? Well, what if my laptop is stolen and my entire life is on it? That becomes less of a nightmare if I've created a hard drive designated to be a clone of my laptop. I can boot up from the clone, and it's exactly like booting up from my laptop—the same dock, same applications, same email—a mirror image of my laptop's hard drive. Some software authorizations won't work, but many of them will. For me, it's worth it to spend $100 to keep a hard drive for cloning.

A few programs are available that do this. For the Mac, the most common is a $5 piece of shareware called Carbon Copy Cloner. (You can download it from versiontracker.com.) To use it, you select the source hard drive that you're cloning, select the target hard drive that you're cloning to, and just click Clone. Fast and simple.

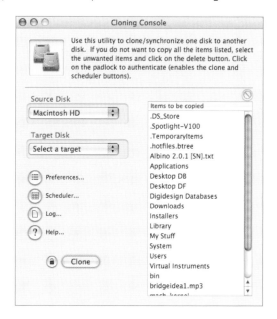

A new software application called Synchronize Pro for the Mac costs $99; it does scheduled back-ups and has more features than Carbon Copy Cloner. I haven't used it myself, but I've heard positive things about it.

For Windows, there's a $159 commercial product called PeerSync, and a few smaller shareware apps such as ShadowBack and Cobian Backup. Acronis True Image ($49.99) is also good.

Creating Disc Images

When you create a disc image of a CD, you're saving the contents of that CD as a single file onto your hard drive. On a Mac, when you double-click the file to open it, the CD is mounted on your desktop exactly as if you had physically inserted a CD. On a PC, it does the same thing, but you have to mount the disc image from an application such as SoftDisc and then open up My Computer or Windows Explorer. There, you will see the disc mounted as a virtual drive.

Here's how disc images can be helpful. I'm a bit of a software junkie and I buy a lot of software, virtual instruments, and loop libraries. My CD drawer is quite full after many years of collecting. Rather than having to dig through a drawer full of CDs when I need one, I create disc images of all my CDs and keep them on a hard drive for easy access. I have a hard drive called Installer CDs, and I keep this handy in case I ever need to install any CDs or DVDs. When I travel to other studios, I take it with me in case I need any of my loops or instruments. I don't have to worry about traveling with fragile CDs that can get lost and scratched and which are painfully slow to install. (Besides, if I take a CD, I'm always leaving it in someone's drive, never to be seen again.)

Creating disc images is a good way of backing up software as well, and as I said, when you need one of your CDs and go looking for it, having them all on a hard drive makes it fast and simple to find the one you want.

There are two simple ways to create disc image on a Mac: with Toast, or with the Disk Utility application. Windows users have a little more work to do.

Create a Disc Image with Toast (Mac)

Many Mac users use Toast. Let's create an image of the Pro Tools installer CD, in three easy steps.

1] Insert the CD you want to copy.

2] Open Toast and click on the Copy tab.

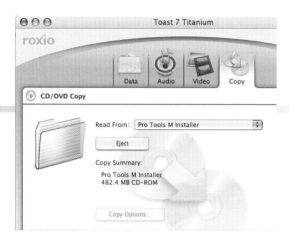

3] Choose Save as Disc Image from the File menu.

Be sure that you know where you're saving your disc images. Also, it's best not to rename them.
I have my CDs organized in folders called Disk Utilities, Audio Applications, Virtual Instruments, and so on.

To mount a CD image, just double-click the image.

Pro Tools M Installer.toast

This opens Toast to the Image File window and gives you a Mount button.

When you mount a cross-platform CD image on a Mac, you'll see two CDs. One is for PC and one is for Mac. To eject an image, just like a real CD, highlight it and hit ⌘+E or drag it to the trash.

Create a Disc Image with Disk Utility (Mac)

A cool shortcut in the Finder is ⌘+Shift+A, which opens the Applications folder. You can also use ⌘+Shift+U to open the Utilities folder. Open the Utilities folder now, and open the Disk Utility application. You may want to keep Disk Utility in your dock. The application comes with the Mac and is found here: Macintosh HD/Applications/Utilities.

1] Highlight the CD in the Disk Utility window.

2] Click on New Image. Name the CD so you'll remember what it is, and then choose where to save it. Click Save. This will take a minute or two.

On your hard drive you'll now have a .dmg file.

PTInstaller.dmg

3] To mount a .dmg file, just double-click it and the virtual drive will mount on your desktop. To eject it, just highlight it and press ⌘+E.

I use Toast images out of habit, but .dmg seems to be the better format because you don't have to have Toast to mount them. And they use compression, which saves hard drive space.

Disc Images for Windows Users

As usual, Windows users have to jump through a few more hoops, but it's worth the steps required to create and use disc image files. You may wonder, "Can't I just copy my CD to my hard drive?" The answer is no. Installer CDs are very picky and require the actual CD to be inserted. Creating a CD image simulates an actual CD but allows you to save the CD as a file to your hard drive. When you mount the disc image, it shows up in My Computer as if a real CD were inserted. I don't know why, but Easy Media Creator does not create or mount standard disc image files, and nothing that comes with your operating system does this, either. So you need yet another piece of software.

I use a $19.95 program called SoftDisc. Many applications save and mount disc images, but this one seems pretty straightforward and affordable.

1] Insert the CD you want to image, and open SoftDisc. Go to the File menu and choose Make CD/DVD Image.

2] A small window asks where you want to save your disc image. Choose where to save it, and click Make.

This creates a disc image on your hard drive that shows up like a CD.

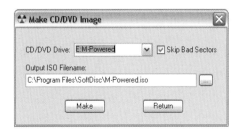

3] To mount a disc image from SoftDisc, find the image file, right-click, and choose Mount Image File.

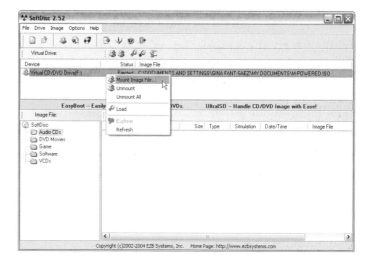

4] Look in My Computer or Windows Explorer, and you'll see that it looks as if you have an actual physical CD inserted in your computer. You can use this image as if it were a physical CD.

INTERNET COLLABORATION

B

Pro Tools is used by musicians at all levels, from weekend hobbyists to serious professionals. No matter what your level, I hope *Pro Tools for Musicians and Songwriters* has helped you solidify your skills so you can make better music. That said, this book was not written just for the hobbyist who wants to email an mp3 file to a colleague every now and then. I also had in mind professional musicians and songwriters who have spent years honing their craft and now want to bring their careers into the twenty-first century.

Buying and learning Pro Tools is a huge commitment, and I sincerely honor your efforts. But just as important as knowing how to record your work is learning how to collaborate with other people. In this day and age, that means being able to send your work to anyone, anywhere, at any time. Knowing how to do this can open up a whole new world for you creatively—not to mention saving you a lot of travel expenses and Federal Express bills.

So let's talk about sending your files across the Internet and collaborating with anyone regardless of their hardware or software. Collaborating over the Internet has been a passion of mine for many years. Over the past seven or eight years I've tried and tested every method available. I love to work with great musicians, songwriters, and engineers, but I also love living in Austin, Texas. Although we have some amazing talent here and it's great to work in person, many of my longtime colleagues and cowriters are in New York, Nashville, Los Angeles, Germany, and other places. These people use different operating systems, different software, different hardware, and different plug-ins. The good news is, I've learned a lot about Internet collaboration as a result. The bad news is, there are drawbacks in every solution.

In this final appendix, we'll take a look at various methods I've used, including FTP servers, chat applications, DigiDelivery, and iDisk. We'll start with a brief tour of my new online collaboration company, eSession.com.

What Is eSession.com?

eSession.com is an Internet-based portal for booking talent. Some of the music industry's top musicians, engineers, and producers participate. The website is created to help clients around the world hire these artists, communicate with them, and even work with them in real time. The site handles file transfers and financial transactions between the client and the talent.

With eSession.com you could hire Peter Gabriel's bassist to work on your music, or Alanis Morissette's guitarist, or the guy who mixed Coldplay's latest album. Sending a work request to any of these artists costs only $25.

Two other versions of eSession will debut in 2006—eSessionIndie.com and eSessionLite.com. While eSession.com is geared toward the mainstream professional market, eSessionIndie.com will be for the indie music sector, and eSessionLite.com will be for anyone who wants to play on anyone else's music. eSessionLite.com is being built with the music hobbyist in mind.

All versions of eSession will essentially work the same way. There are five simple steps: First, choose a musician or engineer with whom you'd like to work. Next, negotiate fees and schedules. When you've reached agreement, send the artist your stem files. At this point, you'll be able to record a session with them in real time using a special plug-in or let them record on their own and send you files with which you can create your own composite. Finally, after payment is received by eSession, you'll be able to download their files and import them into Pro Tools.

This is an example of an eSession database page:

Each talent member has a profile that shows you their discography, computer setup, bio, equipment, and so on. You'll see photos of engineers' studios and musicians' instruments. You'll also be able to listen to audio samples of their work.

Chat Applications

My entire world is my chat application. I don't use my chat app to banter and gossip with my friends. It's an invaluable business tool that I use every waking hour. I use my chat app to receive files from my Web designers, send chapters to my editors, collaborate with cowriters, save money on phone calls, send mixes to clients, and send Pro Tools sessions to musicians. I also recently used video chat to keep an eye on my building contractors while I was traveling.

Most chat apps work exactly the same way. They require that you set up an account. Most accounts are free—except for Apple's iChat, though it does allow you to sign up for a 90-day free trial. An iChat account costs $99 a year because it's part of a very versatile collection of tools called .Mac (dot Mac). With a .Mac account, Macintosh users get tools to back up their files, synchronize their calendar and address book, publish their photos online, and create a simple but slick website. You get a .Mac email address and another service called iDisk that gives you one gigabyte of virtual disk space, which is accessible from a Mac or PC. iDisk provides a place to post your files for anyone to download from or upload to. All of the software required for using .Mac is installed with OS X.

Using Chat Apps to Collaborate

There are many chat applications to choose from, including MSN Messenger, AOL Instant Messenger (AIM), Skype, Yahoo Messenger, and ICQ. Google has just introduced a brand-new chat application called Google Talk. Since it's still in beta testing as I'm writing this, it's hard to know what the final product will be like, but it looks very promising.

I've tried all these chat applications. For ease of use, file transfer speed, and aesthetic design, nothing holds a candle to iChat, but then again, I'm partial to the way Apple designs everything. I find Apple's applications very user-friendly and rather sexy, if I may say so. The worst application for collaboration is Skype, because of its slow file transfer speed.

The great thing about Apple iChat and Google Talk is that they both support an open protocol called Jabber. What is Jabber? Here's the deal: Most chat applications such as AIM or MSN only allow you to talk to other people on AIM or MSN. But when Jabber is built into a chat application, it allows that chat application to communicate with most other major chat apps using your preferred application.

In addition to iChat and Google Talk, there are several multiprotocol Jabber chat applications worth checking out, including Fire, Psi, Coccinella, Adium, Paltalk, Miranda, and Trillian.

Some applications now support audio and video chat as well. In iChat, if a user has a microphone input and an audio output port on their computer, a small telephone icon is shown next to their name, letting you know that you can audio-chat with that person. If you have a video camera plugged into your computer, the telephone icon next to your name becomes a video camera, and the icon will also change for anyone else who has a video camera connected to their computer.

For videoconferencing, I'm a big fan of the Apple iSight. This little FireWire camera has a built-in microphone, gets an excellent picture, and attaches easily to your computer. For less than $150, it's one of the best videoconferencing tools available.

Before you can chat with anyone, you'll need to decide what chat application you're going to use and create an account. Unlike email, where you'll only be able to attach relatively small files (5 MB or 10 MB in most cases), with chat apps there's no limit on file size. This comes in very handy when sending stems or Pro Tools sessions. To send a file to someone, you simply drag and drop a file on their name in the Buddy List. Here is the file transfer window in Skype:

The person to whom you're sending the file receives a pop-up window letting them know they have an incoming file, and they can accept or decline it. If they accept, then your file starts sending. I use the file transfer capabilities on a daily basis for sending and receiving small and large files.

Using Audio Chat Applications Within Pro Tools

Here's a cool trick I've used to successfully cowrite using iChat and Pro Tools at the same time. (Any chat application will work as long as it supports audio chatting and your computer has its own separate audio inputs and outputs.)

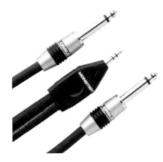

My laptop has an audio output, which is a 1/8" jack, also called a mini-phone jack. My laptop also has a 1/8" line-level audio input. You'll need two simple Y-cables that you can find at any Radio Shack or Best Buy. Each cable has a 1/8" stereo mini-phone jack on one end; on the other end are two 1/4" connectors, also known as phone jacks. You plug the audio output of your computer into the input of your Pro Tools interface, and plug the audio input of your computer to the output of your Pro Tools interface.

You'll need to open up your chat application preferences or properties and make sure your microphone input is set to the line input of your computer.

In Pro Tools, you create a stereo aux input and set the input to 1–2 (or whatever input ports you're using). Now everything coming out of your computer is going into Pro Tools, and everything coming out of Pro Tools is going into your computer's audio input.

Start an audio chat with the person you're working with.

◆ If your interface only has two inputs and two outputs, you'll need to plug in one input of the stereo Y-cable and then use the other input for your microphone so that you can talk to your collaborator.

◆ If your interface only has two outputs and you normally use these outputs for your speakers, you'll have to unplug your speakers. Then you use the outputs so that your collaborator hears your tracks in stereo, and you'll have to use your headphones to listen.

This type of link is better suited to cowriting than to actual recording of tracks. Due to the unavoidable time lag, getting two computers to sync up when connected via the Internet is not possible. Also, real-time audio transfers via chat are in a compressed format, so tracks played by your collaborator and streamed to you would have reduced quality.

It's possible to work around the time delay by measuring it and then compensating for it. Create a click track and print it to an audio track for a few bars. Then record your collaborator's click and measure the distance between your clicks and those that arrive remotely. After your collaborator plays a track, you can advance it by the correct number of ticks to line it up with your other tracks.

Using iDisk

The iDisk service that comes with .Mac is a virtual hard drive that you access with an Internet connection. Think of a virtual hard drive as being like a storage unit that you rent. If your neighbor then wants to borrow your lawn mower, which is in storage, you might give him the key so that he can go get it himself. If your neighbor asks if he can store his ice chest, again you might give him the keys to your storage unit. iDisk is a lot like that. It's a file storage unit where you can put your own files for others to access, and it's also a place to which others can copy files for you to access.

You'll need a .Mac account to use iDisk. With this account, you get 1 GB of storage, upgradeable to 4 GB.

Once you have a .Mac account, you simply go to the Go menu of the Finder and choose iDisk > My iDisk. Your iDisk will mount on your desktop just like a hard drive.

For others to have access to your files, you must copy them into your iDisk's Public folder. For example, if you have a Pro Tools session that you want a cowriter to download, you'd copy this session into your Public folder and give the cowriter your .Mac login name. If they're on a Mac, they'd go to the Finder and select Go > iDisk > Other User's Public Folder. Type in your .Mac login and click Connect. Your iDisk will show up on their desktop, but the only files they'll see are the ones that you copied into your Public folder. They can also copy their own files into the Public folder, which you can then access.

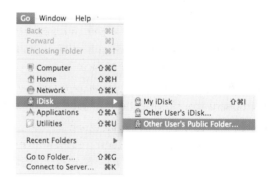

You can access your iDisk from the Internet by going to www.mac.com. You'll have to log in and then click on iDisk. You'll be asked to log in again, but from this page you can upload and download on any browser in Mac or Windows.

Apple has also created the Windows iDisk Utility, which works very much the way iDisk works on a Mac. You'll need to download this utility from www.mac.com, or go to Google and type in "Windows iDisk Utility." After you download and install the utility, if you have your own .Mac account, you'll type in your .Mac login and password. If you need to access someone else's iDisk Public Folder, choose Public and type in the login name. Then look in My Computer, under Devices with Removable Storage, and you'll see iDisk show up as another hard drive.

Other sites, such as Xdrive.com, Box.net, and i2drive.com, offer virtual disk space. Many PC-based virtual disk services are not cross-platform, which limits Windows users to only working with other Windows users. Here again, I think Apple has the simplest, slickest, and most versatile virtual disk solution.

Many other sites charge around $9.99 a month. That's about $120 a year. In contrast, a .Mac account costs only $99 and gives you an email account, an iChat account, 1 GB of iDisk space, a Web page, and more.

There are many benefits to using something like iDisk rather than setting up your own server. Setting up an FTP server (see below) can be complicated and requires the monthly expense of a fixed IP address. A fixed IP can cost $25 or more a month. That's $300 a year to set up your own server.

Overall, iDisk and other virtual disk services are a good solution for ease of use, affordability, and cross-platform versatility.

FTP Servers

FTP is the most common way in which people send and receive large files. FTP means File Transfer Protocol, but don't let that scare you.

Think of using FTP as being like using a telephone. In order to call someone, you need their phone number. When you're calling someone at a company, you'll also need to give your name to the receptionist. It's the same with FTP: To connect to someone's FTP server, you need to know their number (the *IP address*). And to get into the server, you also need to give a login name and password. So accessing an FTP server requires that you have three things: the FTP address, a login/username, and a password.

You need a phone to call someone, right? Well, you need an FTP client application to send files and get files from an FTP server. You can use a Web browser to download files stored on an FTP server, but the browser can't upload files to the server. Rather than use a browser, it's much better to download and install an FTP application.

There are literally dozens of FTP applications for both Mac and Windows. Most FTP apps are shareware or require a minimal fee for a serial number. Some are even free, but I'm a big believer that you get what you pay for. On the Mac, for many years people used a program called Fetch. Though many people still use this, Transmit seems to be the application of choice these days. Transmit costs $29.95. A very common FTP app for Windows is CuteFTP ($39.95). Brixoft Source Edit, which is free, includes an excellent FTP app called File Courier.

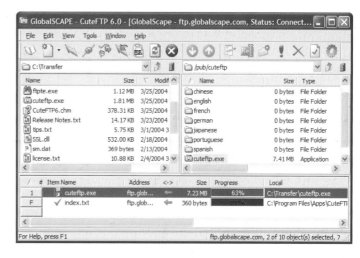

All FTP applications are pretty much the same. You start with a window that asks you for the server address, your username, and the password. After you log in, this same window usually becomes the directory of the server you're connecting to. On the left side of the window is your own computer's directory. You find your own files on the left and drag them over to the correct folder on the remote server on the right, or click an arrow button to transmit them. Of course, you drag from right to left if you're downloading rather than uploading.

Setting Up Your Own FTP Server

If you're doing a lot of collaboration with musicians who live and work elsewhere, you may want to set up your own FTP server and allow your friends to log in and drop files into your computer. Mac users who establish their own FTP server have it easier than Windows users; the process is far simpler.

The key ingredient is what's called a fixed IP Address. As I mentioned earlier, an FTP client application requires that you know the IP address, just as you need a phone number to make a phone call. When you first get service from the phone company, you get a phone number, and that phone number will normally be one fixed number for as long as you have the service.

Internet service does not, unfortunately, work the same way. As you use your computer for browsing the Web, receiving email, and so on, you have a constantly changing IP address. When you log onto the Internet, regardless of whether you have cable, DSL, or even dial-up, you're given an IP address, and this number changes each time you restart the Internet hardware. Some Internet companies even reset your IP address themselves every 24 hours. Technically, you might be able to set up a server without a fixed IP address, but if you did, you'd have to keep giving people whatever address you had for that day.

The benefit of an FTP server over a virtual disk solution is that when someone copies a file to your server, the file is now on your own computer. Using a solution such as iDisk, you have to log in and download files to your computer from iDisk, rather than just opening up your hard drive and seeing the files. And when you're dealing with really large files, downloading takes time. So an FTP server would eliminate the download time required on your end. Also, with your own FTP server, there's no limit on the maximum file size of data transfers.

DigiDelivery

Created by Digidesign, DigiDelivery is a system for safe and secure large file transfers. You can receive files free from anyone sending from a DigiDelivery system, just by downloading and installing the free DigiDelivery Client software. I receive DigiDelivery files frequently from clients.

In order to send files, however, you must have an account on a special DigiDelivery hardware server, which costs between $3,200 and $10,000. This system is intended to be used by large corporations, commercial studios, film and video companies, mastering studios, and so on, that need to send and receive large files to and from clients on a daily basis.

WebCargo.net is an online service like DigiDelivery. They specialize in encrypted digital file transmission. They charge 10 cents a megabyte per transfer, so a 1 GB session file would cost $100 to send. For artists who are ultra-sensitive about their material being intercepted or at risk and who don't want to invest in a DigiDelivery system, paying for WebCargo.net transfers may be worth the peace of mind.

For more information about internet collaboration, see this book's companion web site (www.protoolsformusicians.com).

INDEX

Workspace, 289
zooming in/out, 33, 57, 70
kHz (kilohertz), 126
Killen, Kevin, 178, 347
Knee value
Compressor plug-in, 174, 176
instrument compression, 178
Kumpel, Teddy, 285

L

Langevin and Manley, 34
latency compensation, 38, 361
Level Trimmer tool, 399
Levin, Tony, 285
limiters, compression, 175
Line Pencil tool, 244
Line settings, 34, 36
location indicators, 54
Main indicator, 62, 63
Sub indicator, 63
Loop Playback
enabling, 72
versus Loop Recording, 215
1-Band EQ II plug-in, 128
recording MIDI tracks, 215
Loop Playback (Options menu) command, 72
Loop Recording (Options menu) command, 320
loops. *See also* multi-track loops
downloading, 21–22
drum loops, repeating, 31–33
duplicating, 300
importing, 24
options, 25
from Workspace, 291, 298–299
locating downloaded loops, 23
loop recording, 318–322
creating composite from looped recording, 322–325
versus Loop Playback, 215
meter, 293
playing continuously, 72
Region Groups
assigning colors, 307–309
creating, 305–307
tempo, 293, 294
selecting, 295
TCE Trimmer, 296–297, 302–304

M

M-Audio FireWire 410
Buffer Size settings, 38
Mic or Line settings, 34
M-Audio FireWire Solo, 161
M-Audio Project Mix, 387
.Mac accounts, 509, 510
Macintosh
audio tracks, recording in Tiger OS, 42
cloning hard drives, 496
default settings, 16, 27
disc images, 499
file compression, 23
file sizes, backups, 442
importing, loops, 25
markers, creating on PowerBook, 261
MIDI tracks
tempo settings, 204
troubleshooting, 193
Option key, 27
Pro Tools
finding on hard drives, 3–4
hiding *versus* minimizing, 7
returning to, 8
Roxio Toast
burning CDs, 415, 417
disc images, 497–498
SampleTank Free
downloading, 183
installing, 184, 186
switching applications, 189
Mackie mixer, bussing, 150–151
Main Counter submenu, Bars and Beats (View menu) command, 12
Manley, Eva, 494
markers. *See* Memory Location/Marker window
Markers ruler, 18, 114–118
Massenburg, George, 494
Mastelotto, Pat, 263–264, 285
Master Fader, 408, 411
Renaissance Compressor insert, 409–410
Maxim plug-in, 347
Mbox
Buffer Size settings, 38
Mic, Line, or Instrument settings, 34, 36
measurements for music, 62
Medium Delay II plug-in, 163, 166–167
Memory Location/Marker window
information provided, 317–318
locations
creating, 115
deleting, 117
moving, 118